SYMBOLIC LEADERS

OBSERVATIONS

A series edited by HOWARD S. BECKER, Stanford University

SYMBOLIC LEADERS

PUBLIC DRAMAS AND PUBLIC MEN

by Orrin E. Klapp

ALDINE Publishing Company / *Chicago*

First published 1964 by
ALDINE Publishing Company
64 East Van Buren Street
Chicago, Illinois 60605

Library of Congress Catalog Card Number
   64-23369
Designed by David Miller
Printed in the United States of America

To Evelyn, Merrie and Curtis

Preface

This book seems, at first glance, to be merely about celebrities and their doings. Actually, it is a study of an important form of leadership, one that has not, I believe, been sufficiently recognized, by scholars at least (the masses, of course, have always recognized it). A symbolic leader is one who functions primarily through his meaning or image (for example, Gandhi meant much as a person to the masses of India—indeed, of the earth—regardless of his official status). Thus I make a distinction between a symbolic leader and an organizational leader; the latter works within a certain social structure or organized group and may not mean much to people otherwise.

The book discusses the "burdens of fame," not merely as the celebrity's problem, but in terms of the pressures and demands that tell him he is *doing* something for people, even that he has what amounts to a profession. It tells how symbolic leaders emerge, that is, how hitherto unknown people become symbolic by a "hit," usually a lucky accident, in which they find their function, and it analyzes the kinds of dramatic encounters that are likely to make "heroes" or "villains" or

7

"fools." The book portrays the ups-and-downs of public images, crises and role reversals, in which parties of a public drama may exchange roles without meaning to. It then describes some practical problems of "role strategy" in public relations. A final chapter deals with the public drama, its implications for change and instability in modern society.

I cannot properly acknowledge all my indebtedness to those, including many college students, who have helped me with this book, but I wish particularly to mention Herbert Blumer, Anselm L. Strauss, and Howard S. Becker.

ORRIN E. KLAPP

Contents

SYMBOLIC LEADERS

LIVING
WITH A PUBLIC IMAGE

It might be a relief to be finished—
fame may go by and—so long, I've had you.
MARILYN MONROE

THE AGE OF CELEBRITIES

A celebrity does not have an easy life these days. He has his part
to play, just as does the policeman and the doctor. He has to
be a Symbol for a great many people that he does not know.
He cannot tell exactly where his private life ends and his public life begins. He has to worry about his "image" or hire
someone to manage it for him. He is a central figure in a great
modern institution—the cult of celebrities[1]—built around the
personalities of people who have for some reason been glorified by the image-making and fame-building processes.

The age of celebrities began with the development of the
American movies and the appearance of Hollywood as the
star capital of the world. Before that we knew fame, to be sure
—and the theater had its Ole Bulls, Sarah Bernhardts, and
Jennie Linds—but never before had such a mass shrine been
constructed as the movie, with its many opportunities for very

1. I have described this in *Heroes, Villains and Fools: The Changing
American Character* (Englewood Cliffs, N.J.: Prentice-Hall, 1962), pp.
142–45.

ordinary people (like Rudolph Valentino, Greta Garbo, and Fatty Arbuckle) to "make it" to fame and popular idolization. Later, radio, phonograph records, and television became magic pumpkins for the ride to fame. As a result, our celebrity elite is today so vast that Cleveland Amory has edited its *Register,* a volume resembling a telephone book listing alphabetically all the people who have become famous in America. Special commentators and magazines watch their doings closely and keep the public informed about them.

One result of this focus of society is that the young man of today might be described as a born celebrity-watcher. He has been brought up on a diet of star dust since he was knee-high to a television set, which was probably his baby-sitter. He is likely to be a mass-communication addict, who keeps one eye on the television while his ear is tuned to a radio if possible. He is a member of some audience—at home, in a theater or stadium, or parked in his car—seven nights a week.

That is why the celebrity himself has such a big job. He must rise to the demands made on the symbol. He must be prepared for a life that is in many ways a contradiction of old-fashioned ideas about privacy and integrity—for example, that a man should "be himself." A few illustrations from the careers of public figures will present the problem from the professional celebrity's point of view. On the other hand, many who are thrust before the public eye are amateurs, puzzled, sometimes indignant, at the demands made on them.

THE BURDENS OF FAME

The attraction of fame is a built-in part of the American dream. Yet one of the most characteristic symptoms of having actually become a celebrity is a certain disillusionment, which sets in—after the first thrill of seeing one's name in headlines —upon discovering the obligations and inconveniences of being known by everybody everywhere. A cliché among artists is that the hardest thing to survive is success. Marilyn Monroe spoke for all entertainers in a classic statement in which she described herself as a stage-struck girl fitting her shoe into actors' footprints before Grauman's Chinese Theatre in Hollywood, her subsequent surprise at seeing her own name in lights for the first time, and finally her disillusionment. These symptoms are not the tragedy of a particular person. It might be said that the stresses of fame are fairly constant, though the ability of people to bear up under them varies. If some seem to thrive in the limelight, it does not follow that conflicts are not present.

Disillusionment with being a celebrity is, in fact, a result of many irritations, large and small, that dissipate the charm of a public role. One of the most important is difficulty in maintaining a "private life." The person who suddenly becomes famous rarely abandons his privacy with good spirit, to accept life in a goldfish bowl. Rather, he wants to have it both ways. He will complain of intrusions, perhaps, as did Frank Sinatra in his courtship of Ava Gardner—feuding with reporters, angrily dodging them with fisticuffs and camera-breaking. Lindbergh, too, was hounded by the public; reporters pried into the secrets of his household; people came up to him while he was eating in a restaurant and counted the peas on his fork. Harry Truman, even while President, liked to think of himself as an ordinary man and once refused to revisit a church where the minister had "made a show" of his attendance. Perhaps Truman *was* an ordinary man, and perhaps it is to a man's credit to refuse to get a swelled head, but is it realistic to insist that the public treat a celebrity like an ordinary person?

Frustrating the public's legitimate interest in famous persons is more likely to pique than to curb curiosity. The industrialist-financier Howard Hughes went to fantastic lengths to keep his life secret, in spite of his association with a series of glamorous actresses and his control of huge enterprises. He retired to a gun-guarded, fenced, patrolled "castle," never revealing his location when he made telephone calls and usually working through intermediaries rather than in person. Yet all he managed to do was build up an image of a "mystery man," whose life was the more fascinating because of his efforts to guard it.

Along with loss of privacy there come pressures to live up to various public expectations that are irksome, unreasonable, and even impossible. Movie actors complain of having to conform to the American notion of perennial youth, even when they have reached middle age. A public leader will have trouble with the moral ideals of various groups scrutinizing him: Franklin Delano Roosevelt was once severely criticized for saying "damn" in public; at a banquet he would sometimes hide a row of cocktails discreetly behind flower vases. (Joseph Stalin, it might be noted, had a reverse difficulty: he drank sauterne wine from small glasses at banquets, pretending it was vodka.) Athletic stars find that they are supposed to be models for youth and lead exemplary lives (which was difficult for Babe Ruth, no matter how hard he tried, and even more difficult for Bill Tilden, who had an embarrassing fondness for young boys). When an intellectual becomes famous, he is expected to assume a public role—to make speeches, defend his position, attend social gatherings—even if doing so is inconsistent with his own personality or an interruption of his creative work. Cases in point include Madame Curie, Einstein, Dylan Thomas, and Rachel Carson, whose book *Silent Spring* embroiled her in controversy and the unwelcome duties of public advocate.

Movie stars, with alert public relations offices to guide them in deportment, often have the feeling of being "managed," of not having a "life of their own."[2] Their names and personalities may be revamped arbitrarily. The star of a teen-

2. The control over television stars is apparently more stringent than that over movie stars because of the nature of the audiences, public pro-

age television drama, "Dobie Gillis," complained that he was not allowed to date whom he pleased but had to appear with someone the studio picked out for him. Kim Novak cried because she was treated like "public property." Marilyn Monroe said, "I'm invited places to kind of brighten up a dinner table —like a musician who'll play the piano after dinner, and I know you're not really invited for yourself. You're just an ornament."

This feeling of being public property is not an illusion; it reflects the truth that the public has adopted the celebrity as an image of a certain kind and expects him to perform the functions of that image. He is no longer just a person but has become an institution. Since he is "our" Will, "our" George, "our" John, the public assumes the right to criticize, guide, and make demands. Celebrities often complain of requests made of them by strangers, who ask for loans, gifts, or advice or claim relationship of one kind or another. The status of the celebrity as public property also helps explain intrusions on his privacy, familiarities by strangers, people who crowd into photographs with him, and even the curious "touching mania." The Duke of Windsor remarked that while he was Prince of Wales, people used to try to touch him by any means, prod him, even hit him with folded newspapers.

The enormous demand of the public for communication with its celebrities also creates a staff problem: handling fan mail by the sack, answering letters that ask for photographs or advise the celebrity to "drop dead," receiving and acknowledging gifts. Some gifts are odd and constitute a storage or disposal problem; Lindbergh received so many gifts that he filled a museum with them, and women knitted hundreds of pairs of socks for Rudolph Valentino.

The "rights" of the public over its image include the

tests, sponsor trouble, and fears that the network will drop the show. The stars lead "colorless, circumspect private lives" and make dull copy compared with movie stars. There is no sex goddess on TV. (Lloyd Shearer, *Parade,* October 14, 1962, p. 8.)

privilege of using a celebrity as a scapegoat. He may be the target of unexpected animosity from people he has not knowingly harmed. One baseball star was shot by a lovesick girl whom he did not know. Again, Marilyn Monroe, whose testimony is eloquent on the whole problem of being a celebrity, provides a relevant quote:

> When you're famous you kind of run into human nature in a raw kind of way. It stirs up envy, fame does. People you run into feel that, well, who is she—who does she think she is, Marilyn Monroe? They feel fame gives them some kind of privilege to walk up to you and say anything to you. . . . One time here I am looking for a home to buy and I stopped at this place. A man came out and was very pleasant, very cheerful, and said, "Oh, just a moment, I want my wife to meet you." Well, she came out and said, "Will you please get off the premises?"

Many great men—Lincoln, Washington, Jefferson, Nelson—have suffered from the caprices of a public that made heroes of them one moment and villains the next.

The celebrity may feel guilt or embarrassment because he is not the person the public thinks he is.[3] This attitude was so common among fliers coming back after war service that it got to be known as the "hero's neurosis." Vince Edwards, star of "Dr. Ben Casey," a television series about a heroic surgeon, became uncomfortably aware of the discrepancy between his own life (including a devotion to betting on horse races) and the "godlike" image he had come to present to the public. "I won't do anything to destroy the image," he said, and tried to keep his private life subdued and separate. Yet it was not

3. "My craving for good repute among men . . . made me profoundly suspect my truthfulness to myself. Only too good an actor could so impress his favourable opinion. Here were the Arabs believing me, Allenby and Clayton trusting me, my bodyguard dying for me: and I began to wonder if all established reputations were founded, like mine, on fraud." (T. E. Lawrence, *Seven Pillars of Wisdom* [Garden City, N.Y.: Garden City Pub. Co., 1933], p. 562.)

easy; magazines published pictures of his horse-playing, the public watched him every possible moment, and even his close friends began to be affected.

> Some of my old friends begin to weigh their words when we get together now. They don't see me as plain old Vince Edwards. What they see now is the Image. They see Ben Casey. It makes a difference, believe me. Their attitudes change. They stiffen. I can't say I like that. And I'm not so sure I like losing a little privacy. I wish it were different in some ways, the whole success thing. But that's how it is and how do you fight it?

The irony was that as a result of Edwards' very efforts to protect the public image by keeping his private life separate, people began to accuse him of being a snob.

Many celebrities rather sportingly accept the burdens of fame and try to avoid disappointing the public. If they are symbols, they find out what kind of symbol they are and try to live up to it. Mae West and Tallulah Bankhead illustrate such a sporting attitude; they do not seem to mind being cast by the public as "queens of sex" and "bad girls." They play up to the role whenever they can (for example, Tallulah called to a man in a hotel lobby, "Dahling! I didn't recognize you with your clothes on!"). Marilyn Monroe, too, accepted the burden of being a sex symbol, though perhaps not quite as enthusiastically:

> I never quite understood it—this sex symbol—I always thought symbols were those things you clash together! That's the trouble, a sex symbol becomes a thing. I just hate to be a thing. But if I'm going to be a symbol of something I'd rather have it sex than some other things they've got symbols of!

A certain *noblesse oblige* characterizes the celebrity who will not let his public down. Marlene Dietrich is careful to wear expensive gowns, display her legs, and project glamor, though in private life she is described as being like an "old German shoe." Jack Benny puts on his "tightwad" character like an old soldier's uniform. Some entertainers go into special poses or acts, such as the grunting and grimacing of the jazz musicions Gene Krupa, Lionel Hampton, and Louis Armstrong. As the comedian Sammy Davis put it, expressing the trouper's *noblesse oblige*: "Whenever you step outside, you're on, brother, you're on." Comparatively few celebrities are fortunate enough to have real characters so like their public images that they feel no strain or difference in being "on." (Will Rogers was apparently one of these. His character remained the same whether talking to a stagehand or before a Ziegfeld Follies crowd; those who knew him said that even his everyday conversation was publishable.)

There is a point, however, at which, for all the intentions of a celebrity, good-natured or not, the public image gets out of control. It may begin to live a life of its own. A vast number of anarchic rumors may circulate about almost anyone in whom the public is interested (for example, of the sex perversion of movie stars, that Franklin D. Roosevelt used to wake up in the White House screaming and was mentally unsound, that General Douglas MacArthur deserted nurses and soldiers during the Japanese invasion of the Philippines). All this is part of the price of being famous. Some men, by virtue of the multitude of stories about them, become living legends—for example, Al Capone (who became a kind of Robin Hood to the poor of Chicago) or Ivar Krueger, the colorful "match king." At the death of the celebrity, if interest continues, the dam of anecdote opens up. The celebrity cannot rise to confront his image. People like Abraham Lincoln have a veritable river of legend about them (as shown by Basler[4]) that will never be fully sorted out into fact and fiction.

The celebrity and his image belong to the public that creates them. This book is concerned with how one becomes a

4. Roy P. Basler, *The Lincoln Legend* (Boston: Houghton Mifflin, 1935).

public image through participation in dramatic encounters. It is concerned with the troubles the celebrity meets when he loses touch with his image or violates some feature of it. It is concerned with the kinds of images it is possible to have—heroic, villainous, or foolish—and with how the image can change. Finally, it is concerned with the meaning of the phenomenon of images in a changing society.

However, before these things are considered, some of the ideas on which this book is based should be explained. Political scientists, even sociologists, may be puzzled by an approach to leadership that minimizes organization and focuses on dramatic concepts like "heroes" and "villains." Psychologists may be puzzled by an approach that, to a great extent, ignores the personality traits that make one person more dominant, decisive, or extroverted than another. How can one talk about leadership without describing either organizations of those who follow or personality traits of those who lead? Yet the paradox of the kind of leadership that I call "symbolic" is that it operates in such a vacuum. To explain what, indeed, fills this vacuum, it is necessary to use concepts like the "audience" and "drama," especially applicable to a mass society, and also to explore the part played by "social types" in informal social structure. The latter is usually invisible to newcomers and outsiders, but, as they come to "know the ropes," they also see things they have not seen before.

The study of social types was begun by Robert E. Park and his colleagues and students in a well-known series of monographs, of which Nels Anderson's *The Hobo,* Clifford Shaw's *The Jack-roller,* and Harvey Zorbaugh's *The Gold Coast and the Slum* are representative. A "social type" is a kind of person or role found in a certain milieu—for example, playboy, tightwad, schussboomer (skiing), jackroller (underworld). It is not, however, a mere occupational category but usually refers to a kind of *character* found in one or several occupational categories or social levels. Nor is it a personality type, in the sense of a psychologically adequate description of an individual, yet it does often refer to an outstanding trait accurately enough to identify individuals for people who know the milieu. It therefore deserves better than the somewhat derogatory name of "stereotype."

I can draw upon the study of teen-agers to illustrate social types. High-school students are found to have an elaborate informal social organization, much of which is not visible to those outside the high school, even to parents. A clue to this organization comes from teen lingo, which includes many names for social types (in San Diego, California, types like "surfer," "cool head," "brain," "soc," "S.A.," "ivy-leaguer"). These terms are found to be important to teen-agers for classifying one's position in the youth status system and may refer to leaders or leading "crowds" and cliques. Some types, like "cool heads," are "heroes" (models of the way to be and vehicles of identification) for many schoolmates. Thousands of San Diego teen-agers in late 1963 and early 1964 adopted the title, pose, dress, and behavior of "surfers"; this type rapidly became one of the leading personality models. The rise of the surfer shows what is meant by symbolic leadership and the part played in it by social types. The orientation of teen-agers was drastically shifted by this identification model. Some boys bleached their hair (in conformity with the tradition that a surfer is supposed to be blond) and changed their dress so that friends hardly recognized them. They rode to the beach in droves with surfboards on top of their cars. Their new leader, the "surfer" hero, seemed a kind of Pied Piper calling them away from school, home, and community for many hours of each free day. Soon organizations grew up—surfers' clubs, dances, tournaments—reflecting the new orientation, but much of the basic change in way of life had occurred before formal organization.

Symbolic leadership works on masses and audiences prior to, without, and in spite of organization. The "leader" may merely be one to whom many people respond emotionally by identifying with or hating him (the scapegoat, too, is a kind of leader) or a prestigious social type that people imitate. A symbolic leader moves people through his image, the kind of man he seems to be, the style of life or attitude he symbolizes. People respond to him in the mass and in audiences, so he does not need bureaucratic or other status to be effective. He can combine organizational with symbolic leadership (as did Gandhi), but a symbolic leader is likely to have functions far beyond those of particular organizations and structures (as with people like Gene Autry, Elvis Presley, Will Rogers). Similarly, persons like Winston Churchill, Queen Elizabeth, Eleanor Roosevelt, and John F. Kennedy have important symbolic leadership functions in addition to their official roles—alive or dead.[5]

If we look for other than organizational concepts to explain how a symbolic leader works, we find the dramatic ideas of the "hero," "villain," and "fool" very useful. Indeed, as I have held in another book,[6] they seem to be the three most important roles of symbolic leaders. Many particular social types can play such parts. For example, a "good Joe" can be a hero, a "chiseler" a villain, and a "playboy" a fool. The hero dominates the action and has the job of winning for the audience. If a person is cast as hero in many public dramas, or in only one good one, he begins to have an influence on the personalities of thousands of people—for example, the "great lover"

5. Perhaps it will illuminate the subject (at least for sociologists) if I explain that such an approach might be called "neo-Durkheimian" since it assumes that any image—widely held, on which there is consensus— is a "collective representation," which has a function in maintaining (or changing) the social order. It assumes that any important change in images of institutions or leaders means a change in the social order. Of course, as I have pointed out, symbolic leaders do not always have organizations. But the moral order and "structure of action" may be affected very much by their images. Émile Durkheim, I think, did not fully appreciate the dynamic—as opposed to the structural—side of collective representations nor, of course, could he have appreciated the dramatic internalization of roles within the self as explained by George Herbert Mead.

6. *Heroes, Villains and Fools.* The dramatic approach to society can

role of Rudolph Valentino, or the presumable effect of Edward G. Robinson and George Raft starring as gangsters, or the way the "playboy" is coming to be cast more and more as a hero (in movies) and in careers like those of Errol Flynn, "Ruby" Rubirosa, and Rafael Trujillo, Jr.). What is this doing to our concept of leisure and the good life? This book does not investigate the psychological effect of particular heroes on individuals and audiences, but it assumes that they have such effects, manifest or latent.

Another way of looking at social types, then, is to talk about the public drama and its effect on audiences and our changing society (see chap. ix). Perhaps it will suffice here to explain that drama is treated as a social process in which things happen to audiences because of parts played by actors; the function of the actor is to transport an audience vicariously out of everyday roles into a new kind of "reality" that has laws and patterns different from the routines of the ordinary social structure. Of course, drama cannot occur unless images are projected and parts played that an audience can use psychologically, and drama does not become really "dramatic" unless it develops suspense from crisis—from a turning point or unexpected outcome that has the audience on the edges of their seats, so to speak. These critical "events,"[7] occurring largely

---

be found in various studies, such as Kenneth Burke, *Attitudes toward History* (New York; The New Republic, 1936), and *A Rhetoric of Motives* (Englewood Cliffs, N.J.: Prentice-Hall, 1950); Charles H. Cooley, *Human Nature and the Social Order* (New York: Scribner, 1922); George H. Mead, *Mind, Self, and Society* (Chicago: University of Chicago Press, 1936); Thurman Arnold, *Symbols of Government* (New Haven: Yale University Press, 1938); W. Lloyd Warner, *The Living and the Dead* (New Haven: Yale University Press, 1959); Erving Goffman, *The Presentation of Self in Everyday Life* (New York: Doubleday, 1959); Hugh D. Duncan, *Communication and Social Order* (New York: Bedminster, 1962). However, public leadership has not yet been sufficiently treated by this approach.

7. Daniel Boorstin calls "pseudo-events" those which seem to be manufactured by mass communication more than by the realities of what is happening (in *The Image* [New York: Atheneum, 1962]). I agree that they have an effect far greater than they "ought" to have, whether one calls them "pseudo-events" or dramatic "reality."

through mass communication, I call the "public drama." This drama provides the scenes within which important changes are occurring in our society that cannot be accounted for by ordinary organizational leadership. In the last chapter of this book, I explain why I think the public drama has increased its scope and changed its function in modern life and why, by its tendency to transcend social structure, it favors a fluid, masslike—and unstable—society.

But let us, before dealing with these implications, look at celebrities, what they do, how they look to people, how they get to be famous, and how dramatic roles change their images.

CHAPTER TWO

BECOMING
A SYMBOL

So . . . you want to be a star. And who
can blame you! It's exciting. It's glamorous.

ED SULLIVAN

The chance of becoming famous might be called the great
American jackpot. To be a celebrity, to appear on television,
to be applauded, to have necks crane when you enter a room
—that is the warm and not-so-secret dream of countless Americans in a society that is becoming more and more an audience
directed by mass communication. And, looking at the American favorites of past decades, the Buffalo Bills, Annie Oakleys,
Billy the Kids, Rudolph Valentinos, Huey Longs, and Babe
Ruths, it may be hard to avoid the impression that almost any
kind of person can be a celebrity in America. He need be
neither a great man nor a good one in the usual sense. Nor do
the higher echelons of aristocracy offer barriers to crashers
from the elite of the flashbulb; as Cleveland Amory has copi-
ously shown, "high society" is being invaded by celebrities.[1]
This is the irony of Richard Nixon's failure in the Presidential
election—and that of Adlai Stevenson and others; they had

1. *Who Killed Society?* (New York: Harper, 1960).

every right to feel that they could become the nation's popular choice. Why not? Look at the others who made it.

We should not be misled, however, by the apparent catholicity of the public in choosing its favorites. It is true that at times the public seems almost to snatch at someone to make him a "hero," but public taste seems indiscriminate only because we are usually not aware of the number who have been passed over and because we disapprove of the taste displayed in some selections. Let someone *try* to be popular, and it is likely that he cannot find the key to unlock the door. I believe that the public is highly selective, even at times finical. Sometimes the door seems to open accidentally to someone who, one might say, leaned on it, not intending to please people, while, another time, a performer struggles earnestly before apathetic audiences and cannot get a hand. But this "apathy" is as much an illuson as the supposed lack of discrimination. When the public sees what it really wants, it is so delighted that it snatches—literally—at its favorites.

Even after a favorite has been chosen and installed on his throne of votes or "box office," we may not feel that we really understand *what* has been selected. Phrases like "love goddess," "it girl," masculinity symbol," "father image," "favorite son," "personal magnetism," hardly answer the question, and, even if not mere rationalizations, they are only hindsight. In Hollywood a belief and an institution have developed known as "the buildup" or "the system," by which, it is supposed, experts can tell "star" material in advance and even manufacture it outright. A case like that of Kim Novak shows this process at work. Maxwell Arnow, an executive of Columbia Pictures, tells how she was "discovered."

> I sensed something. She had an unusual personality which we can spot in one of five hundred girls who are sent to us. I think it was those fantastic eyes that sold me—the eyes and the Slavic cheekbones. I told her to lose twenty pounds and come back to see me.

Miss Novak was taken over by the studio. A crew of dramatic coaches, photographers, dress designers, cosmeticians, and directors went to work on her. Each took credit for making her into a star, typically referring to her as a "dumb blonde," who owed everything to him. This appears, at least, to have been the myth maintained by the studio to keep control over starlets ("We'll drop you and get another if you're not good"). Considering the number of people who claim credit for making a star, and the large number of starlets who fail to have contracts renewed, it is hard to believe that "buildup" is as effective as its proponents suggest. Regarding the notion that stars can be manufactured artificially, film producer Jerry Wald says:

> This is absolute nonsense. There is no Geiger counter you can hold up to a girl and then say, "This one I can make into a star." Sam Goldwyn spent a million dollars trying to make a star of Anna Sten and failed. Cohn himself tried it with fifty girls and succeeded with only two—Rita Hayworth and Kim Novak. Why, there were six other girls who came to Columbia at the same time as Kim. They were all given the same opportunity, the same build-up. None of them is setting the world on fire . . . [But] the minute she [Kim] appeared on the screen, people began to put their money down to buy tickets—and nobody could manufacture that.[2]

The implication seems to be, then, that experts play hunches but do not themselves really know who will become a star.

Another aspect of the Hollywood "buildup" is that for years it produced stars—or so everybody thought—at a minimum cost of two hundred thousand dollars in grooming and promotion for a major star; then, suddenly, as a knowledgeable writer on the film world observed, the process ran dry. "Hollywood has stopped making stars. The belt-line is out of order." What caused the inexplicable stoppage of a supposedly reliable process, in spite of the high demand (as proved by the

2. Both quotations are from Bill Davidson, "Kim Novak: A Woman Who Can't Be Free," *Redbook*, March, 1959, pp. 84–85.

exorbitant salaries of reigning stars)? Shearer gives two answers: first, based on the condition of the industry, major studios no longer make enough motion pictures to give sufficient exposure (five or six films in a year) to a new actor; second, the public "simply will not go for" the results often enough, so the studios have decided not to stand the expense.[3]

The conclusion, I suggest, is that the power of the "build-up" was largely an illusion that could be maintained as long as the public was actively selecting stars from a certain medium. When, for some reason, interest shifted or what the public happened to seek was not there at the time, the "power" suddenly ceased. Studios did not know what was making stars. They were only disguising their guesswork by an expensive procedure.[4]

Let us look at the case of Charles Lindbergh, whose as-

3. Lloyd Shearer, "Is the Star System Finished?" *Parade,* January 20, 1963, p. 12.

4. I suspect that much the same thing is true in advertising and efforts to merchandise to the popular taste. As long as there is an avid public appetite, goods move and sales pitches "sell"; almost any restaurant can make money without knowing what people really like. According to J. F. Merriman, manager of marketing research for Campbell Soup Company, the failure rate of new products in the United States is a "marketing disgrace," between 80 and 90 per cent in the first year. (*Saturday Review,* June 8, 1963, p. 54.)

A modest example of how promotion is overrated is provided by the sale of a razor blade. In 1962, a British firm, Wilkinson Sword, Ltd., introduced a new blade to the American market. It was done without fanfare and without advertising to the general public, as a gimmick for distributors to help the sale of garden tools. To the astonishment of everyone, the blades were snapped up; word quickly got around that they were several times as good as American blades; dealers were forced to ration them; a black market sprang up in New York, which raised the price considerably over list; the giant Gillette Company found itself challenged by a tiny, practically unknown, competitor (*Consumer Reports,* July, 1963, p. 328). All the power of advertising could not prevent a switch of consumer loyalties; very little publicity was necessary for the Wilkinson blade because it was something men really wanted. Rumor was quite enough publicity.

A similar situation in fad and fashion merchandising was long ago pointed out by Herbert Blumer in the myth of fashion dictatorship: of hundreds of dress designs only a few are selected by buyers, and of these only some are selected by the public. What dictator fails most of the

tounding success as a popular idol in 1927 is a classic illustration of the mystery of public choice and the unimportance of "buildup." As a hero, he was a young man not perceptibly different from thousands of others; in fact, his ordinariness was said to be part of his appeal, in that it made him a "typical" American youth. As a flier, he was not the first but the twenty-seventh man to cross the Atlantic by air.[5] He had no publicity agent. What, then, explained the astonishing national and world response to his flight? Lindbergh was surprised and stunned by the sea of faces at Le Bourget Field, the crowds that swarmed over him and almost wrecked his plane (and for years followed him and poked into his private affairs), the emotional attitude of men and women toward him, the sentimental poems (over five thousand published) that hailed him as Icarus, Galahad, and Columbus. Writers groped for the mysterious "charm" of his personality, which turned out to be not so charming as he became aloof and unco-operative with the press and the public; but the fact was that nobody really knew him, and he stayed unknown. How, then, could it have been his "personality" that made him popular? Can his modest demeanor and refusal of commercial offers after his flight explain such a hero? We must rely on a dramatic analysis of the flight itself (which in practical terms was not a greater contribution to aviation than the flights of Byrd, Chamberlain, and a dozen other contemporary pioneers), its Cinderella plot, the "dark horse" entry upsetting the favorites, the pathos of aloneness, the psychological timing of the flight, and the mood of the audience at that moment.[6]

---

time? Likewise for popular song "plugging," which seems to be of little help in making songs popular. See Gerhart Wiebe, "The Effect of Radio Plugging on Students' Opinions of Popular Songs," *Journal of Applied Psychology,* XXIV (1940), 721–27; reprinted in R. H. Turner and L. M. Killian, *Collective Behavior* (Englewood Cliffs, N.J.: Prentice-Hall, 1957), pp. 185–87.

5. Dixon Wecter, *The Hero in America* (New York: Scribner, 1941).
6. This case has been analyzed in Orrin E. Klapp, "The Hero as a Social Type" (Ph.D. dissertation, University of Chicago, 1948).

With other favorites—Will Rogers is a famous example—personality seems to have had much more to do with their popularity or at least explains why they were able to play certain roles. Rogers had unusual warmth, combined with a unique ability to ad lib and aim pungent witticisms at important people. Others also, such as Oscar Levant and Groucho Marx, seem to have this remarkable ability. But it is not so easy in most cases to identify such an unusual and outstanding personality trait. More generally, we are unable to find anything very "different" in a hero (apart from what he does or is supposed to have done) to distinguish him from others. Often the favorite himself does not know what people see in him. For example, Marcello Mastroianni, the Italian star of "La Dolce Vita," had been acting for twelve years in over forty-five movies before stumbling upon the part that made him a world favorite and Italy's highest-paid male movie star. Neither a he-man nor a great lover, he was genuinely puzzled about what he symbolized. He thought it might be his worried look; "they like me better with wrinkles," he mused. Labels like "the frustrated intellectual" or a "symbol of ennui and sophistication" did little to clear up the mystery. All Mastroianni could do was go on making money as fast as possible and hope that his luck would last.

In short, I have been suggesting that experts in the "personality market" do not really know why a person becomes a mass symbol. Once a choice has been made, there are endless learned speculations about his "personality," "magnetism," and so on, but usually these views overlook the dozens or hundreds of others with similar qualities who failed to "hit" or "sell," even with as much publicity. It is no use minimizing a problem that has baffled some of the shrewdest minds in show business. And if some, like Billy Rose or Irving Berlin or Franklin Roosevelt, solved it, they have kept the secret.

This is a problem not of show business alone, obviously, but of leadership in almost any field—religion, business, education, or politics. Certain persons have enormous effect, not because of achievement or vocation but because they stand for certain things; they play dramatic roles highly satisfying to their audiences; they are *used* psychologically and stir up followings. Let us call them "symbolic leaders."

THE DIALECTICAL PROCESS OF SELECTION

I cannot offer an easy answer to the enigma of why certain people are symbolic, but I can point to a clue. The symbolic leader is an emergent phenomenon, and that is why we so often do not know in advance—nor does he—what he will become. It is typical of a dialectic—an argument or other prolonged give-and-take in which interaction is creative—that neither party knows the outcome; it is a discovery for both. In the present case, the parties to the interaction are the public and the actor or leader. Sometimes fame bursts upon a person; by luck he has hit immediately upon what the public is looking for, so there has not been a prolonged process of discovery. But very often a performer "finds himself" by using cues from audience responses and making himself into what people want. He may do so by painful trial and error, or he may hit it quickly. In any case, sensitivity is crucial—sensitivity to the feedback that helps him perfect his style. In thus interacting with the public, he is performing a public service; he is searching out latent functions that need to be fulfilled.

This kind of feedback was manifested to me in an incident —a modest experiment—in which I, a "nobody," was able to type myself as a small symbol of a popular trend. The incident shows the sort of thing that could happen to an important person in a matter of more consequence. I was in the habit of walking to and from work, two miles each way. My route took me through a suburban neighborhood filled with children, tricycles, and dogs. There was very little traffic other than local.

My daily trip did not go unnoticed. I knew I was attracting attention the day I heard children call out: "Here comes the Walking Man." I realized then that there was something a little odd about walking (at least in a community of two-car garages). I was a character! This idea of the "Walking Man," however, intrigued me. What did it mean? What could be done with it? I decided to carry the act a little further. I managed to "leak" the anecdote about children's calling me "Walking Man" to a newspaper columnist, who saw a human-interest angle in it and published a squib about it. I also purchased a Swiss walking hat as a prop for my role. Soon a feature writer from the newspaper sensed a story and interviewed me about the opinions of the "Walking Man" with regard to health, the merits of exercise, why Americans do not walk more, what is happening to American society, and why I was regarded as an oddity. A photograph showed me starting out from home in my Swiss hat, with my daughter and her girl friend accompanying me (which they did not usually do). The story publicized me throughout the area; motorists recognized and hailed me, sometimes apologetically offering lifts. People around town whom I did not know sent me clippings. But more, a short version of the story went out over the Associated Press wire. Soon, from all over the country—Maine, Vermont, Louisiana, Texas, Kansas, Montana, Oregon—came letters from people encouraging me to go on walking, saying that they, too, were walking, and hoping that the "cause" would not be abandoned, that it would grow.[7] My local status as the "Walking Man" persisted for years.

What had happened? Had I created anything or had I merely discovered something? It seems to me that the first public response to the "Walking Man" showed a green shoot;

7. Several years later, President Kennedy provoked a 50-mile hiking fad in Washington, D.C., by wondering whether the Marine Corps was still up to this requirement established by Theodore Roosevelt. Where this trend could go, what kind of organization could be made of it, remains unknown.

I was merely co-operating with a trend, perhaps a potential movement. To attract attention, however, I had to do something a little odd that would symbolize the trend. The Swiss hat had no creative value but added a detail to the public's own image; the wrong prop (say, a bicycle) would have had little effect except to confuse the image or diminish my chance of becoming a symbol. Nor was press publicity creative; the columnist and the feature writer sensed public interest, but they only facilitated communication, and if interest in walking men had been sufficiently intense, rumor alone might have been enough. My opportunity to type myself and become a symbol came, in short, only from seizing the cues offered by public response and moving in the direction indicated. I could not arbitrarily decide to be a cycling man, a whistling man, or a Swiss yodeler unless the public were equally interested in these types. I had to accept what was "there" in the popular mood; it was my mandate, as it were, from the public.

Every leader of a social movement, every big star of entertainment and sports, every really popular statesman or church leader, has to make a discovery of this kind. People like Senator Joseph McCarthy and Doctor Townsend made such discoveries, not knowing in advance what they would do or become.

The dialectic might be summarized as follows: (1) Social typing is a co-operative process in which a person has the initiative of hitting the first ball, as in a tennis game. (2) People (the audience) return cues to him that give him a view of his "image."[8] (3) All shots, however, are not returned. There is both perceptual and functional selection. People see only what interests them and respond only to images that "do something" for them. (4) The actor can accept or reject the cues returned, but he cannot make a shot from a position different from where he was when the ball came to him, that is, he cannot project a

8. This corresponds to the process of finding a self in the response of others, the "looking-glass self," as in the theories of Charles H. Cooley and George H. Mead.

totally different image. (5) Indeed, even if he dislikes what is
happening, he may not be able to prevent the game from going
in a direction he does not choose (he develops image trouble);
his lack of co-operation may make matters worse, and he may
lose the game. (6) But he can always capitalize on an existing
situation; he can play it up, do trick shots, elaborate on the gag,
or try to improve or change the trend, so long as he works
within the general framework in which the public will play ball
and within the dimensions and rules of the court. (7) His
status—the symbol or image that emerges—is always a product
of the game and cannot be surely set in advance. He may become a star, a hero, a laughing-stock, a villain, or a scapegoat,
but he must wait until the game has been played to find out.

We often see a dialectic like this in the careers of entertainers who "find themselves" and develop successful styles.
In show business, to hit the bull's eye of public attention is
called "clicking," "making a hit," "wowing" an audience. This
is the "break" that every entertainer hopes will make him a
star. He knows that established styles will work, but it is not
his goal to become a second Bob Hope, Frank Sinatra, or Bing
Crosby. He wants to have a trademark, a "sound" of his own,
perhaps summarized by a nickname like "The Voice," "Schnoz-
zle," "The Great Profile," the "It Girl." But, although he wants
to be different, it is hard to know in advance what this difference will be; he must grope for the "gimmick," the "formula."

Such a discovery may come by accident. Betty Hutton,
widely known for her explosive vocal style, began as an ordinary nightclub singer. One night she heard that she was about
to be fired. In desperation, she grabbed the mike with a strangle
hold and began to "belt out" songs in a rather unladylike manner. The audience reacted enthusiasticaly. Her contract was
renewed; a major bandleader hired her. Her style developed
from elaborating on this idea of dynamism; at the climax of
her performance, for example, she might grab the curtain and

swing out over the startled customers. Such renditions became her style and account for her success.

A similar accident started Will Rogers on his remarkable career. He had found indifferent success as a rodeo cowboy and rope-twirler. One night, while twirling his rope, he made a mistake, and with it an impromptu wisecrack: "Swingin' a rope's all right so long as your neck ain't in it!" The audience laughed. Soon he had abandoned his rope and horse and was using instead the daily newspaper as a source for jokes. The comedian had been born from the cowboy. He kept the folksy manner, however; a twenty-dollar blue-serge suit became his most important prop, as the epitome of the "homely" image. One of the criticisms of Rogers was that he went with the wind and was always on the side of the majority. Was this because he just happened to be the same kind of man that the majority were or because he was very sensitive to the cues that his audience gave him?

If accident does not provide the cue for an emerging leader, perhaps painful trial and error will do so. Glenn Miller, the American bandleader who was a favorite in the forties, found his "sound" only after heartbreaking years of experimentation with orchestration and instrumentation. Finally, putting a clarinet instead of a trumpet as lead instrument over five saxophones, he got a unique sound to which young people reacted markedly. In the history of American popular orchestra music, this was a discovery that in a small way bears comparison with the incandescent bulb and the fogged X-ray plate.

Very often, for movie and theater stars, it is the "break" of finding a play or scenario that is a perfect vehicle for a particular personality—not acting talent per se—that makes for success. Again, the star-to-be cannot know in advance which will be his lucky role. This was notably true for Rudolph Valentino in "The Sheik," for Edward G. Robinson and George Raft in "Little Caesar," and to some extent for more accomplished actors, such as Raymond Massey as Abraham Lincoln,

Charles Laughton as Captain Bligh, Vivian Leigh as Scarlett O'Hara, and Peter O'Toole as T. E. Lawrence. Finding such a role, the actor who seizes cues will return soon in a sequel or will allow himself to be cast in similar parts until the public tires of the type (whether or not he enjoys being so typed).

Whatever the field in which he emerges, a marked audience response tells the performer that he has become a symbol. For a writer, it might be the phenomenal sales of a book, resulting in social lionization or making him a center of controversy. For others, the response might be drawing power as evidenced in the "screaming" of fans, the conversions and "miraculous" cures of an evangelist like Aimee Semple McPherson, or the strange power over crowds that Hitler found in himself when he spoke. Marilyn Monroe said:

> The people made me a star—no studio, no person, but the people did. There was a reaction that came to the studio, the fan mail, or when I went to a premiere, or the exhibitors wanted to meet me. I didn't know why. When they all rushed toward me I looked behind me to see who was there and I said, "My heavens!" I was scared to death.

From such reactions, the celebrity finds out what he must do to continue his success. He develops and refines his "style." His props become standardized. Audiences ask for more of the same—songs, speeches, love scenes, antics, whatever it was that made him popular. They say, "Pour it on, Huey!" or "Knock him out, Jack!" whenever he appears.

Theoretically, such enthusiastic responses mean that he has found a hitherto unrecognized, or at least unsatisfied, function for which the public was yearning without knowing exactly what it wanted. But, after a symbolic leader has emerged, the people "know" what they want. They want "him," or to be like him, and this is a societal discovery, although they may still be unable to say in rational terms what he supplies. It may well be that he has helped crystallize a social type, as did the late James Dean, depicting the rebellious adolescent in the movie "Rebel Without a Cause,"[9] or Elvis Presley as a guitar-playing rock-and-roller. Indeed, one of the prime functions of popular favorites is to make types visible, which in turn make new life styles and new tastes visible.

But if our analogy is hitting the bull's-eye of a target, then we must add that it is a hidden and moving target. The archer is not allowed to see it and knows only the general direction of its movement. Continued audience reactions tell him how near he is to the center and how to correct his next shot. We might view politics, entertainment, and all such fields as games in which hundreds of archers are shooting at hidden, moving targets. What, for example, does a new President like Lyndon Johnson mean to Americans and to the world, aside from his manifest functions as chief executive, that his predecessor did not? It is in the area of changing, latent functions that all the blind shooting occurs, for there seems to be no way yet to find out in advance what the public, inarticulate about its symbolic needs, wants. A formerly successful archer may find himself suddenly missing his shots, a "has-been." His image remains clear enough, but he no longer has a function. Censure of Joseph McCarthy by the United States Senate showed that the door had closed to his kind of role—or, to retain the previous metaphor, that the target had moved.

The moral of this for the practical politician who wishes to become a popular symbol is that he must try to improve his perception of popular moods and the dialectical processes that offer a glimpse of what the public is waiting for. He should be alert to audience reactions, a master of trial balloons, and a student of group dynamics. He might well have a staff of analyzers of the public mood. Fan mail would be only one

9. Dean received thousands of fan letters a week for long after his accidental death while driving a sports car at one hundred miles an hour. The type of the adolescent rebel-without-a-cause not only appealed in the United States but was diffused widely in Mexico as *rebelde sin causa*, coming to stand for "juvenile delinquent."

part of the feedback in which he would be interested. There are few public opinion analysts sufficiently gifted to divine these moods consistently, nor is there a method at hand that takes the place of the "hard way" of dialectical selection. But an aspiring popular symbol can certainly avoid the mistake of imagining that he can shove anything down the public's throat just because he has a staff of public relations men, or prefabricate an image according to his own ideas of what to "project" to the public. We do not yet have even a reliable vocabulary with which to describe the popular moods, tastes, and yearning for latent functions that are important in making popular symbols.[10]

I have not, then, given an answer to the riddle in terms of a formula that will sum up public demands of the next popular favorite. But I shall at least try to explain why it is a riddle and to outline some of the things that the public seems to want done by symbolic leaders.

The first reason for the enigma is, as has been said, shifting popular moods. We have no reliable, precise, prompt way of finding out the underlying popular temper at any given moment. Polling, it seems to me, is too matter-of-fact and does not get at nuances of feeling. The psychological "weather" changes from complacency to anxiety, optimism to gloom, austerity to self-indulgence, fun to "no nonsense," tolerance to scapegoating, without clear demarcation. Unique moods may appear, such as despair over the future of the human race as a result of the H-bomb or the unwillingness of American Negroes to tolerate further delay in receiving civil rights, to which we have no guidelines from past moods.[11]

10. The language of psychoanalysis is in terms of individual rather than group or mass psychology and, at least, will have to prove itself in competition with other vocabularies to be devised or discovered by social scientists. It appears to me that the language of social types is already at hand to elucidate what a leader means to his public.

11. While in one mood, one cannot tell how things will look in another. There is no simple rational translation, any more than a despondent person can be made cheerful by being told that "things aren't so bad."

At the time of the Lindbergh flight, for example, a rather subtle mood was said by some commentators to exist: the country was disgusted by the Harding scandals and was just waiting for a fine, clean young man who would turn down commercial offers while achieving an idealistic success. Norman Mailer tried to describe the mood with which many Americans greeted President John F. Kennedy in 1960:

> It was a hero America needed, a hero central to his time, a man whose personality might suggest contradictions and miseries which could reach into the alienated circuits of the underground, because only a hero can capture the secret imagination of a people, and be so good for the vitality of his nation.[12]

This is a rather vague statement, but who is in a position to make it more specific or to say that Mailer was wrong? Surely there is such a thing as a "season for heroes" (and perhaps for scapegoats) of a certain kind. We are in the indeterminate realm in which any analyst's guess is as legitimate as another's; the best indicator we have is the conjecture of sensitive people, expert in a field.[13] But the acid test is to be able to state the mood so precisely that one can deliver what the public wants better than anyone else can, today and tomorrow.

Of course, some needs are so plain and urgent that it is relatively easy to guess in general what is wanted—a martyr or delivering hero in time of war or someone to blame after a great crime or disaster. But this is picking cases in which the threshold is low and there is little selectivity; demands are generous, and dozens or hundreds of leaders may be acceptable. When there is a fire, no one much cares who puts it out.

12. Quoted by Alfred Kazin in *Contemporaries* (Boston: Little, Brown, 1962), p. 450, who held that Kennedy met the hope of educated Americans for an intellectual hero.
13. Thus *Time* tries to "take the temperature of the U.S. economy" by interviewing 200 key businessmen, economists, and public officials, compounding insight with numbers to conclude that a "new mood" has replaced the mood of the previous year.

A second major reason for the enigma is that emergent types have no prototypes from which we can judge the need.[14] We do not know in advance but only *ex post facto*. Who could have said that the leather-jacketed motorcyclist would suddenly become important in the early 1960's? Or the "glamor girl debutante" in 1937?[15] Who could have predicted that daughters of high society would then turn from their standard prototypes and create this fusion of debutante, model, and actress? The emergence of a type or a life style (and the favorite who embodies it) may be the flowering of a trend, perhaps its last stage. It may lead nowhere, or it may provoke a reaction that will change the direction to its opposite.

A third important reason for the riddle of popular favorites (and villains) is that the dramatic principles creating "good guys" and "bad guys"—of projecting such images by what happens—are not clearly understood either by public men (as actors) or by the audience. The logical good guy may become a villain or fool because he violates some basic dramatic principle, by acting too late, too soon, against the wrong party, or in the wrong company. An "inner-directed" actor is likely to make a fool of himself because he disregards the way he appears to audiences. Nations, being subject to group egocentrism,[16] often play a role to the world that they cannot see because they are wrapped up in their own points of view. Later chapters will explore some of these dramatic principles, which a public actor will ignore at his peril.

There is, fourth, an elusive thing called "color," which enables certain actors to catch public attention and steal the show from others who receive the same amount of publicity.

14. This is in contrast with such well-defined categories as the Christian saint, Hebrew prophet, Hindu holy man, Dalai Lama, or beauty-queen contest winner in the United States. When routes to such institutional statuses are set up, one usually can reliably predict more of the same.

15. Cleveland Amory, *op. cit.*, p. 173.

16. See Reinhold Niebuhr, *Moral Man and Immoral Society* (New York: Scribner, 1960).

Their greater piquancy as persons means that, although not necessarily offering the public better nourishment, they reach its taste buds more effectively. Certain actors, artists, athletes, writers, politicians, and so on—no better than others—become stars because of "color." But who has a recipe for this ingredient? Zany publicity stunts, "gimmicks" such as those tried in boxing and wrestling ("Gorgeous George," who wore long platinum hair and sprayed the ring with perfume before a wrestling match), may or may not succeed. Some well-known "characters," like Alexander King, have color almost to excess, but they cannot tell the secret. To call it an instinct for self-dramatization adds little to understanding. One characteristic of color, however, is that it invites imputations; it is the kind of thing that acts as a cue to imagination, speculation, gossip, and legend-building. It is not, in other words, merely acting curiously or interestingly; it is symbolism of a special kind.

These four elements (undefined popular moods, types without prototypes, disregarded dramatic principles, and color) are quite enough to make the emergence of popular favorites a mystery; nor am I implying that these are all. But let us turn to another area in which we need a good deal more information: the kinds of things that symbolic leaders *do* for audiences. It is possible to distinguish some of the most important of these functions without extensive psychological data.

KINDS OF SYMBOLIC LEADERS

How does the public use symbolic leaders? His psychological use distinguishes a symbolic leader from practical leaders who *do* things for groups by way of active command, management, contributions, works, and the like. The pure symbolic leader may "act" in a dramatic sense, but it is quite possible for him to be otherwise inert and passive.[17] He does not actually lead; the public uses him. Even in action he is a vehicle. Such a leader does not ride his following as though it were a horse; rather, the horse, it might be said, rides him.

1. The Hero

The most obvious way in which a person can be used in this manner is for him to act as a vehicle for identification and a model for imitation by audience and followings. What he "does" (his dramatic role) he gives to the audience as a vicarious experience. What he is or does he also gives to the group as a pattern for imitation. But many more people will identify with a hero than will imitate him overtly, so identification is the basic relationship with a hero. When people identify with a hero's role, they usually experience a thrilling sense of uplift, triumph, or achievement. If the hero plays a role that serves the group or its values, they also derive a sense of security and well-being. It is not necessary to describe all the types of heroes here: several hundred are distinguished in the American language.[18] We can, however, mention the following: the champion, defender, crusader, martyr, moralistic hero or moral leader (who provides a model of rectitude), splendid performer (who "shines" before audiences), fashion plate or style-setter, "smoothie" or "cool cat" (who always knows the right thing to do), great lover, and self-made man, among many others.

When people use a hero psychologically, his meaning is translated into such functions[19] for social organizations as the

17. As John M. Mecklin observed, the monastic saint was often for all practical purposes useless. (*The Passing of the Saint* [Chicago: University of Chicago Press, 1940].)

18. See the survey of American hero types in O. E. Klapp, *Heroes, Villains and Fools* (Englewood Cliffs, N.J.: Prentice-Hall, 1962), Chap. ii.

19. Of course, if the role with which people identify runs counter to mores or the needs of a particular organization, such as romantic desperadoes and other "corrupted heroes," then its effects can be dysfunctional. See *ibid.*, Chap. vi.

following: boosting morale, providing institutionalized role models, providing group self-images, dramatizing causes and thus crystallizing and mobilizing movements, and developing hero-cult followings.

2. The Incorruptible

If such figures do for people vicariously what they would like to do but cannot, then we may set apart another kind of hero who stands for what people ought to do but are not really trying to do. Let us call this the role of the "incorruptible." These symbolic figures bring satisfaction and comfort to people because they are really so different from what might be called the "working models." Take, for example, the special place of Mary Pickford among other movie stars of her time, or the purified, almost prudish, image of George Washington as it contrasts with the image of other political leaders (even Lincoln), or the special position of the late Senator Robert Taft among contemporary politicians. It seems plain that such favorites do not represent the dominant tendency of the masses or even of their own admirers. The same can be seen in certain conservative bankers, prized by the business community but not typical of the way business is carried on, or in ministers, school presidents, and the like, who stand as pillars of respectability and security within a community (including even their own institutions) to which the same descriptions do not apply.

Occasionally such a figure is elected to a major executive office (perhaps as a reform mayor), but, in general, people prefer that he not be in charge—not because he would be a figurehead but because he would be *too* active. The point is that his job is to represent a minority tendency; he helps direct and stabilize the ship but does not set its course. You can count on "Old Faithful" to behave in a certain way, but it does not for a moment follow that everybody is supposed to do what he does. Everybody is making money, but "Old

Faithful" reassures us that credit and honesty are being maintained. His job, then, is not to inspire everyone to be like him but to compensate for different roles.

There is nothing especially cynical or hypocritical about this; highly differentiated and changing societies must develop many kinds of roles that do not fit a common code of morality. People might become alarmed that "the world is going to pieces" were it not for the incorruptible, secure in his place, saying "No" to temptation, holding the line when others are crossing. It may well be that dynamic societies require an incorruptible to slow down the apparent pace and give people a sense of security. At any rate, it seems plain that modern societies like incorruptibles, even when they do not represent dominant trends (which are expressed by other heroes), and, where one is lacking, there is an opening for a symbolic leader to emerge. (This may be, as suggested, a key to the phenomenon of Lindbergh.) Such leaders do not usually move people to action, unless it be bursts of reaction and reform, but they do help stabilize what otherwise might well be the excessive dynamic of new heroes. They hold the line and maintain the center against centrifugal tendencies.

3. The Object of Desire

Let us now consider a kind of favorite who functions in a way different from either the dramatic hero or the compensatory incorruptible. This favorite gives the public directly what it wants but does so through his person rather than in a role that could be played by others. Many favorites are themselves desirable and satisfying. The audience wants to experience them as directly as possible—through sight, sound, touch, or imagination—as objects[20] that are to be contacted, possessed,

20. This distinction parallels the familiar one made by Sigmund Freud between a "cathectic object" and a person with whom one identifies—two different mechanisms for emotional ties of groups. (*Group Psychology and the Analysis of the Ego* [London: Hogarth Press, 1949, trans. James Strachey], pp. 48, 59–61, 64.)

and, if possible, literally consumed. This may apply to vo-
calists who tease the audience with a certain "sound," to
charmers, magnetic speakers, certain kinds of humorists, pin-
up girls, sex queens, love goddesses, romantic "pashes,"[21] and
the like. I realize that such favorites may also play a role
that is a vehicle for identification, but it is not necessary for
them to do so, and the analytical distinction is here important.
To use a crude example, you may like apple pie but you do
not have to identify with it. One may distinguish between Babe
Ruth, who was nothing in himself but had a very exciting role
to identify with, and Marilyn Monroe, who was very much
something in herself, regardless of the dramatic parts she
played.

Such favorites not only draw followings but easily become
commodities for which the public is willing to pay directly. Thus
one of their important social effects is to organize mass demand
into institutions like the theater and the movies, burlesque,
beauty contests, talent contests, and so on, as part of the "personality market." On the other hand, it is more difficult to create
this personal-object type of hero; it is more likely that he must
be "found," whereas almost any kind of person can be cast in
a role with which the public will enjoy identifying. (Thurber's
"The Greatest Man in the World" tells of a hero whose role was
exactly what society wanted but whose personality was so un-
acceptable that he was finally pushed out of a window.)

21. *Mademoiselle* magazine lists some of the great "pashes" (sheiks,
feminine heart-throbs) of the twentieth century: Rudolph Valentino,
John Barrymore, Clark Gable (who "made them feel that he had their
number and knew exactly what to do with it . . . So all-man that if he
hadn't existed, Hemingway would have invented him"), John Gilbert,
Cary Grant, Errol Flynn, Gary Cooper, Charles Boyer, Marlon Brando,
Frank Sinatra, Rock Hudson, Robert Taylor, James Dean, Ramon
Navarro, H. R. H. the Prince of Wales, Rudy Vallee, Wallace Reid,
Douglas Fairbanks, Sr., Ronald Coleman, Fred Astaire, Gene Tunney,
Gregory Peck, Charles Lindbergh, John Wayne, Marcello Mastroianni,
Peter O'Toole, Humphrey Bogart, Elvis Presley, and others (Leo Ler-
man, "The Pashes," June, 1963, pp. 86–89). I do not claim, of course,
that all these men equally well illustrate the type of male object who is
desirable in himself apart from dramatic role, but I am not inclined to
quarrel with *Mademoiselle's* general judgment.

4. Popular Villains

Many favorites are villains. They draw attention, not because people like them or identify with them, but because hating is at times enjoyable and people will turn out to see the bad guy lose as well as to see the good guy win. Westbrook Pegler and Walter Winchell were columnists with large followings who disliked them intensely and read them mostly to gnash their teeth. Clure Mosher, a popular Miami television sportscaster, was known as "Scrooge." He insulted nearly everyone he interviewed, disparaged players and even the sports themselves. Angry telephone calls after his show might last forty minutes, but people waited to hear what he would say next. His sponsor, General Tire and Rubber Company, though fearful that he would go too far, found that their sales in Mosher's area had almost tripled. He maintained continual feuds to keep up interest, though wit and practical jokes took some of the sting out of his nastiness. Actually, his proportion of malice to "nice things" was only 20 per cent, "that tiny 20% that arouses the masses."[22]

A similar drawing power was found in Sonny Liston, world heavyweight boxing champion, described by newsmen as "a prehistoric beast," a "brute without feeling." After his second knockout of Floyd Patterson, a record crowd in Nevada booed him "as no world champion has ever been booed." He remarked to a reporter as he climbed into his Thunderbird after the fight, "They came, and sold out, didn't they, the jerks."[23]

22. John Underwood, "In Miami Nearly Everybody Hates Clure Mosher," *Sports Illustrated,* July 15, 1963, pp. 54–64.

23. Hal Pawson, *Edmonton Journal,* July 23, 1963. Liston's personal deportment was partly to blame for this response. He was rude and bullying to such people as waitresses, porters, maids, and bootblacks. He openly scorned the NAACP. Members of his own race said things like this about him: "Sonny Liston is just too mean to be allowed around decent people. They ought to ship him back to Africa. No, make that Mississippi." "Liston has no feelings. He doesn't care about anyone or anything, just himself. I hope Patterson kills him." (Robert H. Boyle, "Sonny Slams Ahead," *Sports Illustrated,* July 29, 1963, pp. 12–13.)

Oddly, Liston's next match was with another fighter whose drawing power also consisted largely of people wishing to see him beaten, "The Lip," "Gasseous Cassius" Clay. The public dislike of Clay came, however, from his egocentric proclamation of himself as "The Greatest" and his confident predictions of the round in which he would knock out opponents, which meant that he cast himself more as an impudent clown than as an outright villain. "Please," said an old lady to one of his unsuccessful opponents, "Knock out this Clay fellow in the first round!"

Thus we have the paradox of popular unpopularity, or the favorite villain. The power of the villain to draw, to move people, to organize audiences and followings, is plain. One of his important leadership functions is to set the stage so that someone else can play the hero. His own part, of course, is to be a scapegoat for aggression while we identify with the one who (we hope) will bring him down. As Eric Hoffer said, the organizing power of hatred is at least as great as that of love. The only thing that may require explanation is the willingness of some people to take this role, when for most it is a misfortune. A public man such as J. P. Morgan usually becomes a villain not by seeking cues from the audiences but by ignoring them. Thus "poor little rich girl" Barbara Hutton asked plaintively, "Why do they hate me? There are other girls as rich, richer, almost as rich. Why do they especially dislike me?"[24]

5. The Comic Figure

We do not ordinarily think of a clown as a leader, but (as with the villain) we must revise this notion if we take account of the vast influence and popularity of some funny people. To say that Bob Hope or Charlie Chaplin were not leaders

24. In 1939, pickets ouside her hotel bore signs, "We live on $16.50 a week. Could you?" A man shouted. "You rich bitch. I'd like to throw acid in your face." (Amory, *op. cit.*, p. 170.)

would ignore their following and drawing power. To say that Will Rogers or Groucho Marx or Mort Sahl were not leaders would ignore the way their witticisms have shaped our thought. The clown himself seems least leader-like (who follows a fool?), but, if we consider that clowning has helped many leaders (from Huey Long to Abe Lincoln) rise to power, we must definitely regard it as a dimension of leadership.

The role of funny man is not always helpful to status, of course; it was not altogether an asset to Adlai Stevenson, and it would do no good whatever for a pope. But there are conditions under which the funny man's role gives influence and immunity to attack and criticism; the conditions under which it may cause loss of dignity and influence will be considered in a later chapter. Here it is sufficient to point out some of the main symbolic functions of funny men as leaders: (1) acting as butt or scapegoat (or initiator) of comic aggression; (2) stating daring insights under the immunity of the jester's role; (3) in both these capacities, serving comic justice, which is part of social justice; (4) giving audiences comic relief, vacation from serious aspects of life (obligation, routine, discipline); (5) giving audiences a feeling of unity and superiority to "the fool." Such psychic and social values help explain why funny men can be very popular and, through their popularity, powerful. And, even if we are not impressed by the leadership of fools and villains, we should be impressed by (6) their power to bestow power on heroes, for whom they "set things up."

Another function of clowning is sometimes (7) to draw sympathy and following to an underdog. Comedy can turn the tide for a loser, not by making him a winner but by turning his lemon into lemonade. In 1962, the New York Mets lost 120 out of 162 baseball games. They were unquestionably the poorest team in the National League, possibly in modern baseball history. They had a strange knack for making preposterous errors, for losing in spite of the best intentions and the most ardent efforts. But the more games they lost, the more people came to see them. By the end of the 1962 season and in the early part of 1963 they were drawing larger crowds than the New York Yankees, winners of the World Series. It was more fun to see the Mets lose than the Yankees win. Their first-baseman was accident-prone, "Marvelous Marv" Throneberry. After particularly bad errors, his fan letters mounted to one hunded per day. People wore T-shirts to the games marked with his name spelt backward, "VRAM." The Mets did not, at first, try to clown; they were serious, but everything they did came out like a Marx Brothers comedy. Apparently people were identifying with them as losers and were getting pleasure from their errors. The Mets seemed to symbolize humorously the troubles and failures of the ordinary man,[25] and this, I think, is the appeal of the "sad sack." The crowd can be with the one who never does anything right not only because they feel superior to him but also because they get relief from their own troubles by identifying with a clown who has worse. The emotional color of the "sad sack" is just one of the many hues in the spectrum of folly, and we may properly consider it one of the most important kinds of symbolic leadership.

6. The Popular Victim

The person who evokes sympathy and not much more is in some sense a symbolic leader, though he could not properly be called a hero and is surely not a fool. Not all unfortunate people draw popular sympathy, but when they do—usually by a dramatic role—they can arouse deep sentiment and focus attention for a considerable time. They may even persist in group memory (Mary Queen of Scots and Helen of Troy),

25. James Breslin, *Can't Anybody Here Play This Game?* (New York: Viking Press, 1963). Another conspicuous example of the drawing power of clowning for an athletic team is the Harlem Globetrotters basketball team; but here the clowning is only incidental to a phenomenal capacity to win, and in no sense could the Globetrotters be considered "sad sacks."

and even if they do not stir people into action to help them, they can act as symbolic leaders. A sad story, bullying or oppression, certain kinds of illness, a child's misfortune, even an animal in an unhappy predicament—these can engulf the public in a wave of sympathy and concern. However, the most practical effects of victims are to stir movements for aid and reform and to help develop welfare institutions.

I have presented six types of symbolic figures who can properly be said to be leaders, in the sense that they initiate feelings, orient multitudes, and are used psychologically so that audiences or followings can move to a state of mind, if not a course of action, that would not be possible without the leader's help. I do not claim that this typology is exhaustive or that important functions have not been overlooked,[26] but these types illustrate the targets of those who seek popular favor. To hit the bull's-eye as a dramatic hero, an incorruptible, a desire-object, a villain, a clown, or a victim,[27] is a sure route to certain important kinds of influence.

It is interesting to note that most of these classes of sym-

26. For example, nothing has been said of the tragic hero. See O. E. Klapp, "Tragedy and the American Climate of Opinion," *Centennial Review,* XI (1958), 396–413; reprinted in John D. Hurrell, *Two Modern American Tragedies* (New York: Scribner, 1961). See also, for comparison, Fritz Redl's typology of affective leader roles in "Group Emotions and Leadership," *Psychiatry,* IV (1942), 573–96.

27. Hugh D. Duncan treats under the general head of "victimage" various types that I am distinguishing here: martyr (hero), villain, comic butt, victim, and tragic character. "Victimage," says Duncan (following Kenneth Burke), "is the means by which we cleanse the group of tribal or 'inherited' guilt." (*Communication and Social Order* [New York: Bedminster Press, 1962], pp. 125–28.) While it is true that various of these types can be, and are, used as scapegoats by audiences for cathartic or cohesive functions, I think the distinctions among the various types of symbolic leaders should not be blurred. The tragic character is a very different symbol from victim, villain, martyr, and fool. Each has his own constellation of functions. "Victim," as I define it (a mere object of pity), has presumably little of the guilt-cleansing function Duncan attributes to "victimage"; at least, it remains to be proved that when a crowd is sorry for a dog or child in trouble it is "cleansing" itself of guilt. Nor can all the types of fool be equally considered under the head of "victimage"; this is especially the province of the comic butt.

bolic leaders work toward some kind of reassurance to audiences—the dramatic hero by triumph; the incorruptible by standing firm; the villain by being punished; the clown by saying (in effect), "I'm a jerk, you look good in comparison!"; the victim by saying, "It happened to me, not you." Such symbols, then, have an effect like that of white magic, and the psychic relief from anxiety that they give to individuals can easily be translated into the stability of institutions.

A symbolic leader can also function as a story, drama, film, song, or other representation and does not have to be present as a real person. There seems to be no direct relationship between the degree to which a symbolic leader is true or real and the degree to which he can move people psychologically. This paradox can be understood better by considering a range of symbolic leadership, from zero symbol to zero man.

LEVELS OF SYMBOLIC LEADERSHIP

We can distinguish three levels of leadership, ranging from the commonsense idea of practical doers who work within social structures to those whose influence is entirely symbolic and may not be "real" at all. Each level has different thresholds and laws of operation.

1. Practical Actions of Real Men in Social Structures

The first level of leadership is that of practical leaders who do things, or fail to do things, without achieving popular images (or at least for whom the popular image is not important in analyzing their influence). A football coach, corporation president, church minister, political boss, boys' gang-leader, prime minister—all these have definite roles to perform in social structures. They work through groups, and groups act with their help and under their command. It is true, in a sense, that they have "images," or their followers could not take account of them, but it is not necessary that they have special meaning as persons apart from their status in their organizations. Such a leader need not be a "personality," a "symbol," a "hero," a "legend," to do his job. This is the matter-of-fact realm in which a man of affairs usually operates. If a man "does" anything, it is because he has actually moved some group through a status relationship that can be specified, and, if he departs or dies, his work ceases. Such matter-of-fact analysis would not work, of course, in analyzing the influence of a saint or other true symbolic leader, but it is quite applicable to the job of an army colonel.[28]

It applies also to a producer of ideas—a writer, artist, or other intellectual; a producer of symbols need not himself be a symbolic leader. So long as a man communicates ideas or directives to society (even if he is creative rather than a mere transmitter) and so long as he works on society through what he produces (perhaps a scientific contribution or a musical composition) rather than what he means as a person, he is not a symbolic leader. The distinction can be made between the books of Thoreau and Thoreau as a symbol of a style of life, between the theory of relativity and Einstein as a symbol of genius. In other words, the symbolic products of a man should be classed along with other practical works; he is still only a "doer" until he starts to mean something other than the mere effects of his work itself, until *he,* as well as his work, lives on in society. The public man can remain at a practical level or pass on. Some public men mean far more as symbols than in terms of anything they have really done.

2. The Dramatic Actor

Our concern here is not with this practical level but only with the moment at which a person leaves it to enter the

28. The work of the English Crown can be analyzed into two components: its official acts, which I would call leadership at the practical level, and Queen Elizabeth's personal meaning (different from that of each of her predecessors), which I would call her role as a symbolic leader. See Percy Black, *The Mystique of Modern Monarchy* (London: Watts, 1953). The same is true of the American President.

dramatic domain. At this level he escapes from the limitations and laws of practical achievement in social structures. He need satisfy no bureaucratic or other job requirements to perform symbolically as a popular image. It may be, of course, that his practical job helps him to achieve symbolic status; but he might, on the other hand, get a very important role without having a definite place in a social structure. He may have been a drifter, a nobody, yet now he has a starring part.

The requirements he must satisfy at this level constitute the dramatic threshold, the most obvious aspect of which is that he must capture an audience, make a "hit" as a person or by a role especially meaningful to a great many people. Since this book is mainly concerned with the dramatic level, I shall do no more here than note that peculiar laws seem to govern it—peculiar, at least, from the matter-of-fact viewpoint. When an audience views a dramatic event, it does not do so matter-of-factly; it does not say, "Here are so many men exerting so many foot-pounds of energy in space-time." It views it with a special pathos, and a tear may be more meaningful than an ocean, a feather of feeling may weigh a hundred pounds. All the nice bookkeeping of physical forces and of social obligation and credit seems to be of little account in deciding who does or gets what. The important or worthy man in an organization may be passed over in favor of some outsider who "steals the show."[29] A person whose traits are not very satisfactory may serve very well as a popular hero (Pancho Villa, John Brown, Adolf Hitler, General Custer) for the time, perhaps for all time.

29. Stealing the show may be made easier by the failure of practical leadership. Richard H. McCleery has shown how the failure of formal and informal leadership in a prison was associated with a rise of heroes who "dramatically asserted the ideals of toughness and resistance" and encouraged rebellion among inmates. ("Policy Change in Prison Management," in Amitai Etzioni [ed.], *Complex Organizations* [New York: Holt, Rinehart and Winston, 1961], p. 397.) Such "transfer of influence from the leader to the hero" illustrates the distinction I am making between how the practical leader works within and by means of social structures and how the symbolic leader works outside them or when they collapse (perhaps to crystallize new structures).

In this peculiar realm, to lose, to die (perhaps as a martyr), is sometimes to win. The importance of anything is measured by its impact on an audience rather than by real outcomes or historical effects. Personal images tend to take the form of heroes, villains, fools, or other sharpened, perhaps exaggerated and sentimentalized, types that have a part in dramatic plots and can serve as vehicles for audiences. Actions (or at least their interpretations) tend to be exciting, vivid, colorful, and simple. A great moment, whether magnificent or despicable, is more important than the whole career or life of a man.

> The automobile at the head of the procession of saffron-robed Buddhist monks in Saigon suddenly choked to a stop at an intersection. The occupants of the car lifted its hood as chanting priests began forming a circle seven or eight deep around the vehicle. Prayer beads clutched in his hand, a phlegmatic, 73-year-old monk named Thieh Quang Duc sat down cross-legged on the asphalt in the center of the circle. From under the auto's hood, a monk took a canister of gasoline and poured it over the old priest. An expression of serenity on his wizened face, Quang Duc suddenly struck a match. As flames engulfed his body, he made not a single cry nor moved a muscle. "Oh my God," cried a Western observer, "Oh my God."[30]

Roles are "thrust upon" men rather than being simple results of character. There can be sudden reversals. The issue of the event, more than the input, determines it. The situation governs. What an audience sees in an event such as a bullfight cannot be determined by an outsider (a Kansas farmer or a member of the Humane Society) from what is physically there.

That laws *do* govern this peculiar realm is, of course, the thesis and problem of this book. One of the most obvious simplifications to be avoided is to say that publicity alone can create a symbolic leader. You can be on center stage in the

30. *Time,* June 21, 1963, p. 34.

full glare of the spotlight and have nothing to hold an audience. You can be in the chorus, among the extras, even on the floor in the audience, and by the mysterious osmosis of public communication people can become interested in you— if there is anything to be interested in. There are important symbolic leaders who received practically no publicity and yet became dramatized, almost, so it seemed, in spite of themselves;[31] on the other hand, a battery of PR men, even a Hollywood buildup, can be ineffective.

This book is a search for whatever it is beyond mere publicity that enables some men to become symbolic leaders. Certain men with a capacity for "natural drama" find it easy. Mayor Fiorello La Guardia of New York read the comics to children over the radio during a newspaper strike and had no difficulty making himself more interesting than others who were playing a more important and more practical part at the time. Winston Churchill's melodramatic outlook and instinct for taking risks and seeking confrontations likewise made him more interesting than other prime ministers, such as Clement Attlee. Churchill was, of course, genuinely a great man in the practical sense, but in addition he had what it takes to be a great symbolic leader. Rather than call this "personality," which is vague at best, let us call it "a talent for self-dramatization." A nose for conflicts and confrontations puts such men in the spotlight, and, once there, they have at least a chance to enter the dramatic domain and seize some of the better parts. There is also the enormous importance of a *beau geste,* which is not a great deed but a highly significant gesture that seems to contain everything the public wants, dramatically and meaningfully. It may come out of an action—Raleigh

31. One such case, which I analyzed in "The Hero as a Social Type," was St. Thérèse of Lisieux, an obscure nun with a passion for anonymity, who hid herself away in a convent. Quite suddenly, through the limited circulation of a routine biography at her death, she became a candidate for sainthood and one of the best known of modern saints. She reached the public not by promotion but by rumor, and despite her deliberate effort to avoid publicity for herself.

spreading the cloak, Babe Ruth announcing to a baseball audience, "I'll knock it out there for you!" and then doing it—or a memorable utterance, a joke or piece of repartee, or a perfectly timed deed. In trying to assess its historic importance, a *beau geste* (whether real or legendary[32]) is worth a thousand men and a million bullets. A "great man" is made by such things as well as by his real achievements.

3. The Durable Symbol

But dramas are transitory. The limelight fades, the spotlight shifts to new actors who challenge the place and memory of the old. However vividly an actor has penetrated popular consciousness, however widely his fame has spread, he may be a hero (or other symbol) only for a day unless he can keep repeating his "hits" or unless his image has developed staying power.

This step is illustrated by the career of Harry S. Truman, who did not attain his full stature as a public image until well after he was elected President in 1948. He came finally to be affectionately regarded as "Harry," a kind of public character, an outspoken champion of the plain man, expressing opinions freely on any subject and willing to tell anybody off. He retained this status as a private citizen; it might be said that he had found a niche. Years after his retirement from the Presidency, a newspaper described him as follows:

> Mr. Truman still wanders the land, as he has ever since leaving the White House, dividing the people into big bad guys and good little guys, and holding at bay the enemy from which only he can protect the "little" people.[33]

This special and durable status distinguished Truman from

32. For example, the quotation attributed to Secretary Stanton at the death of Lincoln ("Now he belongs to the ages") was apparently not said by Stanton at all); and note Whittier's inaccuracy about Barbara Frietchie (apparently General "Stonewall" Jackson's army did not pass down her street).

33. *San Diego Union,* September 15, 1962.

many contemporaries of equal fame at the time. Once attained, it did not have to be proved continually; everyone knew what to expect from "Harry."

Will Rogers also had a special niche—that of "unofficial ambassador" and "court jester" of the United States for many years. It is interesting to speculate whether Truman has to some degree stepped into this rather different niche.[34]

Finding such a niche means that an image has been consolidated and that a symbolic leader has hit upon a permanent function. He has, in other words, become institutionalized. Once he reaches this status, he may be referred to as an "immortal," the "one and only," the "grand old man," or perhaps a classic villain.[35] It is felt (true or not) that no one can replace such a leader. Bing Crosby, "The Old Groaner," goes on singing in his sixties; John Barrymore and Clark Gable played great-lover roles in middle age; Mae West in her fifties was still a symbol of sex. Babe Ruth acquired this kind of status, which explains the tremors that were felt when two players, Roger Maris and Mickey Mantle, almost broke his home-run record in the same year. But the fears were groundless; even if they had broken the record (in terms of number of games played), Ruth would still be the home-run hero of all time. The same applies to Jack Dempsey, still "The Champ" though defeated twice by Gene Tunney. Albert Schweitzer has become to the world a symbol of service to man and reverence for life. Crowds come by airplane to visit the "great white doctor" in his jungle hospital. *Time* magazine complains that he is an anachronism because he has not changed and "a continent and a century have passed him by."[36] But why should he change? Is he not exactly what the public wants? Let new symbols express the emerging needs of Africa. The point is

34. See my case study of Rogers in "The Clever Hero," *Journal of American Folklore*, 1949.
35. After almost two hundred years, Benedict Arnold is still the Great American Traitor.
36. June 21, 1963, p. 37.

that a symbolic leader who has found his niche is not in competition any longer. The public is satisfied with him the way he is. Even in retirement (like the race horse, Man-o-War) he keeps his status.

A "war of succession," such as develops among movie stars when a "great lover" or "love queen" dies, means that the niche is an abstract type—one might say an informal office —that must again be filled by a living personality. The holder of office had not created a unique personal niche but had only occupied one established by a predecessor. Even for the first in a particular niche, there is a question whether *his* image will live on or a successor will inherit his place. But if a favorite has fully established an image of his own, successors displace but do not replace him; he is still remembered as an "immortal," the "one and only."

Death forces the question whether there is anything in an image that can persist and function after the living man has ceased to perform his role. Does the image have viability as an image? Has it separated from the personality? If the image is still attached to the man—if it still depends on his personal appearance or performance—then it must, of course, perish with the man. This is the death knell for many aging film lovers, athletes, singers, and speechmakers, about whom no one can remember anything except that they were "great." But if the image has separated from the man and lives a life of its own, then it may get on very well without him. His death or non-performance is not a crisis. Indeed, the person ceases to be an embarrassment to the image; he is not around to contradict it; it is liberated and can develop in the way the public wants (biographers permitting). A death in the form of martyrdom is not only no end to the image but gives it impetus by a final gesture. But if the crown of martyrdom is added, it should be remembered that this is a very abstract role, and the same question of the persistence of a personal image remains: Will he be remembered as a known person who died in an especially memorable way, or only as an unknown soldier?

Separation of the image from the man, its viability in its own right, means that a third threshold has been passed. The first was achieving a "hit" as a dramatic actor (with the possible subsequent perfection of style by feedback from audiences). The second was finding a niche as a living "immortal." The third is conversion of a dramatic (personally enacted) role into pure symbol.

This means generally that taking the place of the person and acting for him is (1) a likeness that can be duplicated (for example, a statue), (2) a story that can be told and retold (or sung or printed), or (3) a drama that can be re-enacted (danced, ritualized, filmed, historically commemorated, etc.). At this stage, the stuff of the hero, the infamy of the villain, color, and good story ingredients, all have been abstracted from real life. Art may represent the leader as greater than life-sized. This kind of selection goes on in rumor and the growth of legend and, to some extent, in biographies, as writers look for those details that will make their subject interesting and omit the prosaic about him. As examples of conversion from personal drama to pure symbol, we may cite figures like Columbus, Paul Revere, or Robin Hood. Whatever they were to audiences of their time, they are now stories of a particular kind. Nothing much is left in them to help or embarrass the symbol. In this step to pure symbol a kind of funneling has occurred, in which anything that was needed to make a good story or a perfect hero, villain, or fool has been abstracted from all the information available to society (news, rumor, art, conjecture, etc.) and translated into social function. Was the person tall, short, ugly, fat, humorous, mean, good-natured? Let us forget anything that is not necessary to the story and make him into a little more of what we want.

In this third stage, society plainly must do most of the work. It is no longer a matter of what the leader does but of what the people do. Not only are there all those things that go under the heading of *legend-building*—such as anecdotage and imaginary imputations—but some machinery must be created for perpetuation of the symbol. The commonest is ritual drama, which may involve the commemoration of historic events (Washington crossing the Delaware, Moses leading the Exodus, the Mormons reliving their trek to Utah under the leadership of Brigham Young, the annual re-enactment of Jesse James's holdup of the bank at Northfield, Minnesota). Much of theater, in the broad sense, is really ritual drama— for example, passion plays, morality plays, soap operas,[37] horse operas,[38] crime and mystery movies, slapstick comedy, and tragedy[39]—which repeats standardized roles (whether or not originally enacted by real persons). Similar consequences ensue from the institutionalization of certain actors in favorite parts, such as Lionel Barrymore's annual radio performance of Scrooge or revivals of Chaplin, Garbo, and Valentino films.

Besides drama itself, another kind of institution for supplying symbolic persons might be called the "personality market" (to use C. W. Mills's expression) or, better, the "type market." After the need for certain social types becomes recognized (possibly because a symbolic leader has established it), people organize economically to supply them as the occasion demands or to make it possible for imitations to appear. To cite obvious examples, Christmas produces innumerable Santa Clauses, appropriately costumed, and clowns and clown costumes are always available for a public event. When the beatnik type became fashionable, New York theatrical agents

37. See Herta Herzog, "What Do We Really Know about Daytime Serial Listeners," in Paul Lazarsfeld and Frank Stanton (eds.), *Radio Research 1942–1943* (New York: Duell, Sloan and Pearce, 1944), and W. L. Warner and W. E. Henry, "The Radio Day Time Serial: A symbolic Analysis," *Genetic Psychology Monographs,* XXXVII, 3–71.

38. See Peter Homans, "Puritanism Revisited: An Analysis of the Contemporary Screen-Image Western," *Studies in Public Communication* (University of Chicago), No. 3, Summer, 1961, pp. 73–84.

39. O. E. Klapp, "Tragedy and the American Climate of Opinion," *op. cit.*

recruited "professional beatniks" for hostesses to hire for their parties. "Cowboys," with silver-studded chaps and saddles, shooting from the hip, can be produced in any community in the western United States. In Canada and the United States a "professional pioneer" has developed, an actor skilled at imitating Old West characters like Wild Bill Hickok or Yukon celebrities like Dangerous Dan McGrew, for community festivals such as Cheyenne's Frontier Day, the Calgary Stampede, and Edmonton's Klondike Day. The entire entertainment industry might be looked on as a vast type market, ready to supply anything the public demands. We may class with entertainment those industries which equip people to portray current social types. For example, we find suppliers of western-style clothing (including gun and leather-goods manufacturers), of aqualungs, bathing-suits, sun-tan ointment, water skis, and motorboats; ski-equipment makers; and the guitar industry, providing props for countless imitators of Elvis Presley and various folksingers. The list continues to grow because merchandisers are quick to organize for the profit in helping to supply any fashionable type.

There is yet a fourth threshold that can be analytically distinguished in the process of becoming a pure symbol. When a new generation confronts an image created by their parents, will they, too, accept it and find it useful? Or will they feel it necessary to create new types? Let us call this the "intergenerational threshold." In some cases, a favorite entertainer who has aged with the older generation is also popular with the new generation. This was the case of Eddie Peabody, the "Banjo King," who, having delighted a generation in the 1930's, was lucky enough to hit a banjo fad in the early 1960's, which made him once again a favorite with a new crop of young people, still cutting the same apparently youthful figure.[40] Again, the story of Babe Ruth is apparently still

40. Not so, apparently, for Rudy Vallee, whose audiences consisted then mostly of middle-aged people who could still remember the original rendition of "The Stein Song."

meaningful to boys who have never seen him. Once this in-tergenerational barrier has been passed, very possibly because a pure symbol (story, drama) has been perfected, there seems to be no necessary limit to the life of the symbol. We are in the realm of legend and myth, ranging from the river of literature and anecdote about historical figures, such as Lincoln, Parnell, Napoleon, Caesar, St. Patrick, or Robin Hood, to abstract symbols like Buddha and Krishna.[41] Even minor stories, like those of Barbara Frietchie, Betsy Ross, or King Alfred and his cakes, seem to have all the earmarks of per-fected symbols that can last for centuries, pleasing each gen-eration anew. Nor is there any strict limit on how much society can transform a symbolic figure in accordance with its needs. Stories like that of Buddha have undergone many changes that scholars find difficult to document. But, at such a point, the historical reality of the man may become a rather academic question. If we have the symbol, why do we need the man?

To sharpen the concept, we might say that a pure symbolic leader would lack everything not essential to his function. He would do nothing in practical terms, contribute nothing in the way of ideas or intellectual products to society, act alone and outside of social structures, not communicate directly with or

41. See the literature on legends as symbols and the processes building them, such as: Friedrich Gundolf, *The Mantle of Caesar*, trans. J. W. Hartmann (New York: Vanguard Press, 1928); Roy P. Basler, *The Lincoln Legend* (Boston: Houghton Mifflin, 1935); Arnold van Gennep, *La Formation des légendes* (Paris: E. Flamarion, 1910); S. G. Fisher, *Legendary and Myth-making Processes in Histories of the American Revolution* (Philadelphia: S. G. Fisher, 1912); A. L. Guér-ard, *Reflections on the Napoleonic Legend* (New York: Scribner, 1924); George Willison, *Saints and Strangers* (New York: Reynal, 1945); H. G. Creel, *Confucius: The Man and the Myth* (New York: Day, 1949); John T. Flynn, *The Roosevelt Myth* (New York: Devin-Adair, 1948); Hamilton Basso, "The Roosevelt Legend," *Life,* Novem-ber 3, 1947, pp. 126 ff.; Keith Sward, *The Legend of Henry Ford* (New York: Rinehart, 1948); W. E. Woodward, *George Washington: The Image and the Man* (New York: Penguin Books, 1946); Richard J. Walsh and Milton S. Salisbury, *The Making of Buffalo Bill* (Indianapo-lis: Bobbs-Merrill, 1928); Bernard Mayo, *Myths and Men* (Athens, Ga.: University of Georgia Press, 1960).

try to appeal to any group, be outside the stream of historical causation as an "event-making" man,[42] be a perfected dramatic figure (e.g., a hero, villain, or fool); he might not even exist, except as story, drama, or myth, and he would function solely as a collective idea.[43]

I have been sketching a process that, if completed, would remove a man from the action of everyday life not only to a firm position in history but as a timeless and placeless myth. This, as I see it, is the true role and path of the symbolic leader who goes the whole course. A man in public life often has a choice whether to follow the path of the practical doer (who may fail to become an acceptable symbol though his material achievements are important) or to act as a role-player with maximum impact as image on his society. Sometimes a man is fortunate enough to do both, but he will find that a dramatic sense of symbolical requirements is a very different thing from practical requirements. This book, of course, is concerned with the dramatic role.

Several stages along this route have been distinguished. They are:

1. Making a personal-dramatic "hit," which creates demand for a function and may lead to dialectical perfection of style of performance
2. Becoming a durable symbol
   a) Getting a niche as a living "immortal"
   b) Separating the image from the person so that it becomes viable on its own
   c) Converting the role actually performed into pure symbol (likeness, story, drama)
   d) Institutionalization by ritual drama and/or the type market

42. Defined by Sidney Hook as one who, by his actions or decisions, really makes a difference in historical outcomes. *The Hero In History* (New York: John Day, 1943).

43. Or "collective representation," in the terminology of Émile Durkheim, which means that social organizations would be built around him and his image would be vested with authority.

e) Passing the intergenerational threshold to become a
potentially deathless symbol or myth

I do not say that these must be passed in this order, but if
a man passes all these thresholds, we are justified in making
at least the following assumptions: (1) he has hit the bull's-
eye of audience function at the beginning; (2) the needs he
has served were permanent; (3) people have helped perfect
him as a symbol or legend; (4) a ritual institution for perpetuating and duplicating his image has been built; and (5) he
has not violated his image at early personal-dramatic stages (a
matter that will be dealt with in a later chapter).

The concern of this book, however, is not with all stages
of symbolic leadership but with the crucial early thresholds.
When a man is still alive, what he is or does matters greatly
in making or breaking his image, and dramatic factors are
most important. The next chapter will deal with dramatic encounters.

CHAPTER THREE

DRAMATIC ENCOUNTERS

Some are born great, some achieve greatness, and some have greatness thrust
upon 'em.

SHAKESPEARE

Public men are understandably wary of dramatic encounters—televised debates, pointed questions, and personal challenges. In one city, twelve mayoralty primary candidates were
invited to the same banquet to explain their positions. Of
those who came, we can imagine that some had mixed feelings
and poor digestions, for they knew they would not only get
publicity but be put "on the spot"; they knew, also, that such
a free-for-all was potentially very dangerous; but they came.
A public man has to pretend to like confrontations, or at least
he must not seem reluctant to face them. Yet the question is
fair: Why should a program or a reputation, perhaps the
work of years, be casually jeopardized merely to satisfy some
person or group? There is always more risk for a "big" man
than for a small one in challenging encounters; the former has
much to lose, while the latter may have everything to gain.
The trouble with a dramatic confrontation is that, unlike a
mere "appearance" or "presentation,"[1] one puts himself and

1. Compare Jacqueline Kennedy's famous televised tour of the
White House, which, though a smash hit, was not a confrontation but
a solo performance and therefore comparatively safe. Had she under-

his prestige into the scales for a contest or comparison with somebody else, and in so doing may confer the gift of prestige on his opponent and meanwhile subject himself to a role crisis.

A political candidate is aware of this vast difference between a speech or a TV appearance and a confrontation. People with unstable personalities may expose themselves recklessly, so their careers are a tapestry of scandalous and ludicrous, albeit interesting, incidents;[2] politicians are more likely to try to try to avoid dangerous encounters and to accept only those that are favorable, meanwhile maintaining the pose that they would meet anyone anywhere. Their wariness comes from their recognition of the risks in the dramatic domain; they know that peculiar laws operate in it and that great role changes can come from minor incidents. Perhaps this throws light on criticisms that were made of President John F. Kennedy for failing to take a stand on certain issues,[3] although he came forth in some notable confrontations. How are these facts to be reconciled? Is the truth that he did not really avoid confrontations (his temperament, as shown by *Profiles in Courage,* being to seek them) but, rather, picked his issues? Was he trying to throw the weight of his

---

taken a discussion or an argument with another lady about the history, art, and style of the White House, she might have glorified her partner and also subjected herself to a confrontation that could have meant "win or lose" for both.

2. See Myrick Land, *The Fine Art of Literary Mayhem* (New York: Holt, Rinehart and Winston, 1963).

3. Walter Lippmann said: "One of his . . . weaknesses as a public leader is that he does not want to be unpopular anywhere—with anyone, and I think that a public leader, at times . . . has to get into struggles where somebody gets a bloody nose." James Reston, of the *New York Times,* criticized his coolness on the racial question: "He is a tactician but not a teacher. He plays touch government. He seems to touch everything and tackle nothing" (June 10, 1963). The *New Republic* said: "Kennedy is a cool, hard intellectual type who doesn't care to display passions in public. He got where he is by . . . manipulating the levers of power and . . . instinctively works . . . for deals and bargains" (June 15, 1963).

person and office into an issue only when the circumstances were right? "There is no sense in raising hell, and then not being successful."[4]

What are these circumstances? This chapter will analyze some of the things that any good tactical politician may be considering: the peculiar laws of the dramatic domain, some types of dramatic encounters, and the principles that seem to govern their outcome.

PECULIAR LAWS OF THE DRAMATIC DOMAIN

One of the peculiarities of the dramatic domain is that a public drama cannot be confined to the billed performers; almost anyone can steal the show. Nor does it require remarkable abilities or achievements. Even a lunatic threatening a crowd or a desperate man about to jump off a roof is, for the moment, the star (if not the hero)of the show. Someone who is merely antic or colorful can take the spotlight away from a dull man, however important the latter may be. Entertainers are alert to such possibilities[5] and often object to being billed with animals or children or people who are funnier than they. Subtle theatrical techniques can be used to command attention,[6] and a public man, if he does not use them, should at least be sure that they are not used against him. The gist of this is that the star can be forgotten by a shift of at-

4. Quoting President Kennedy, *ibid.* When Kennedy visited Arkansas to dedicate a dam in the "New South," he heard his civil rights proposals branded as "civil wrongs" by Governor Orval E. Faubus, speaking in the same ceremony. The President, noted the *New York Times,* "chose not to respond to the attack" (October 4, 1963).

5. In the movie, "The Road to Hong Kong," starring Bob Hope and Bing Crosby, Peter Sellers had a small part as a doctor in a delightful five-minute scene. During the shooting, Hope wisecracked, "Get rid of this man. He's too funny." (*McCall's,* August, 1963, p. 42.)

6. Richard Burton found early in his career that by standing absolutely still on stage he could draw attention to himself and away from other actors.

tention. How can a public man protect himself from losing attention just when he needs it most? Will expensive TV time and full press coverage guarantee that the audience will not be watching something else?

Another peculiarity of the dramatic realm is that an insignificant person can easily challenge and jeopardize a more important person. The considerateness with which a public speaker answers a person in the audience—or, on the other hand, the sharpness with which an apparently innocent questioner is "put down"—is likely to result not from the innate courtesy or discourtesy of the speaker but from his awareness of threat and his defensiveness. Every teacher knows that a small person can challenge an important person in a way that has a curious advantage for the smaller. The "upstart" or "smart alec" has no prestige to lose, and any score he can make on the "big shot" benefits him tremendously. On the other hand, the most the bigger man can do is "put down" the upstart and return things to the status quo; he gets little credit for his victory. While the big man may have experience, power, and self-confidence on his side, he has to put into the wager more than it is worth to him. Politicians, knowing this, avoid confrontations that can do them no good and only benefit their rivals. Franklin Delano Roosevelt, as is well known, refused even to mention some rivals and critics by name. Why should he allow them to benefit from an acknowledged relationship with him? To take notice of them would, at the very least, recognize their importance and dignify them.

This danger to the big man and advantage to the underdog is sometimes attributed to democratic ideology, or to the fact that the common man finds it easier to identify with someone at his own level than with someone above. But even people of high status and aristocratic bias can identify with underdogs. More fundamentally, then, a dramatic prejudice in favor of upsets seem to be a built-in feature of drama itself.

A third peculiarity of the dramatic realm is that there

are no strict logical limitations on what can become important to audiences; almost any kind of contest, struggle, predicament, or contretemps can be meaningful, even a frog race.
It would be a mistake to suppose that incidents have to be
significant in a moral, intellectual, or material sense to hold
the attention of the public. The only requirement is that a
person (or animal) in whom the public is capable of being
interested engage in an action that has conflict, suspense, and
other features of "human interest."[7] This means that trivial
events—a movie scandal, a personal feud—can be blown up
out of proportion to their true merit, can become *causes
célèbres,* that mere gestures (Thoreau refusing to pay a one-
dollar tax, Sewell Avery being carried out bodily from the
Montgomery Ward plant, Khrushchev banging his shoe) can
be as important as real deeds. Pygmies then become giants.
Dramatic encounters double the magnitude of any event;
people who have no tangible stake in what is happening become aroused and inflamed by the fate of a hero, villain, or
victim; things that would ordinarily have been insignificant
suddenly become terribly important. On the other hand, bureaucracy suffers from want of drama (unless it, too, becomes
a fool or villain.) However important it may be intrinsically,
it usually seems uninteresting or comic; therefore it cannot
get a fair hearing in the court of public opinion. Because of
such disproportions, we may say that the scale of public
events is topsy-turvy.

The very essence of drama—the high point of its most
important scenes—is usually a confrontation in which parties
are thrown on their mettle, reveal and expose themselves, drop
their defenses, call on their personal resources to meet a crisis.
Spontaneity is maximized. On stage, a script takes care of
this, but in real life spontaneity means unexpected behavior
and consequences; no one knows quite what will happen; mis-

7. See Helen M. Hughes, *News and the Human Interest Story* (Chicago: University of Chicago Press, 1940).

takes, contretemps, or foolish roles are likely. A demagogue tries to create encounters that he can handle and his opponent cannot; witness Khrushchev, clowning, blustering, browbeating, probing into his enemy's defenses looking for a soft spot.[8] Huey Long was uncomfortable to deal with for this reason; a reporter caught this scene with Calvin Coolidge:

> "What part of Louisiana are you from, Governor?" inquired Mr. Coolidge.
>
> "I'm a hill-billy like yourself."
>
> "The hills are a good place to come from," Mr. Coolidge responded.
>
> "Are the Hoovers good housekeepers?" demanded Huey.
>
> "I guess they are," answered Silent Cal cautiously.
>
> "Well, when I was elected I found the governor's mansion in such rotten shape I had to tear it down . . . When I'm elected President I don't want to have to rebuild the White House."[9]

It was hard to hold a "safe" conversation with Huey in public, for he was always ad libbing for the crowd; he was, to use an expressive phrase, always "on the make."

Another potent risk-producing factor of drama is the close-up—not merely of audience with actor (made embarrassingly intimate by modern photography and high-fidelity equipment) but between the parties in personal encounter. Two giants can exist in separate fables, but bring them together and one is likely to appear smaller than the other. It is so for public men; their scale is changed by mere juxta-

8. Premier Nikita Khrushchev of Russia has been called "the man of many faces." Whether making a toast at a banquet or joking with factory workers, he usually shows a nice consistency with the Soviet propaganda line of the moment. He is said to be a natural actor who can assume with zest the role suited to the occasion: the homespun, tipsy *muzhik*, the hard-headed businessman, the tough guy, the genial buffoon, the outraged puritan. He tries to force opponents into situations in which they look bad. (Eugene Lyons, "The Many Faces of Nikita Khrushchev," *Reader's Digest*, August, 1959, pp. 49–54.)

9. Webster Smith, *The Kingfish* (New York: Putnam, 1933), pp. 216–17.

position. Actors know this well and choose partners and positions on stage accordingly. If two persons stand chest-to-chest or eye-to-eye with each other, it is likely that one of them will suffer; whereas, if they perform at separate times and places, only experts can rate the differences and a "match race" to settle things is avoided. So public men should take care about whom they are matched with, billed with, or even stand next to.

Yet another hazard is the enormous importance of timing, of the right role at the right time. One can "play the hero" a moment too soon or too late and be the biggest kind of fool. The successful hero steps into a situation at exactly the moment when audience expectation and the plot call for such a part; things have gotten as bad as possible for the victim, and the crisis has been properly developed; suspense and interest are at a maximum, so no one is tired of the situation; and the balance has become so precarious that it can easily be tipped in his favor. If a man manages to do these things, it is hard to imagine how he can fail to become socially significant. On the other hand, many good deeds and worthy enterprises have failed because the time was not ripe or the ratio of forces was unfavorable. Both tragedy and comedy hinge on precarious considerations like these.

In addition, the pressure of the audience favors certain parts and outcomes. If conflict arises, people need to define a "good guy" and a "bad guy"; they will look for cues or merely cast these parts arbitrarily (as we often do at sporting contests). An audience also usually favors underdogs and victims and is very quick to find a fool, to laugh at anything funny. The man who steps into a situation, may find a part handed to him—he may unexpectedly find himself on stage, as a performer or as the subject of a joke he had not anticipated. Such pressures may seem "unfair," but it is hard to keep the proceedings sensible and objective when the atmosphere becomes dramatic.

The more general observation follows, then, that in drama

outcome does not equal input. One man alone, however sincere and even if he is physically successful in what he sets out to do, cannot guarantee what his act will mean or what roles will be assigned to him and others as a result of his action. The factors that determine these consequences are outside the scope of any individual actor and do not bear a precise relationship to the physical forces mobilized or the real nature of the elements employed. A very large army, for example, could seem small and belittled in spite of its power or a noble deed could emerge as villainy. There is a capricious power in drama that might almost be called magical, for it produces astounding results from apparently insufficient means and causes changes in character like a chameleon.

We see this capriciousness in examples of "quixotic" characters, whose historical roles have unexpected outcomes. I refer here to a man of independent will and idealistic purpose who goes to an extreme that society defines as villainous or foolish, though he is in his own eyes a crusader doing good. His determined adherence to principle throws him out of joint with his times and leads him to the extreme necessary to produce a villain or fool. Certain men, we know, whether from idealism or hot-headedness, are likely to go to excess in fighting for what they believe. They will stand against public opinion even when there seems to be no hope,[10] they become diehards and fanatics, and they are ready to act on their own view regardless of what others think. Harry S. Truman's statement suggests that he could easily play such a role: "I shall continue to do what I think is right whether anybody likes it or not."[11]

The important thing, however, is that though quixotic characters are ready to act as heroes, they cannot determine the

10. John F. Kennedy's *Profiles in Courage* (New York: Harper, 1956) deals with cases like this.

11. H. S. Truman, *Mr. President* (New York: Farrar, Strauss and Young, 1952), p. 288.

role that history will thrust upon them. For one thing, they are either blind or indifferent to others' definitions; they see the drama only in their own terms. When their good intentions carry them to extremes that others will not follow, they cannot understand why the world becomes angry or ridicules them. When such men are "lucky," like John Brown and General Custer, they are approved by history with a sort of grudging recognition of their admirable stubbornness. But when they are unlucky, their very persistence and idealism provide some of the worst desperadoes and most laughable fools, such as John Wilkes Booth, who has often been compared with Brutus,[12] except that his drama had a different outcome.

The comic extreme of such behavior is seen in the "Peace Ship" of Henry Ford, who personally took a boatload of pacifists to Germany to talk the Kaiser out of World War I— one of the most astoundingly quixotic roles ever undertaken by an otherwise level-headed businessman.[13] This made Ford the laughing-stock of the nation, indeed, of the world. Woodrow Wilson also suffered ridicule for his quixotic mission[14] to

12. "Many, I know—the vulgar herd—will blame me for what I am about to do, but posterity, I am sure, will justify me." (John Wilkes Booth, quoted in Izola Forrester, *This One Mad Act* [Boston: Hale, Cushman and Flint, 1937], p. 228; Francis Wilson, *John Wilkes Booth* [Boston: Houghton Mifflin, 1929], pp. 114, 116, 139, 183, 192, 193n.; Philip Van Doren Stern, *The Man Who Killed Lincoln* [New York: Literary Guild of America, 1939], pp. 70, 99, 135, 382–83.)

13. "I don't care what the critics say, I have believed other things were possible, and they were." (Henry Ford, quoted in Gareth Garret, *The Wild Wheel* [New York: Pantheon, 1952], p. 145; see also Keith Sward, *The Legend of Henry Ford* [New York: Rinehart, 1948], pp. 88–89, 93; and Dixon Wecter, *The Hero in America* [New York: Scribner, 1941], p. 420.)

14. One account describes Wilson's landing at Brest in 1918 in these terms: "Down the gangplank walked this Yankee knight errant followed by a desperate crew of college professors in horn-rimmed glasses, carrying textbooks, encyclopedias, maps, charts, graphs, statistics, and all sorts of literary crowbars with which to pry up the boundaries of Europe and move them around in the interest of justice, as seen through the Fourteen Points. Of course, these invaders were trying to implant an ideal. At the bottom of the ideal was an attempt to institutionalize the Golden Rule—a big job." (William Allen White, *Woodrow Wilson: The Man, His Times, and His Task* [Boston: Houghton Mifflin, 1924], p. 377.)

Versailles for a League of Nations to be set up on his own idealistic terms. The French regarded him as a man of *candeur noble* (an idiom meaning stupid simplicity), and not only Europeans but the American Senate rejected him, which led to his tragic death. Albert Schweitzer, in contrast, was another determined idealist, who started with just as apparently foolish and impractical a scheme as Ford or Wilson[15] but emerged as a saint in world opinion. We may finally cite still another dedicated man, Cotton Mather, to whom history has given the back of its hand by stereotyping him as a villain, the witch-hunter par excellence, though he was a pious man who "lashed himself continually with guilt and zeal in the Lord's work."[16] In Mather's case, it was the following generations rather than his contemporaries who cast him as a villain; the social climate changed to one unfavorable to a witch-hunter as a hero.

The widely varying social definitions of such men show, I think, that heroes, villains, and fools can be created of substantially similar personal materials. It would not take too much imagination to see a man like Custer or Brown in Booth's shoes—or any of them in Brutus'—or Cotton Mather in Schweitzer's position. In another situation, Wilson and Ford might have been smashing successes with the same kinds of deeds (even though practical failures, they might have been seen as gallant fighters for a good cause—as, indeed, Wilson has come to seem). The point, in any case, is that the historic roles of hero, villain, and fool could not be predicted from such men's characters, intentions, or behavior, but only by knowing

15. "My relatives and my friends all joined in expostulating me on the folly of my enterprise. I was a man, they said, who was burying the talent entrusted to him and wanted to trade with false currency. Work among savages I ought to leave to those who would not thereby be compelled to leave gifts and acquirements in art and science unused." (Albert Schweitzer, *Out of My Life and Thought* [New York: Holt, 1933; Mentor ed., 1953], pp. 73, 77.)

16. Barrett Wendell, *Cotton Mather, the Puritan Priest* (Cambridge: Harvard University Press, 1926), p. 2; see also Kenneth Murdock, *Increase Mather* (Cambridge: Harvard University Press, 1924), pp. 287, 312–13; and *Columbia Encyclopedia* (New York: Columbia University Press, 1950, 2d ed.), p. 1241.

the particular dramatic and social situations in which they chose to act. The wide variation in dramatic results shows that, at least as far as character and motivation are concerned, outcome does not equal input in the making of heroes, villains, and fools. All we need conclude from this argument is that difference in definitions is far out of proportion to actual differences in men, that even the line of action is no key to what they will become. A little change in circumstances might allow us to see the same men and deeds in opposite parts—Custer as a villain, Ford as a hero of peace, Schweitzer as a fool, perhaps even Booth as a daring hero of self-sacrifice.

The real question of dramatic outcome involves factors having little to do with personal input, with what a man is or intends to be. The pertinent questions are these: Did he act at the right psychological moment? Did he have the spotlight? What was the mood of the audience? Did he carry his role well before the audience? Was he suitably cast for the part? Was the plot pattern favorable? Who played the parts against him, and how did they carry off their parts? If these factors are changed, all kinds of remarkable things can happen to the public character of a man.

In brief, the peculiarities of the dramatic domain are these: (1) almost anyone can steal the show, (2) a small part has an advantage over a larger one, (3) almost any kind of struggle or issue can become important, (4) spontaneity in dramatic crises and encounters favors unexpected outcomes, (5) there is great risk in close-ups, (6) timing is enormously important, (7) audience need and expectation can press hero, villain, fool, and victim roles on people and favor certain kinds of outcomes, and (8) the same kinds of character and motive (especially those called "quixotic") can elicit widely varying definitions, depending on the situation. Because of such peculiarities in the dramatic domain, outcome is not equal to input in any realistic, logical, or personal sense; one cannot predict from the input of a drama (character, deeds, or intentions) what the outcome will be. The power and "magic" of drama originate from other sources.

Let us now look more closely at several types of dramatic confrontations and their outcomes.

TYPES OF DRAMATIC ENCOUNTER

For most practical purposes, there are seven important role alternatives for a public man in dramatic confrontations, ranging from a popular "hit" to downright defeat. Once he commits himself, he may come out in any of these ways.

1. Honorific Ceremonial Meetings

The safest encounter is an honorific ceremony where important people, such as the heads of states or other organizations, meet under conditions of elaborate courtesy. Thus, John F. Kennedy met Paul VI in the first historic confrontation (said *Life*) between a United States President and the head of the Catholic Church; and Premier Nikita Khrushchev of the U.S.S.R. embraced U.S. Undersecretary of State Averill Harriman "warmly" after concluding a nuclear test-ban treaty. "Face" and rank are carefully maintained. No one does anything out of place; if an exchange occurs, it is all positive, with no loss to anybody; it involves mutual compliments, recognition, gifts. The audience warmly identifies with one or both parties.

But it is easy to imagine how such a ceremony could become more dramatic by the introduction of unexpected elements. Suppose that two dignitaries bump heads during an exchange of honors or that Khrushchev starts banging his shoe; then the formal encounter deteriorates into a more risky type.

2. Hero-making Confrontations

Hero-making confrontations are inherently risky but potentially more rewarding than honorific meetings. Three common modes can be distinguished: the benefactor, the winner in a test, and the defeat of the martyr.

The safest confrontation for a hero is with a needy party, to whom he generously makes a gift and who is in an inferior position and is showing gratitude. There is no contest between principals; indeed, the recipient may be a helpless victim. Leaders, patrons, aristocratic classes, and political bosses try to play such a role to the public. In Argentina, Eva Perón played guardian angel to working girls, unwed mothers, and the like, establishing herself as a kind of patron saint as well as reinforcing her husband's regime. Franklin Delano Roosevelt won such a role by passage of the Social Security Act and the historical accident of coming into the Presidency during the Great Depression.

Yet even such relationships between benefactor and recipient can get out of hand. One major risk is that the needy party will not show appropriate gratitude and thus make it hard for the benefactor to play his role without incurring suspicion that there is something wrong with him rather than with the recipient. (This has apparently happened in nations that view American foreign aid in terms of "ugly" Americans.) Another risk is that a competitor will steal the show with an even more exciting gift, thus making the would-be benefactor look reluctant or cheap. (To cite American foreign aid again, several times the Soviet Union has come forward with small but immediate and well-publicized token aid to a needy country and stolen the show from a larger but slower program by the United States.)

The second type of hero-making confrontation—the test —is of course more risky because it requires the subject to emerge as victor in a show of strength after committing himself fully. Such an encounter is safe only with a "setup," an opponent who looks dangerous but really is unable to compete effectively. Thus, a famous news picture shows Mayor Fiorello La Guardia of New York smashing slot machines in a police raid in 1934. He cuts a fine figure, poised over the wicked machines wielding a sledge hammer, rather like Richard the Lion-Hearted with his two-handed sword. Though there is no reason to suppose that La Guardia avoided real encounters, it was much safer for him to attack machines than publicly to rebuke a live gambler.

Within the test category are at least three subpatterns: (1) the battle of rival champions, (2) the defeat of a villain (whose wickedness points up the goodness of the hero), and (3) a David-Goliath encounter in which a little man upsets a big man.

The battle of champions is illustrated by President John F. Kennedy's historic confrontation with Roger Blough, chairman of the board of United States Steel Corporation, on April 12, 1962. The chairman called on the President to inform him of an arbitrary raise in the price of steel. The President soon thereafter, in a press conference, denounced the steel industry for irresponsibility and selfishness and threatened legal and political reprisals. Within forty-eight hours, the steel industry backed down, cancelling its price increases. Said *Time:*

> The ferocity of his attack on steel alienated and angered many a businessman . . . [but] there could be no doubt that John Kennedy had won a popular victory. Beyond question, the great majority of Americans reacted angrily to U.S. Steel's price-increase announcement. That reaction was instinctive, and Kennedy exploited it skillfully. . . . He had made the steelmen look like Milquetoasts.[17]

Though Kennedy charged villainy on the part of the steel industry, actually this was a contest between champions of rival corporate power blocs—big government versus big busi-

17. April 20, 1962, p. 25.

ness. It had all the qualities of a good contest; a personal encounter between two powerful men, a conflict of wills, and a test of strength and prestige. Kennedy acted with the sturdy stance of King Arthur swinging his great sword, and Blough was obliged to back off. Blough's dramatic alternatives were to act as a villain (which he did not accept; his behavior was in no way discreditable, though some blamed him for bad timing and judgment), as the rival champion of equal strength who loses, or as the weak knight[18] who is disgraced and made a fool. While his role had aspects of all these alternatives, it was mainly the second that emerged. Kennedy also risked failure, which could have made him look like a fool (risking the power of the Presidency against a mere group of corporations and being outfoxed); the wrong tactics might have cast him as a bully, coward, swaggerer, or stuffed shirt. Blough had to be big enough to test Kennedy's mettle (there is no glory in an encounter with a stooge, a weak or humble person, or a fool) yet not big enough to overthrow him. It was very important also how Blough reacted; a more colorful man —a cantankerous Sewell Avery, a big-talking Diamond Jim Brady, a wisecracking Will Rogers—might have stolen the show. And, of course, the whole thing might have happened in some other way (by committees, trial balloons, or private correspondence) so that no actual confrontation would have occurred.

The second test pattern, the defeat of a villain, is safer for the "hero" because there is no sympathy to swing to the opponent if the tables should be turned. Almost any good effort against a villain receives some credit; a knockout is, of course, a "hit." The badness and strength of the villain make the hero look all the better (whereas to defeat a good man inevitably leaves the audience with some ambivalent regret). When the pattern is at its best, the hero catches a

18. Epitomized in tales of King Arthur as Sir Kay, who is overthrown by boys and fools.

villain red-handed and at the height of a crisis, knocks him down, and carries off the prize or restores the threatened welfare. Ideally, a villain helps by confirming his own status: admitting guilt, fighting unfairly, running away, performing treachery or cruelty, and other acts well known in melodrama. President Kennedy did not have a very good villain in Roger Blough, but he had a better one in Premier Khrushchev, in the confrontation over the missile bases in Cuba in October, 1962, which followed classic lines. Here, it might almost be said, was Perseus arriving to face the dragon or Achilles girding himself to do battle for the Greeks, and the dragon backed off and withdrew his missiles, giving dramatic victory to the hero.[19] Another classic example of hero-villain confrontation was the televised hearings of a Senate crime-investigating committee headed by Estes Kefauver in 1951, which catapulted him into fame and helped make him a Presidential possibility. As chairman,

> he dragged such diverse and unsavory characters as Greasy Thumb Guzik, Virginia Hill and Frank Costello into the bright lights for a classic lesson in morality. Gentle but relentless, Kefauver questioned them with painful sincerity, became to millions a pillar of log-cabin courage and small-town mores because of the contrast between his stolid ruggedness and the squirmy, shifty-eyed hoodlums he confronted. From those hearings came no important legislation, few arrests, nothing very concrete. But his investigation did center national attention on big-time crime—and on Estes Kefauver.[20]

The third hero-making test pattern, that of David and

19. The President personally offered a challenge to Russia by discussing on television the danger to the United States from the missile sites and the encounter of Soviet and U.S. ships. The *New York Times* described the atmosphere in the capital as a "nightmare" during these days. After an unsuccessful bid to swap Cuban for Turkish bases, Khrushchev suddenly backed down, giving dramatic victory to Kennedy, who "emerged in the West as the hero of the crisis" (October 30, 1962).

20. *Time,* August 16, 1963, p. 19.

Goliath, requires that a small hero be pitted against a large villain. It is well illustrated by Martin Luther King's organization of the strike against the bus companies of Montgomery, Alabama, forcing them to modify their "Jim Crow" rules. The success of an obscure Baptist minister against the bus companies and against powerful white resistance put him in the role of David against the Goliath of segregation, which he then hit with the stone of non-violent resistance, again and again.

Ironically, another illustration is provided by an enemy of integration, Governor Ross Barnett of Mississippi, a dull political prospect who managed by a series of confrontations with the United States government to make himself a local hero and thus brighten his outlook. In an article entitled "Now He's a Hero," *Time* tells how his defiance of the federal government, for a time blocking the registration of James Meredith in the University of Mississippi, brought a "dizzying turnabout" in his political prospects.[21] We may analyze this role with profit. Prior to the event, his reputation had been that of a confirmed racist with some reputation for Christian piety (he had taught Sunday school and had vetoed a bill to raise the alcohol limit of wine), but he was a rather disappointing governor, who had a reputation as a "do-nothing." A chance to dramatize himself came with the decision of the Department of Justice to make a test case of James Meredith's entrance at the University of Mississippi. Barnett's transfiguration took place as a series of confrontations in which he defied the Goliath of the federal government as a threat to states' rights. First came a private meeting, on September 20, 1962, in which, as self-appointed registrar of the university, he rejected Meredith and the federal court order supporting his application for admission. This called some attention to him

21. Though he could not, by law, succeed himself as governor, his new popularity at home made almost any other public office in the state seem open to him. (*Time,* October 5, 1962, p. 17.)

as a man who had succeeded in defying the law, but the second encounter, at the doorway of Room 1007 of the capitol building with Chief U.S. Marshall James McShane, on September 25, was more crucial. The door swung open with "theatrical timing" as Meredith appeared, backed by McShane and an aide. There stood the Governor. The officers tried "fumblingly" to hand Barnett some court orders, which he refused. Then he read off a proclamation denying Meredith admission to the university. The federal officer, James Doar, made "one last, limp try":

> "Do you refuse to permit us to come in this door?" he asked.
> *Barnett:* "Yes, sir."
> *Doar:* "All right. Thank you."
> *Barnett:* "I do that politely."
> *Doar:* "Thank you. We leave politely."[22]

Thus the federal government backed down. It is entirely possible that the encounter could have come out favorably for the government with more adroit handling. As it was, the federal officers were made to look inept, clumsy, and even timid; they were apparently balked by the stand of one valiant man. If they had circumvented or defeated the Governor in some way, they could have stolen his thunder.

The third encounter, next day, was also a dramatic loss to the federal forces, though Barnett, because of a missed plane, was unable to capitalize on it personally. Now the man blocking the way was Lieutenant Governor Paul B. Johnson, who stood at the doorway of the university, backed by about twenty state policemen and a dozen sheriffs.

> As before, McShane and Doar tried pleading, urging, arguing, demanding and waving court orders—all in vain. Now McShane tried using his muscles. Several times he pushed a meaty shoulder against highway patrolmen. . . . But he was outnumbered twenty to

22. *Time,* October 5, 1962, p. 15.

one by the troopers, some of them pretty husky too,
and his scufflings with them were utterly futile, merely
adding a dash of absurdity to the proceeding.

The fourth encounter, September 27, was between a motor
cavalcade of marshalls and a small army of some 200 state
policemen backed by sheriffs, deputies, and a mob. Again the
federal forces, seeing the impossibility of making progress
without serious bloodshed, withdrew. "The decision to pull
back was sensible, but it looked embarrassingly like a retreat."
There then followed a lull, during which President Kennedy
made a speech and a federal court found Barnett guilty of
contempt *in absentia,* threatening him with a 10,000-dollar-a-
day fine and confinement. The Governor, seeing the handwrit-
ing on the wall, desisted, and the episode was over. He had
already made himself a hero and "could quit well ahead."
Why should he be a martyr to satisfy a few fanatics?[23]

An appraisal of this episode shows that the four encounters
were defeats, practically and dramatically, for the federal government, that Barnett gained corresponding credit, and that
the court decision lacked the qualities of an encounter and so
was not a defeat for Barnett. President Kennedy, probably
fortunately, stayed out of all this personally, though if he had
confronted Barnett it might have created a new pattern of
drama (though one of doubtful advantage to the President).
The most important thing to be noted was a buildup of forces
on each side from one encounter to another that continuously
operated to the disadvantage of the government. The federal
forces were not strong or adroit enough to win easily. Yet, if
they had built up their power and overridden the Governor
and his forces, they would have offered a good opportunity
of martyrdom to the rebels; while by backing off, they looked
weak, hesitant, even foolish (in the comic frustration of a
large by a small force). How could they have won without
seeming to be Goliaths (bullies) who overcame valiant little

23. *Time,* October 5, 1962, pp. 15–17.

men? Almost any kind of private or indirect dealing, it seems, would have been dramatically better for the federal government than allowing Barnett to benefit from these favorable scenes. I am not qualified to suggest alternative diplomatic tactics, but clearly the public ratio of forces was dramatically bad for the government, even though Barnett in his relation to Meredith (as a single man without federal support) was a bully oppressing the weak (at least in northern eyes). The public encounter with Barnett should have been managed with a ratio of forces that did not offer heroism or martyrdom to the defiant party. You cannot win dramatically by flouting this ratio.

Following this episode, Governor George C. Wallace of Alabama tried to carry off a similar confrontation between himself as a hero of states' rights and the federal bully. His first attempt, on June 11, 1963, was a moderate success. He stood in the doorway of the University of Alabama, "in almost pitiable solitude," opposing federal officers. (The two Negro applicants were kept out of the way in a waiting car.) Deputy Attorney General Nicholas Katzenbach asked him to "not bar entry" to the students. Wallace then read off a five-page proclamation denouncing the illegality of the central government. When he finished, Katzenbach asked him to step aside. Wallace "simply stood there" silently, "glaring with melodramatic scorn." "Very well," said Katzenbach, and then turned away to escort the students to a dormitory. The second scene followed on the same afternoon. This time General Henry Graham of the Alabama National Guard confronted the Governor to inform him that the National Guard had been federalized. Wallace read off another statement, then walked away. He had held off the federal juggernaut for four and one-half hours, then given way to superior force. Though not without certain comic features,[24] the scene, on the whole, was his.

24. The comic touches included a lectern and chest microphone, which gave an air of pomposity to Wallace's stand; also, he was "visibly pale and trembly." (*Time*, June 21, 1963, pp. 15–16.)

He had managed to look a bit like David by merely slowing Goliath down. Again the ratio of forces favored the underdog and worked against the big man. (But the second time Wallace tried "standing in the doorway," the results were different, as I shall point out below in discussing villain-making encounters.)

If you cannot win, you can lose heroically; and this sometimes makes a better symbol than a victory. This is especially the case for the martyr role, the third and most costly hero-making route. The defeat or suffering endured by the hero is taken as a sign that, although he has lost, the cause itself will win, if only out of the loyalty of such men or the improved morale of those who remember and follow him. In contrast, a victim role, though it gets public sympathy, is not nearly so valuable; the essential difference is that it comes by accident. The martyr role must emerge from a seemingly voluntary choice for the good of the cause. One could not, for example, impose martyrdom on a fleeing victim, though if he turned and stood he might easily win the role.

The great advantage of non-violent resistance, as practiced by Hindus under Gandhi or Negroes following Martin Luther King, is that it invites martyrdom, so to speak, as a second choice to victory. It is, then, a dramatic strategy that cannot lose; the resister, being passive, is extremely hard to see as a villain, while the opponent, whether he wins or not, can hardly avoid being cast as an aggressor by an open-minded audience. The catch, of course, as practitioners well know, is in the self-control of the resister, since, if he displays the least aggressiveness, he enters the ordinary arena where he can quite as easily become a villain as a hero, and his advantage is gone.

It is not absolutely necessary to have a villain in a martyr drama; Colonel Gorgas' volunteers in the fight against malaria, for example, were martyrs, though malaria parasites could be called villains only by some stretch of the imagination. But, if the villain is present, he must play his part correctly. For example, if he overwhelms the hero without allowing him time to display fortitude and choice, he is more likely to create a mere victim, or, if he fails to be sufficiently cruel and unfair (as, for example, did Pontius Pilate), he does not make a very good persecutor and robs the martyr of his melodramatic advantage. If we begin to feel sorry for the bad guy, the affair is more likely to seem tragic than melodramatic.[25] From the standpoint of casting martyrs, then, it is partly a matter of finding a suitable villain—one who will accept his part and play it with vindictive glee, showing no remorse and not spoiling the scene by being human.

3. Villain-making Encounters

It is sufficient to point out here two patterns[26] of villainy: the oppression of a weaker party and the cowardly attack.

The behavior of Eugene "Bull" Conner of Birmingham, Alabama, enormously helped Martin Luther King's civil rights cause:

Conner became an international symbol of blind, cruel Southern racism. When King sent out his marchers, Conner had them mowed down by streams from fire hoses. Shocking news photos splashed across the pages of the world's press—of a young Negro sent sprawling by a jet of water, of a Negro woman pinioned to the sidewalk with a cop's knee at her throat, of police dogs lunging at fleeing Negroes. With that, millions of people—North and South, black and white—felt the pangs of segregation and, at least in sympathy, joined the protest movement.[27]

The other villain-making pattern is also conveniently illus-

25. Melodramas are, by definition, black versus white, where the villain takes all the badness on himself and gives all the goodness to the hero; whereas, in tragedy, fault is always shared by the hero.
26. For a survey of American patterns see my *Heroes, Villains and Fools,* chap. iii.
27. *Time,* August 30, 1963, p. 12.

trated from the civil rights struggle in the unseen assassins who shot Medgar Evers, Negro leader, in the back, or those who bombed the Baptist church in Birmingham, Alabama, on September 15, 1963, killing four Negro children. These events, though the criminals were not caught, supplied a vivid image of the kind of person involved in such villainy; nor was there any mistaking the surge of national and world feeling for the Negro cause that followed these acts. The villains could not have done more damage to their own cause if they had used bombs and bullets on their own ranks.

In such dramas, almost any unsuspecting, helpless victim is sufficient. Of course, the height of the villainy is greatly increased if the one attacked is a popular hero; this puts the villain into a status like that of John Wilkes Booth, Judas, Mordred, or Delilah. In Governor Wallace's second attempt to make himself a hero, the federal government, presumably having profited from previous encounters with him and with Governor Barnett, refused to play the role of "Goliath"; the government did not use a superior force of soldiers embodying what Wallace would call "military dictatorship." When the Governor again proposed, on September 6, 1963, to "stand in the doorway" of the public schools of Huntsville, Alabama, the only force present was that of his own soldiers.

> Armed state troopers barred white and Negro children from four public schools . . . on orders of Governor George Wallace, stirring a rising resentment in this . . . city and other parts of Alabama.
> One brigade of determined mothers braved the line of helmeted, club-carrying troopers at one school and took their children in for registration.[28]

Wallace himself did not appear, the state troopers (with the Governor as their absent commander) found themselves in the villain's role versus mothers and children. Local citizens were enraged. The Huntsville Board of Education and town

28. *San Diego Union,* September 7, 1963.

authorities sought to defy the Governor and open the schools despite him. "You ought to be ashamed of yourselves," a mother told the troopers. By not having the superior force of the federal government to oppose and by accepting the wrong dramatic partners, he had made himself look like a tyrant depriving children of their educational rights. Again, this incident illustrates how the dramatic ratio, as much as substantive issues, determines political success. Wallace was doing almost the same thing, before the same audience, but his timing, the ratio of forces, and almost everything else about the situation were dramatically bad for him. Even the Montgomery *Advertiser,* a firm supporter of Governor Wallace, concluded that he had "gone wild."[29]

The sequel to the incident was the second federalizing of the Alabama National Guard by President Kennedy a few days later. This action deprived Wallace of the force seriously to challenge federal force, and it was now unnecessary for the President to use federal force and thus play into the Governor's hand. Cabell Phillips said in the *New York Times:*

KENNEDY AVOIDED A SHOW OF FORCE;
HIS STRATEGISTS THINK THEY OUTWITTED
WALLACE AT HIS OWN GAME IN CRISES.

A strategy hastily devised at the White House between 10 o'clock last night and dawn led to the successful integration of a group of Alabama schools today without reliance upon "a Federal presence."

This was a solution toward which the Kennedy Administration had worked during the last hectic week in the face of defiance from Governor George C. Wallace. Government officials had sought means of avoiding the use of force to carry out Federal court orders to admit Negro pupils to the schools.

Their success, in view of the strategists themselves, obliterates—for the time being at least—the basis of Governor Wallace's complaint today that "I can't fight

29. *New York Times,* September 9, 1963.

bayonets with my bare hands." For there were no bayonets in evidence today as the Negro pupils entered
previously all-white schools in Birmingham, Mobile
and Tuskegee.

National Guardsmen with bayonets, acting under
the Governor's orders to keep the Negro children out,
had taken up their posts at the beleaguered schools
before dawn. But before the school bells rang, President Kennedy had federalized the Guardsmen and they
had been whisked back to their armories, where they
stayed, "awaiting orders."[30]

4. Fool-making Encounters

Another dramatic possibility, of course, is to be made a
fool, either by one's own action or by someone else's. As
noted, Governor Wallace's first, successful role had comic
possibilities. For example, some mishap might have occurred
as he stood before his wired-for-sound rostrum (say, a failure
of power), or a soldier might have made a wisecrack good
enough to report to the nation. Comic mishaps such as these
can rob a performer of serious consideration unless he can
turn them to his own advantage, perhaps by accepting the
clown role, or by turning the tables so cleverly that the audience is more impressed by his agility than by what he intended
to do in the first place. If he takes himself too seriously or
lacks sufficient wit to turn it to his advantage, a public man
can be in difficulty when the show turns to comedy.

While anyone can make a fool of himself merely by acting
in an undignified fashion, he is likely to be made a fool by
somebody else in one of two ways: a joke that he cannot turn
back against the jester or a defeat by a small obstacle or a
grossly inferior party. The first situation is exemplified by a
"hot foot" perpetrated on a sleeping victim or a heckling wisecrack that makes a speaker lose his temper and his good
judgment. The second is illustrated by the comic frustration
of a large force by a small force (the mouse outwitting the

30. September 11, 1963.

elephant, a large man getting himself locked in a telephone booth). A jester can literally try to put his opponents in such situations, or he can depict them by stories, remarks, cartoons, rumors, and so on. In a later chapter some of these fool-making tactics and situations will be examined.

The main thing that keeps comedy from being used more widely in public life is that it requires more wit than does melodrama. And, in general, people protect themselves from comic predicaments rather better than they do from melodramas, where there is a tendency for sincere people to rush in. But if public men began paying gagmen as much as top comedians pay television scriptwriters, we might see a new and livelier era in politics.

5. *Becoming a Victim*

The role of victim falls to many people whether or not they choose it. The role has added pathos to public careers —Franklin Roosevelt's paralysis; the loss of sons by Coolidge, Lindbergh, and Nelson Rockefeller; Wilson's stroke during his battle with Senate enemies. It has pulled some men out of trouble and pushed others into trouble. It is a symbolic advantage of a sort; the least it can do is quiet criticism for a time, since, whether or not critics actually feel sorry for the victim, they do not want it to appear that they are "hitting a man when he is down."

A public man can stumble into a villain's role when the stone on which he stubs his toe is a victim. Thus, John Ciardi, poetry editor of the *Saturday Review,* provoked what he called the "hottest controversy" of his career by what to many readers seemed a needlessly severe review of Anne Morrow Lindbergh's book, *The Unicorn.* He condemned the book as sentimentality, not poetry. Why did he provoke an outraged response in carrying out what he thought was his function as critic? He had, it seems (1) been ungentlemanly to (2) a woman, who (3) was a mother, (4) had lost a son in a great tragedy, (5) was the wife of a national hero, and (6) had revealed herself in various writings as the kind of person with whom readers identified. They did not separate Mrs. Lindbergh from her poetry or care much about the technical difference between sentimentality and poetry. It was clearly the dramatic relation between Ciardi the man and Mrs. Lindbergh the woman that was uppermost in people's minds. And why, indeed should he, as critic, expect to avoid this dramatic relationship any more than can any public man? The moral is, perhaps, that making a victim of someone can be avoided by proper attention to dramatic conditions, but one cannot expect to do so by ignoring them and focusing only on technical or logical considerations. All Ciardi had to do was adopt what Kenneth Burke would call a rhetoric appropriate to the situation, and he could have avoided offending the devotees of Mrs. Lindbergh while making whatever criticisms he thought valid.

If we ask what constitutes a good victim, the first inference from a case like the one cited above is that certain kinds of objects are especially likely to attract sympathy. Differences in culture plainly make a great difference in this regard; perhaps the most shocking thing one can do in England is mistreat a dog, while such action would cause little stir in the Philippines. But, once allowance is made for such cultural biases, the ratio of apparent forces assumes its due importance. The second inference, judging by folktales and dramas everywhere, is that smallness or weakness in anything or anyone that makes it helpless and unable to fight back is a prime quality of a good victim. (If Mrs. Lindbergh had come into the *Saturday Review* office and tongue-lashed Mr. Ciardi, she would have ceased to be a victim, whatever else she might have become.) Third, we may infer that style of encounter is significant—passivity, meekness, innocence, gentleness, feminity, versus aggressiveness and the modes of villainy. Here the villain makes his contribution by taking all the blame on himself and leaving all the sympathy to the other; should the victim have any fault, it is easily forgotten because the villain is so much worse. Fourth, magnitude of misfortune makes a difference. The event must approach disaster; it must not be the kind of thing that happens to us all. Finally, it is crucial that the trouble be suffered but not chosen, since otherwise the public may say that the victim brought it all on himself.[31] The victim should not do much to help himself or seem capable of remedying the situation, otherwise he will rob the misfortune of its disastrous quality—and, incidentally, he may then steal the show from any hero who might try to save him (if the drowning man swims with the lifeguard, neither gets much credit).

The victim, then, has two dramatic partners: a hero, who is going to get him out of trouble, and the villain, who got him into trouble in the first place. The moral is that, if one is going to have anything to do with a victim, it had better be as hero rather than as villain.

6. The Tragic Role

The tragic role is not as important as it might be in American public life for the simple reason that it is too hard to achieve. The popular mind in this country runs along comic and and melodramatic rather than tragic lines, tending most often to create villains, fools, victims, or martyrs out of the potential material.[32] Lincoln, Wilson, and McKinley are sometimes cited

31. Martyrdom, as an alternative, has already been discussed, but, for martyrdom, a significant cause must be evident. A suicide, to the American public, is a person who has lost the dramatic advantages of both victim and martyr. His death is meaningless, so he cannot be a martyr. He brought it on himself, so he cannot be a victim. On the other hand, Medgar Evers, the assassinated Negro leader, was not quite a perfect martyr and more a victim. He was too passive and helpless for it to be said that he had fully chosen his role, though it is true that he had announced his willingness to die for integration and his expectation that someone might kill him. However, comparison with perfect martyrs like Joan of Arc or Socrates, who explicitly chose their deaths and repeatedly rejected their chances to escape, makes it clear why Evers' role was closer to victim than to martyr.

32. I have come to the conclusion that average Americans do not know what tragedy is. My reasons are given in "Tragedy and the Amer-

as tragic Presidents; yet none of the disasters that struck them was strictly tragic. Wilson and McKinley were victims, and even Lincoln's assassination was a classic melodrama, one that could hardly have been more lurid if Harriet Beecher Stowe herself had worked on the script.[33] There is loose talk about the "tragedy" of this or that, especially in newspapers, but actually very few well-known people do achieve tragedy in public images, though we may not rule it out as a possibility.

For a public drama to develop along tragic lines, it would require a hero close enough to villainy to be deeply and consciously at fault for the misfortunes that he brings on himself and others, yet noble enough, for all that—in fortitude and dignity, at least—to command the sympathy if not the admiration of the audience. He must not have a clearly worthy cause or his misfortune will seem a martyrdom; he must come close to the martyr role in choosing his fate or he will seem merely a helpless victim of disaster. Those who oppose or persecute him may be villains to some extent; but if they are too evil— or he paints them so—the pattern descends to melodrama and he loses his tragic character. If he falls off this knife-edge, he becomes one of the simpler types that we have been discussing. Indeed, without a master dramatist to guide him, how is a public person to manage such a role?

The answer may be that it does not matter, that it is academic to try to define the conditions of a public tragic role since there is not enough advantage in it to warrant trying to attain it, though it could come by accident. Such a role, being

---

ican Climate of Opinion," *Centennial Review,* 11 (1958), 396–413; also reprinted in John D. Hurrell, *Two Modern Tragedies* (New York: Scribner. 1961), and in Robert W. Corrigan, *The Form and Vision of Tragedy* (San Francisco: Chandler Publishing Company, 1965).

33. Booth, if anyone, was the tragic character, with his Brutus-like role. The tragedy of Lincoln's career must be found, as Whitman saw, in the choice, direction, and course of the war itself—a nation rending itself and guilty of its own blood. In this sense, he was captain of a tragic ship.

ambivalent, cannot mobilize an audience in the way of simpler types. It may be, indeed, that the only advantage of a tragic role would be to provide interesting material for biographers.

7. *Draw or Loss without Discredit*

Finally, we may distinguish the confrontation pattern of holding one's own, of defeat without discredit, coming off honhonorably without victory, as when knights of King Arthur's Round Table, after breaking a few lances, part without deciding the issue. It is found in the surrender of General Robert E. Lee to General Ulysses S. Grant, for each had made such a good fight that the outcome seemed almost accidental—a Roland and Oliver type of encounter, in which two champions rest on their swords and declare (or discover) themselves friends. Each had proved the other's mettle, and the loser shared honors with the victor. Another version of defeat with honor is for a "comer"—a young aspirant new to professional or public life—to hold his own against a more important opponent. His showing is not only good publicity but indicates his potential for better things.

The famous "kitchen debate" of Vice-President Richard Nixon with Premier Khrushchev at the American Exhibition in Moscow had some features of both these patterns (the young man holding his own against the more experienced, and a battle of champions in which honors were divided). Round 1 was fought in a model television studio. Said Nixon: "We found ourselves by accident, rather than design, standing on a stage with literally millions of potential viewers." Khrushchev denounced the Captive Nation Resolution of the U.S. Senate, and Nixon replied tactfully (in the role of host), trying to change the tone of the conversation.

> As we watched the playback—I could see that he had been aggressive, rude, and forceful. He had gone after me with no holds barred. And I had had to

counter him like a fighter with one hand tied—his attack had shaken me right to my toes. He had been on the offensive and I had been on the defensive throughout. I knew that he had scored heavily and I felt it was imperative that I find an opportunity to strike back. . . . Bob Considine later compared the episode to the first round of the Dempsey-Firpo fight. Khrushchev had started the encounter by knocking me out of the ring. At the end, I had climbed back in to fight again. But the second round was still coming up.[34]

Round 2 took place in a model American home, the "kitchen conference." An argument developed over whether the model was typical of American homes and whether it was better to have freedom of choice or one model for all. It built up to an angry comparison of rockets and to accusations, each man giving ultimatums to the other. Nixon stood "firm without being belligerent" and pointed his finger at Khrushchev: "You are strong and we are strong. . . . But [this] misses the point. . . . No one should ever use his strength to put another in the position where he in effect has an ultimatum. . . . If war comes we both lose." Khrushchev tried to laugh it off and agreed with his American "friend." But Nixon pursued the point that it was "very dangerous" to put ultimatums. "Now we were going at it toe-to-toe." A hot exchange occurred ("using," not losing, tempers) over who was threatening whom. Then it ended by mutual consent. Nixon returned to his pleasant role of host. "I was not sure whether I had held my own. But two widely different sources of opinion buoyed me up on this score." (A United Press correspondent and Deputy Premier Mikoyan both complimented him.[35])

While this encounter was a draw, Nixon gained something merely by holding his own, giving back as good as he took from the more important and powerful man. He had been

34. Richard M. Nixon, *Six Crises* (Garden City, N.Y.: Doubleday, 1962), p. 254.
35. *Ibid,* pp. 257–58.

on the spot and risked much by the possibility that he would make not only himself but all Americans look bad if he failed to stand up to Khrushchev successfully. Indeed, the prestige of both countries was at stake. And no doubt both audiences sighed with relief at the outcome.

CONCLUSION

I have thus outlined seven outcomes of dramatic confrontation: (1) honorific ceremony, (2) hero-making (benefactor, winner, and martyr), (3) villain-making, (4) fool-making, (5) victim-making, (6) tragic, and (7) loss or draw without discredit. (More complex possibilities of role reversal will be explored in a later chapter.) Judging from these, what can be said about the principles that seem to govern? Surely there is more involved than merely the force exerted or the success of the outcome, for one can win materially yet lose dramatically.

The single most important factor in any dramatic encounter is the apparent ratio of forces. This ratio has much to do not only with how the event will actually turn out but with who will be hero, villain, fool, or victim and where audience sympathy will turn. Too great a preponderance of force on one side sets the stage for a villain who is using an unfair advantage or, if defeat looms, for a fool who could not win even when the cards were stacked in his favor. A David-and-Goliath situation is created, and the smaller party gets a role choice of hero or victim; the larger party has the possibility of victory with small credit but runs a very real chance of being villain or fool, and such an encounter is, for him, a poor bargain.[36] Apparent force, of course, is the key factor. It does not matter how many aces you have up your sleeve or tanks

36. Perhaps this applies mainly to countries with the Anglo-American tradition of fair play and sympathy for the underdog, though I suspect that it is much more widespread, since the basic melodramatic and comic patterns can be found throughout world folklore and drama.

or henchmen hidden away; you must not display your true strength too obviously. Too large a display at the outset of a drama may make one look fearsome (as a villain), fearful (as a coward), or grandiose and pompous (as a stuffed shirt riding to his fall). For that reason, the movie hero usually underplays his strength before knocking out the bad guy,[37] and the cartoon Popeye eats his can of spinach only at the last. Buildups at the beginning are for villains and fools.

It seems plain that restraint in the early stages of an encounter has a number of consequences: (1) it avoids having the hero seem overconfident (the public welcomes the deflation of a stuffed shirt); (2) it casts the opponent as the "heavy" or the "bully"; (3) it arouses sympathy for a nice guy getting the worst of it until his wrath, valor, or potency is kindled; (4) it builds up suspense and deepens crisis; and (5) it maximizes the swing from looming defeat to victory, thus giving the audience the most exciting of emotional sleigh-rides. Of course, we presume a "win" or a martyr outcome; otherwise the would-be hero, instead of showing restraint, had better not appear at all.

The practical moral is that the public man, if he wishes to be popular, and regardless of how well laid his plans, how clever his tactics, or how great his resources, should always seem to act with a fair or somewhat disadvantageous ratio of force. He thus avoids being set up as a villain by would-be martyrs or impudent challengers. If defeat comes for him, with a safe ratio of forces he has the dramatic "outs" of the

37. One of the greatest of movie fights occured in "El Cid." It followed classic lines. When El Cid fights the champion of the rival king, he is knocked off his horse, then off his feet. Getting to his feet he backs away, apparently at the mercy of the brute strength of his opponent, who swings a heavy mace. Finally, grasping a two-handed sword at the same time as his enemy, he finds himself on fair and equal terms. A furious exchange follows, in which El Cid knocks down his opponent, then with both hands plunges the sword through his prostrate form (pity is gone). El Cid lost the early rounds and then won by a knockout. Likewise, in classic Westerns, the hero shows restraint and gentility, even acting like a sissy, before he defeats the villain.

martyr or victim or of defeat with honor. He avoids (without being obvious about it) confrontations with small or unworthy antagonists who can only make him look bad as villain or fool. Applying this, for example, to the relations of the United States with Cuba in 1963–64, we see how important it was to avoid a confrontation with Premier Castro in which the ratio of forces would either make him look big enough to bother or challenge the United States or, if he lost, appear a victim or martyr in the eyes of Latin Americans, Communists, and much of the world already disposed to see Uncle Sam as a villain. The President of the United States should never exchange a direct public word with such a leader whose posture is one of defiance. Military efforts against Cuba (from a dramatic standpoint, at least) should be indirect or by small parties. Blockades and similar tactics only create a picture of a great villain throttling the people of Cuba. As Senator George S. McGovern of South Dakota remarked:

> Castro not only occupies the time and energy of many of our top State Department, White House and CIA officials, but absorbs the attention of Congress and threatens to be a central issue in the 1964 Presidential election.
> This animated national debate, considering the comparative weakness of Cuba, scarcely does justice to the dignity of the United States as a great world power charged with global leadership. . . .
> The President, early in his Administration, gave his sanction to the unfortunate Bay of Pigs invasion. This clumsy failure, the embarrassment, the humiliation, the sense of guilt—all these combined to produce a traumatic national experience for the United States. . . .
> We can best diminish Castro's prestige by ceasing to act as though he were the chief object of our concern.[38]

Another principle that emerges from the cases discussed

38. *New York Times,* May 18, 1963.

is that the style of performance is of great importance, though not as important as the ratio of forces. It does not matter what you do substantively so much as how you do it. The advantage of non-violent resistance, for example, is that its style makes it almost impossible to define the aggressor as a villain; the worst he can be called is "troublemaker." He is, however, naturally eligible for victim and martyr roles. Certain qualities of style (unfairness, sneakiness, bluster, arrogance) help create a villain in the mind of the audience, just as other qualities (modesty, fairness, straightforwardness, pluck) set up a hero within an appropriate ratio of forces. Again, pomposity, clumsiness, timidity, levity, or antic behavior cast one—whatever his substantive deeds—as fool, if only because the audience becomes predisposed to laugh at anything that happens to him. But style alone, without an appropriate ratio of forces, cannot govern. Governor Wallace used the same style in both his confrontations with the federal government, but President Kennedy refused to give him the needed ratio in the second.

Seeking key factors should not obscure the importance of the drama as a whole, the mutual effects of the roles of all actors as action proceeds through scenes, development, and turns. A later chapter will take up several public dramas that show how the reciprocal effects of the roles of actors, together with the style and ratio of forces, bring about interesting exchanges or reversals of role.

CHAPTER FOUR

IMAGE
TROUBLE

A New Ailment of Public Men

The age of images has produced a new kind of ailment to worry public men: image trouble. Perhaps it has always existed, but now, like fashionable neurosis, it is more widely recognized; some of the best people have it, and it may even come to be "the thing" to have regular analysis of one's public image. This ailment has two aspects. One is the "hero's neurosis," already mentioned in chapter One. The image a man projects may be much better than he really is; he suffers from guilt or embarrassment at not being what people think he is. The other aspect is the reverse of this. The image a man projects may be worse than the one he thinks he is entitled to; he feels resentment and puzzlement at the unkindness of critics, the fickleness of public opinion, and the disloyalty of fair-weather friends.

It is not a matter of being an outright villain, a laughing stock, or a public disgrace. Rather, image trouble is an obscure symbolic problem. A public figure may become aware that he has a "bad image," but usually he does not know exactly what is wrong with it, how he got it, or what to do about it. He may be a respected man in high office, but he feels an impediment to something he wants to do and has a right to expect. He is at a loss to explain why he is not popular. He may complain of a "bad press," of being "smeared," but the point is that with image trouble it becomes easier for people to make snide remarks and for others to listen to them. His enemies, of course, use this bad image for all it is worth.

Many famous Americans have had image trouble, for example, Eleanor Roosevelt, Adlai Stevenson, Thomas E. Dewey, Harry Truman, Henry Wallace, Henry Ford, John D. Rockefeller (who hired Ivy Lee, a public relations pioneer, to do one of the first professional repair jobs on a public image), Frank Sinatra (who had fist fights to prove that he was not an effeminate crooner). Professions, corporations, even nations, can also have image trouble.[1] We may cite two examples for more extensive consideration here; others, such as Truman, will be dealt with later.

In 1952 and 1956 the Democrats had a presidential candidate with image trouble, and in 1960 the Republicans had one. Let us consider, first, Adlai E. Stevenson, who, says Elmo Roper, had the "thankless task" of leading the Democratic party during a time when there was a surge of public feeling "away from the old symbols . . . toward a personality who had been admired and beloved for a decade. . . . It is likely that no man living could have defeated the popular idol, Eisenhower, in either 1952 or 1956." I am not referring,

---

1. Doctors, lawyers, and politicians are conspicuous examples of professions with "bad images," whether or not deserved, and in spite of public relations expenditures, such as those of the American Medical Association. That a nation can have image trouble in spite of a good opinion of itself was shown by books like William Lederer and Eugene Burdick's *The Ugly American*.

however, to the fact that one candidate is better liked than another. Stevenson's image trouble was a deficiency hard to put one's finger on but a real impediment to his candidacy in both campaigns. As Roper described it:

> He was someone who never entirely escaped from the private world of his own thoughts. His mind was constantly standing a little apart, questioning, judging, reconsidering. . . . There is no question that Stevenson caught on. . . . But the nation as a whole never overcame a certain reluctance to give its full trust to this man whose character was of a mould so different from the average American's. Americans are accustomed to admire men who get things done, men who radiate faith and confidence. If some corners are cut in the process, they are not overly concerned. Americans are not inclined toward doubt; they like to be all for or all against something, right away if possible. Everything about Stevenson discouraged this attitude. Most people felt they understood Eisenhower, as they had understood Truman before him. But though there was recognition of Stevenson's ability and intelligence, awareness of his charm was mingled, for many, with a hesitation to give him their full confidence as a political leader. Ability to inspire confidence was the quality least often ascribed to Stevenson in poll answers.[2]

The essential picture did not change much in four years, from 1952 to 1956. "The consensus still was that here was a highly intelligent man, who somehow did not arouse a feeling of deep trust and confidence." Stevenson was the "victim of his own inability to project the type of personality the public could respond to freely and warmly." The "egghead" label was a wit's memorable way of summarizing the difference between Stevenson and the average member of the electorate.

2. Elmo Roper, *You and Your Leaders* (New York: Morrow, 1957), pp. 209, 219–20, 229, 232.

THE CASE OF NIXON

I have chosen the image trouble of Richard M. Nixon for more extensive analysis because it might be called a classic specimen. I have no wish to dwell unduly on the political misfortune of one man, except for the light it may throw on general principles—the dramatic and typical image problems with which this book is concerned. Such a post mortem has exactly the same justification as a medical one. It is important to try to find out what went wrong.

Let us start with the observation that Nixon is (or was) one of the most admired men in America. A Gallup poll in December, 1960, ranked him fifth, behind Eisenhower, Churchill, Schweitzer, and Kennedy. It stands to reason that his party would not have chosen him as a Presidential candidate had it been otherwise; yet he lost the 1960 election and clearly has declined in public esteem since that time. What was the nature of his trouble? Is it possible, by scrutiny of his public image, to throw any light on the negative components that, in spite of the man's obvious merit, spelled death to his political career? I shall try first to describe the symptoms of image trouble; second, to diagnose the fault of the image; third, to trace some of the sources or causes of these faults; and, finally, to make some tentative recommendations about how such trouble might have been avoided or lessened.

Signs of Image Trouble

Nixon himself would probably be the first to admit that he had failed to reach the public in the way that he wished. He displayed at the end of his political career the attitude of a man who felt that he was misunderstood. Conceding defeat in the California gubernatorial election, on November 7, 1962, he expressed bitterness to reporters, whom he accused of treating him badly. It seems plain that he believed his bad press to be due to the bias of the people who had the job of communicating fairly his image and message to the public.

Almost from his entrance into the political major leagues, Nixon had what might be considered exceptional bad luck. His desperate television defense against imputations of the misuses of election funds, which barely saved his chance to run with Eisenhower, caused rather more difficulty than one would expect from an item of sixteen thousand dollars of expense money in a campaign costing millions to each party, and in a tradition where some mudslinging is expected. After his election as Vice-President, his troubles did not diminish, Nixon said:

> The President . . . seemed to be seeking some way of avoiding another campaign. . . . It was "most disappointing" to him, he said, to see that my popularity had not risen as high as he had hoped it would.

Nixon felt the threat of being "dumped" by his party in the next election. When President Eisenhower's heart attack occurred, he described himself as "walking on eggs"—not just because of the new responsibility on him but because "any mistake, no matter how slight, I might make in public or in private" would be subject to "easy misinterpretation."[3] This is not the predicament simply of a man doing a tough job but of a man who is under some kind of vague suspicion that is likely to damn whatever effort he makes. He is vulnerable to all kinds of charges that would not bother another.

Nixon's bad luck continued. For example, an unfortunate cover picture appeared on *Time* that made him look rather sinister and brutal. His poor appearance on the first televised debate with John F. Kennedy was blamed on the absence of makeup to cover his "five o'clock shadow"; he lost

3. Richard M. Nixon, *Six Crises* (New York: Doubleday, 1962).

in this encounter, and at heavy cost. Such accidents might of themselves mean nothing, but they were part of the Nixon pattern. Long before his defeat in the Presidential race, it became recognized that something was wrong with Nixon's image. Opponents, challenged to explain their dislike of him, often became inarticulate with rage in excess of reasons, and even adherents admitted the problem. As James Reston of the *New York Times* wrote:

> Everything he says or does . . . seems to go wrong.
> . . . Even in his home state . . . he seems trapped by
> that old familiar but vague charge that "there is some-
> thing about him that troubles me."[4]

There were many efforts to explain his "unlove affair" with reporters. Polls tried to appraise the strong and weak points of his image.[5]

There seems little doubt that something people saw in Nixon was standing in the way of his popular acceptance; and it is important to recognize that the trouble, whatever it was, was seen by both Republicans and Democrats, friends and foes, so it could not be attributed only to partisan bias or mud-slinging. On the other hand, it is not safe to conclude that because both friends and foes see a thing, it is necessarily "the truth." Rather, we should conclude that there is an image (or there are images) sufficiently real and objective[6] to be visible to both sides, true or not. This is rather like the pain

---

4. *Time,* April 13, 1962, p. 71.

5. For example, the California poll of August 7, 1962, found that the weakest points in his image were these: mudslinging tactics, hot-headedness, aloof and superior attitude, self-seeking opportunism, anti-labor and pro-big-business bias, changing of his viewpoint for political advantage, indecisiveness, and evasiveness. His strong points as seen by his supporters were political know-how and experience, honesty, hard-workingness and agressiveness, concern with the welfare of the country, attractive personality, conservatism, anticommunism, and a good record.

6. The language of a sociologist, Émile Durkheim, may clarify this point. We might say that the bad image was a "collective representa-tion" and that the problematic status that went with it was a "social fact." *Rules of Sociological Method* (Glencoe, Ill.: Free Press, 1950).

we feel when a friend whom we esteem shows himself in a bad light. It is not the whole truth about him as we know him, but it is there and we can see it. With such a state of things, a newswriter—even a partisan—could be influenced by images that he rejected on rational grounds. And people, against their best intentions, even Republicans wanting their candidate to win, could be influenced by an image that undercut their efforts and the good impressions that Nixon might otherwise have made. No matter what he did, the negative image could rise like a ghost to cast a pall.

Analysis

I shall here try to identify more clearly the negative elements of Nixon's image, with the assumption that when a man acquires a definite popular image he has been *typed*.[7] The question, then, is: What were the main negative social types that had become attached to Nixon by the time of his retirement in 1962? I shall draw on a poll I made just before the California governorship election of November 7, 1962, together with my own observations of the public record, to supply the answer.

The poll, taken from equal numbers of Democratic and Republican voters in San Diego,[8] gives a clue to the most salient negative images. The subjects were given a list of over seven hundred favorable and unfavorable social types. They were asked to go over it conscientiously and pick out all that applied to Nixon.[9] It should be noted that all negative types attributed to Nixon by Democrats were also accepted by a

7. See my *Heroes, Villains and Fools*, pp. 1–24.
8. The sample included 188 voters (94 Democratic, 94 Republican). Data were collected during the week preceding the California governorship election on November 7, 1962.
9. "Will you please go through the attached list and mark *all* favorable and unfavorable types that in your opinion aptly apply to Nixon as people think of him. (Not necessarily your own personal opinion but images you think are rather widespread, whether among opponents or supporters.)"

considerable number of Republicans; the difference was only in proportion. The typing, then, was visible to supporters as well as opponents. Many who voted for Nixon did so in spite of these image handicaps.

As might be expected of a man of Nixon's stature, favorable images outranked and outnumbered unfavorable ones. But we are concerned here with the negative ones that acted, one might say, as excessive ballast in his political balloon. In Table 1, note the following negative items (in order of rank): fast-talker, mudslinger, has-been, politician (dirty), climber, apple-polisher, two-faced, do-gooder, big shot, yes-man, hypocrite, sharpie, propagandist, smart operator, promoter. Offsetting these were more favorable images: diplomat, self-made man, go-getter, 100 per cent American, intellectual, patriot, crusader, and so on.

TABLE 1
TYPES MOST OFTEN ASSIGNED TO RICHARD M. NIXON
(N-188)

Rank	Type	No. of Attributions
1	Diplomat	69
2	Fast-talker	68
3	Self-made man	67
4	Go-getter	60
5	Mudslinger	55
6	100 per cent American	54
7	Intellectual	48
8	Patriot	47
9	Crusader	44
10.5	Has-been	43
10.5	Politician (dirty)	43
12.5	Climber	42
12.5	Apple-polisher	42
14.5	Good fellow	41
14.5	Big operator	41
16	V.I.P.	40

17	Two-faced	39
18	Do-gooder	37
20	Individualist	36
20	Free Thinker	36
20	Big Shot	36
22	Perfect gentleman	34
23	Yes-man	33
24.5	Extrovert	32
24.5	Hypocrite	32
26	Underdog	31
28	Sharpie	30
28	Defender	30
28	Propagandist	30
30	Smart operator	29
31	Regular fellow	28
32	Promoter	27

Such attributes are only clues to faults in Nixon's images and need to be analyzed in the context of his career and the public record. First, however, let us group the negative types for a clearer idea of the main faults that were perceived in his character and political conduct. The outstanding one seems to be insincerity or untrustworthiness—the image of a man who hides his real intentions and is trying to put something over (fast-talker, politician, climber,[10] apple-polisher, two-faced, yes-man, hypocrite, sharpie, propagandist, smart operator, promoter). "Mudslinger" seems to impute malice, the willingness to attack and hurt others. "Has-been" refers to the poor political chances of a "loser," a man who is "through." "Do-gooder," though it has a favorable aspect, rates predominantly as a fool type, a man who gets into trouble or gives others trouble because he is too idealistic, and sometimes rates as a villain who meddles in other people's business.[11] "Big shot" may refer to a man who really runs things but is very

10. The "climber" type can be seen also in favorable terms, such as "go-getter," "self-made man."
11. *Heroes, Villains and Fools,* pp. 48, 85.

likely in America to be used derisively for a man who presumes to a status he does not deserve.

If we are to conclude anything from this modest information, however, it should be that untrustworthiness was Nixon's biggest image problem. Why did people mistrust him so? Perhaps further consideration of his career will help us to understand how this impression arose.

Quick success—vertical mobility—was one of the plainest features of Nixon's career. The public was impressed by his sudden emergence as a fighting senator, the star of the Alger Hiss case, even surprised by his candidacy for the Vice-Presidency. He had gone from the grocery business to the Vice-Presidency in remarkably few years. Nothing, it seems, should delight Americans more than a quick rise of this kind. It is the success story of the self-made man, in which the grocery store is only another version of the log cabin as a symbol of humble beginnings. Those who welcome the quick-rising hero are likely to call him, as they did Lindbergh, a fair-haired boy, a comer, a dark horse, a new Horatio Alger. Was this, in fact, the way the public perceived Nixon? We are forced to conclude that it was not; it did not, at least, emerge as a prominent theme.

If we search for another interpretation, it is possible to say that the very speed with which a man makes his way can sometimes cause him to look odd. "Quick" can have a negative meaning, expressed in terms like "fast" (fast crowd, fast worker), "get-rich-quick," and "upstart." In other words, for all our love of the quick rise, Americans can be quite ambivalent about it. "Climber," "nouveau riche", and "opportunist" are also part of our vocabulary for describing vertical mobility. Many people did, in fact, express resentment of Nixon's rise, with questions such as, "How come he got to be Vice-President?" Resentment might be felt against the manner in which a man climbs (his tactics), his personal attitudes (cheek, brass, brashness, presumption, snobbery), his lack of ability for the position claimed, or it might be a result of simple envy ("If he, why not I?").

In fact, the term "climber" fit Nixon a little better than it fit either of the two men with whom he was most often compared: Eisenhower, as running mate, and Kennedy, as rival for the Presidency. Eisenhower had "earned" his prestige by an impressive military career, and Kennedy was a millionaire following a family tradition of political eminence.[12] More important, there was something about Nixon that made the "opportunist" image develop strongly, that made it possible for people to get the picture of a man who wanted to succeed so badly that he would do almost anything to get there. Surely, the term "opportunist" was heard so often in connection with Nixon that he felt obliged explicitly to disclaim it.[13] It dogged his career, especially his candidacy for Governor of California, when, despite all his protestations to the contrary, many people believed that he would use his position as a stepping stone for another try at the Presidency.

Where did this image come from? Liberal Democratic critics would have no hesitation in suggesting that his vigorous attack on Alger Hiss (putting aside the question of whether Hiss was really guilty) was motivated not by a sincere wish to defend the Republic from Communists but by a desire to win publicity. This, at least, was the burden of a televised "Obituary of Richard M. Nixon,"[14] which generalized the charge to criticize his at-

12. Some society leaders frankly seized upon the snob angle during the Presidential campaign, discounting Nixon for his lack of background: "He isn't really from the best families, you know."

13. "My philosophy has always been: don't lean with the wind. Don't do what is politically expedient. Do what your instinct tells you is right. Public opinion polls are useful if a politician uses them only to learn approximately what the people are thinking, so that he can talk to them more intelligently. The politician who sways with the polls is not worth his pay. And I believe the people eventually catch up with the man who merely tells them what he thinks they should hear." (Richard M. Nixon, *Six Crises,* p. 143.) It is possible that this book itself was written to show the public his sincerity in acting in principle rather than merely to advance himself.

14. By Howard K. Smith, November 11, 1962. This program aroused furious controversy, especially because Hiss was allowed to appear and

tacks on political opponents such as Helen Gahagan Douglas and Jerry Voorhees.

The controversy over Nixon's actual motivation may never be settled, but it seems plain that "Red smears" were the origin of some of the image of his opportunism. This should not be overemphasized, since a charge of "seeking publicity" can be made against anyone who does anything vigorously in the political arena. More important in fixing the "opportunist" image on Nixon was his nimble self-defense on television during the "hound's-tooth" crisis; his use of his dog, "Checkers," as a prop[15] showed that he was able to improvise roles quickly and convinced the public that—whether they liked him or not—he was a skilful showman. *Variety,* the magazine of show business, hailed the show as superb soap opera. It may have convinced the man on the street, but to sophisticated people he was "a little too good." The television appearance boomeranged, making him appear, from his very agility in getting out of difficulty, to be a clever man who was going to use any trick in his bag to get where he wanted to go. To the best of my knowledge, "Tricky Dick" as a nickname first began to circulate after this television appearance.

Such an effect illustrates the hairline that separates a public man from the predicament of being "damned if you do and damned if you don't." Failure to defend himself would have been fatal to Nixon's hopes of running with Eisenhower, but in the minds of many his very success convicted him of opportunism.

Perhaps the "hounds-tooth" crisis was the one that really set Nixon off to a bad start. At any rate, he seems never to

state his belief that he had been used by Nixon. The program implied that Douglas and Voorhees had been smeared by Nixon's charge that their voting records were "parallel" to those of certain left-wingers.

15. Admittedly this dramatic device was from Franklin Delano Roosevelt's similar use of his dog, "Fala." (*Life,* March 16, 1962, p. 118.)

have fully recovered his balance. A certain defensiveness characterized his political attitude—perhaps a real defensiveness, or perhaps people merely saw him that way. His aggressive roles seemed to be compensatory, trying to prove something. At his worst moments he seemed furtive, as though there were something he did not want the public to know. The factor of physiognomy must also be included. Nixon is a good-lookng man, but of the type likely to be cast as a "heavy" in a movie. The fatigue of campaigning and a recurrent problem of "five o'clock shadow" were also blamed for some of these impressions. Any of this may help to explain the issue that was made (and the embarrassment evinced by Nixon), during the 1960 campaign, about a large personal loan made to his brother by the Hughes Tool Company on small security. It may also explain the negative emphasis that was given to Nixon's employment of a public relations counsel, as though this were not the established practice in most major political and business promotional campaigns.[16]

All this occurred to a leader who is an honest American businessman, a good family man, and a Quaker to boot! A vicious circle seemed to have set in from which it was hard for cleverness to escape. No matter what Nixon said, he was damned by a large part of the public. The more convincing his argument, the nobler the deed, the more ingratiating the manner, the more clever seemed the scoundrel underneath. So the logic of suspicion goes.

What more natural than that a man should strive to escape from such a predicament by strenuous efforts to prove his sincerity, to project a good image? Yet James Reston, in *The*

---

16. For example, an article in *The Reporter,* entitled "The Chotiner Academy of Scientific Vote-catching," compared Nixon's tactics with those advised by Machiavelli (September 20, 1956, p. 28). Stanley Kelley has pointed out that public relations staff work is now a standard part of American politics (in *Professional Public Relations and Political Power* [Baltimore, Md.: Johns Hopkins Press, 1956]).

New York Times, blames these efforts more than anything else for Nixon's difficulties:

> What was most obvious about Nixon, particularly to the press . . . was his preoccupation with the machinery of politics. Everything seemed to be contrived, even the appearance of naturalness. He attacked planning but planned everything. He seemed bold and elaborately objective in public, but in private seemed less composed, even uneasy and disturbingly introspective.
>
> This was the real root of his trouble with the reporters: not that they were refusing to report what he said but that they were insisting on reporting all the rest of the picture—not only the words but the techniques, not only the public posture, not only the lines of the play but the elaborate stage directions.
>
> No public figure of our time has ever studied the reporters so much or understood them so little. He thought the reporter should be merely a transmission belt for what he said, not of why he said it. Like the cigarette man, he insisted that "It's what's up front that counts," while the reporter, constantly haunted by the feeling that he might deceive the reader merely by reporting the carefully rehearsed lines in the play, insisted on recording what was going on back stage.
>
> Nixon always resented this. He never seemed to understand the difference between news and the truth. To him what he said was "news" and should be left there.[17]

A subsidiary factor in Nixon's "bad luck" was his relationship to Eisenhower, the national hero. He had to take a scapegoat role for all mud that could not be thrown directly at Eisenhower, either because it would not stick or because it was simply easier to blame Dick. There seems to be no doubt that he was a kind of lightning rod for the Republican Administration. It is to his credit that he accepted this role without complaint—but it was bad luck, rather like being cast

17. November 9, 1962.

in a play with a star who overshadows the other players and takes all the glory. An added burden was that he had to measure up to Ike's image of the plain American hero (the good Joe)—a painful contrast for a man suspected of insincerity. When Ike fell ill, the question became, Would the "opportunist" seize the hero's power?

Six Crises did not repair the damage as Nixon probably expected that it would. Although a very interesting book, which showed vividly the trials undergone in his duties as Vice-President, it did not so much prove the purity of his intentions and courage as, for many people, establish another image: Nixon was "sorry for himself." A reader's letter to *Life* expresses this failure: "I was deeply ashamed as an American and as a Republican. His petty petulances and vain-glorious self-congratulation make a sorry record." Again, he could not win unanimous approval from his own party, let alone support from those who suspected him. The theme of self-pity is the image that Americans have of a "crybaby," a "sissy" who cannot play the game, or an egotist who dwells on his own hurts. Added to this is the effect of the "little boy" role that Nixon unwittingly displayed from time to time. He relied too much in public on his wife and adopted a "junior" attitude toward other men, most notably in the photograph that showed him crying on the shoulder of Senator Knowland. His final rebuke to reporters for having treated him unfairly could hardly fail to fall into the same framework.

Finally, we must give some weight to the psychological impact of the "loser" image, which became prominent after his defeat by Kennedy. Marquis Childs, in the *St. Louis Post-Dispatch,* compared him with Thomas E. Dewey as a man with a losing habit. The *New York Times* wrote: "Everything he says or does these days seems to go wrong. . . . The harder he runs, the more he stumbles." There is a mystique about losers in America, similar to the gamblers' notion about a run of luck. Once a run starts, the good gambler is supposed to increase his bets (if it is a "winning streak") or pocket his money and go home if he is losing. Everyone knows that the chances are the same on every throw of the dice, but the mystique persists. Such an idea depressed Nixon's chances in the California governorship race and produced a kind of reverse bandwagon effect, in which the crowd deserts the loser.

Such negative elements seem to have had a part in Nixon's image problem. They offset such strong points as his role of fighting investigator and hero in the Hiss case, staunch advocate of free enterprise, tough antagonist slugging it out toe-to-toe with Khrushchev in the "kitchen debate," plucky man facing the mobs of South America. As noted, I have not undertaken to balance the account by these assets but have sought the debits which were like a lead weight on his political swim. We may never have a chance to find out more, directly, about Nixon's image trouble, for he has apparently bowed out from the public scene.[18] His final defeat may well have generated sympathy that could mellow, if not erase some of the dislike that he encountered while Vice-President and while campaigning.

How Did the Image Trouble Arise?

Without on-the-spot observation, continual polling, and periodic content analysis of communication media—most of which are usually lacking—it is not easy to identify the precise points at which public images develop and the events that give rise to them. To reconstruct the probable sources of a bad image under such circumstances is conjectural at best. Yet it seems to me that the following episodes were among the crucial dramatic points at which the negative images surveyed above were formed.

Episode	Negative Image
1. Alger Hiss investigation	Red-smearer, publicity-seeker (to some)

18. At this time, August, 1963.

2. Campaigns against Douglas and Voorhees	Red-smearer, opportunist
3. Secret campaign fund charges and "Checkers" speech	Opportunist, slick showman
4. The first television debate with Kennedy[19]	Haggardness, defensiveness, "five o'clock shadow"
5. *Six Crises*	"Sorry for himself," deliberately trying to play the hero
6. Press conference after California defeat	"Crybaby" role confirmed

In no sense should these items be taken as a survey of Nixon's career. They are, rather, a summary of the high—rather, the low—points at which, in my opinion, negative images reached the most people.

Recommendations

To tell Mr. Nixon what he should have done, after this survey, would be as presumptuous as for a laboratory technician to write up a prescription for an unseen patient. This is a question to which even Murray Chotiner, Nixon's public relations doctor, did not have an answer. How, indeed, could anyone tell him to do better than the "Checkers" speech, which everyone hailed as a masterpiece of political showmanship?

Suggestions are especially difficult because Nixon in fact did follow many of the conventional rules of public relations. It adds little to point out that his relations with the press could have been improved or that he could have had better luck in television presentation or better consultants for his autobiography.

19. A survey of 31 independent studies of public response to the four debates shows that the first one was the one Nixon most clearly lost. At least 55 per cent of the adult population heard each debate. The public was more interested in the clash of personalities and analyzing the character of contestants than in the issues. (Elihu Katz and Jacob J. Feldman, "The Kennedy-Nixon Debates: A Survey of Surveys," *Studies in Public Opinion* [University of Chicago], No. 4, Autumn, 1962, pp. 127–63.)

If there is any lesson in the "Checkers" episode, it must be that cleverness and technique do not always pay off even when they "succeed" in the immediate objective. Perhaps the moral should be, as some have implied, that less technique should have been used. Is it enough to say that one should be sincere, be himself (like Will Rogers)—and be lucky?

If what is involved is simply a matter of the kind of man one is, again we are at a loss. No one could with a straight face advise a public man to go back and get another personality— and Nixon, after all, had a good one, and it would not be hard to name a dozen or more successful leaders who had rather obvious personal flaws. If there is anything to conclude from a case such as Nixon's, it is that personality alone is not the key to the kind of public image that develops, because so many other ingredients go into it: "propaganda," on the one hand, and "facts," on the other, and chief among all these things, perhaps, is the drama that takes shape. This drama is a matter of how one looks to various audiences as a result of having played certain roles. If one's roles and audiences are right, he will look good, and if they are wrong, he will look bad. His real character, of course, will have something to do with the kinds of roles he chooses and plays, but by no means does it govern alone. Good intentions can lead to disaster, and bad ones may fail to invoke the villain's role. The relationship is not very much closer than that between the real character of an actor and the parts he plays on a stage. His real character may show through his roles, but is it not more likely that his role will govern the part of his character that the audience sees?

If a public man tries to control the role he plays before public audiences—to use the techniques of public relations— certain difficulties are immediately apparent. First, he is not running the show; others, even minor characters, are playing parts that may overshadow or discredit his. Especially in Amer-

ica, of course, a public person cannot control any large segment
of mass communication media, as was conspicuously true with
Nixon. And, in the last analysis, the public (and its countless
subgroups), not the media, makes the images—decides what
to be interested in, what to talk about, and what slant and
name to give it. Output does not equal input. Characterizations,
nicknames, anecdotes, types, and even legends come out of
the popular imagination for which events are only cues, not
sufficient causes. Most public persons suffer from lack of feedback; they do not have adequate and continual contact with
the images of them that are forming. The usual polls, surveys,
and public relations advice may not be enough to keep them
really in touch. And here, perhaps, is a point of advice for
Mr. Nixon, who apparently did not really know what kind of
image he was projecting and was baffled because it did not
come through better. Perhaps improved ways will be found
for analyzing public images, and perhaps we shall all benefit
if public men stay in touch with them.

Another modest piece of advice for Mr. Nixon might come
from the career of another man who had image trouble, Harry
Truman. Many blemishes can be erased, rather remarkably,
simply by doing forceful things more often and more forcefully.
As Truman discovered, a sadly deteriorated image can be
renovated by following the reckless motto, "Give 'em hell—
and go on giving 'em hell!" There is a risk, of course, of worse,
but, in confrontations, the game is basically "double or nothing." You may lose a series, yet win all in the last round.
Nixon, of course, did seek "strong" roles (the kitchen debate,
the South American tour);[20] but perhaps he did not press
strong roles with sufficient consistency. A real instinct for
self-dramatization, possessed by people like Mayor La Guardia

20. A remarkable series of photographs in *Life* earlier in Nixon's
career showed him flirting with danger by thrusting his hand into a
lion's cage.

of New York or Charles de Gaulle might have suggested to Nixon many other strong roles that would have erased the "sorry for himself" and "Checkers" image.[21]

The purpose of this analysis of Nixon's image trouble is to explore its nature and possible causes, and to find the principles that might apply to other public men. So far, I have tried to suggest that more image analysis is needed to keep public men in touch with themselves, that the analysis might well be in terms of social types, and that the key to shaping images is drama.

As a final qualification, let me say that the idea that a man like Nixon has image trouble is relative; it is the old question of the relation of the frog to the pond. If Nixon has image trouble as a Presidential candidate, it does not follow that he would have similar trouble as a practicing lawyer or even as a congressman. On the other hand, were the position we were concerned with as ennobled as that of saint, then even Abraham Lincoln might be found to have image trouble if he aspired to it. Image trouble is also relative to one's competitors, that is, how good one looks in comparison. On any absolute scale, the man whose image we have been considering in this chapter would rate very high indeed.

Image trouble has other dimensions, which I shall explore in the next chapter. I have tried to show that a man who is aspiring to act well may develop image trouble in spite of good intentions. Another side of the problem is that a man may act very badly and not develop image trouble at all.

21. On the other hand, I would not recommend for Nixon a "folksy" manner such as that of Truman. With an image of insincerity established, such an approach could only boomerang.

CHAPTER FIVE

CRISIS IN THE
IMAGE: TYPE-VIOLATION

All our idols have feet of clay but some
have bigger feet than others.

When Lillian Ross published her candid portrait of Ernest
Hemingway, many of his devotees were incensed. They were
shown an uncouth, bearlike man, boozing with pals, affecting
the manners of a pugilist, mutilating the King's English by a
kind of Indian talk, shocking an old lady in an elevator by
saying, "Good Christ!"

Miss Ross reports that these facts upset Hemingway-lovers
because they violated their conception of what a writer should
be. Not only did her subject outrage the genteel conception of
the writer, he failed in dedication to his craft. He let his readers
down by playing the celebrity and clown rather than sticking
to his work. "They didn't like Hemingway to be Hemingway.
They wanted him to be somebody else—probably themselves.
So they came to the conclusion that either Hemingway had
not been portrayed as he was or, if he was that way, I shouldn't
have written about him at all."[1] The dislikers of Hemingway
were, of course, delighted. It simply confirmed their opinion

1. Lillian Ross, *Portrait of Hemingway* (New York: Simon and
Schuster, 1961), pp. 14–17.

that he really was a bum. Their image of him was not only sustained but gloriously amplified.

We are concerned here, however, with type violation. What happens when a man runs afoul of the image people have of him? Does he lose his status or keep it in spite of violations? Where is the breaking point? What kind of violations cause image crisis? Can an image confer a kind of privilege that lets some men "get away with murder"?

Hemingway was allowed behavior as a celebrity that would not have been permissible to another writer, say, Norman Vincent Peale or Anne Morrow Lindbergh. Some images are sensitive to small things, such as a fist-fight or a bottle of liquor, while others seem to thrive on the very same elements. We cannot formulate a simple rule about public images in absolute terms such as, "Violate common expectations, and people won't like you," or "Do something bad and you will become a villain." Nor can we say that the key to popularity is to behave correctly in public and always do what is expected of a person in a given position. None of these propositions can deal with important exceptions.

The following observations, however, may help to explain some of the trouble that celebrities have with public images and also the times when they should have trouble but do not.

1. Leaving the realm of routine and entering the dramatic domain always throws roles into a crucible of crisis where anything is possible. (This was the subject of chap. iii.)

2. Public images are more fluid in the early stages of their development. A bad part or a violation of type early in the game, when the public image is forming and "on probation," is more crucial and potentially destructive of popularity than it would be later. This applies to the dialectical tennis game, not hitting the ball the public has returned is equivalent to "not playing the game," and knocking it out of the court or kicking the net down is worse. At a later stage, fans may be dis-

gruntled, worried, even outraged by such behavior, but they may remain faithful.

3. The man who is simply bad will probably become a villain. But if he is established as a certain kind of person who does bad things (whether hero, villain, or clown), he may be almost as bad as he pleases. The image gives him a certain privilege and duty. The specific kind of image that the public has formed is the key to what he should do and what he can get away with.

4. Having found a successful image, a celebrity should not too flagrantly violate it or he may lose his status. But a point may come at which he cannot violate it even if he tries. The symbol can be so functionally important that people will put up with deceptions, close their eyes to obvious facts, even insist on preserving what is known to be a legend.

Before considering these complexities, let us look at a few cases that seem to be covered by the simple rule, "Be good and do what everyone expects."

SIMPLE TYPE VIOLATION

As the leading citizen of Pecos, Texas, Billie Sol Estes lived up to the Hollywood concept of a Texas millionaire. He had four Cadillacs, a private twin-engined plane, and a chauffeur-valet. He was also a lay preacher and elder of the church, sponsored youth activities, espoused stern views on morality, and seemed to have a special place in his heart for poor Negroes and Mexicans, for whom he built churches. Then, one day, his façade collapsed. A personal feud with the editor of the local newspaper (whom he had tried to ruin for business and political reasons) brought about a series of articles that uncovered an at first unbelievable gamut of ruthless business tactics and confidence games against his townspeople and even the United States government, culminating in Estes' investigation and conviction as one of the biggest swindlers, if not biggest millionaires, Texas ever produced. "Big Daddy" turned out to be a crook.[2]

This event illustrates a simple kind of type violation. The rule seems to be working: if you want to be popular, be good and do what everyone expects. Failure occurred because a side of Estes' character was revealed that contradicted the façade he had built up. His public image collapsed, to be replaced by another appropriate one, the villain.

Type violation need not, of course, be due to crime or scandal. Almost any public conduct that contradicts an image important to people can be a type violation. Arthur Godfrey, as a popular TV personality and disc jockey, unwittingly violated his own type by feuding with and firing several entertainers (former protegés) on his show. He had built up the conception of a "good Joe," full of genial humor, surrounded by his friends, and taking care of his protegés in a fatherly way. Then he summarily fired several of them. The public was shocked. Indignant letters came in. Godfrey threw up his hands as if baffled by all the fuss. "The last time they complained they didn't like the way I fired the guy. This time I did it like it's done in any organized business and they still don't like it." The trouble was that Godfrey had built up an image of friendship in which businesslike (or simply bad-tempered) behavior had no public place. He could not be a "good Joe" and publicly cast off the people he had befriended. His subsequent illness brought him much sympathy, but it could not be denied that this comparatively minor role violation had cost him considerable popularity.

Fidel Castro alienated the American public by a gross type violation. In his early role, he had been rather a darling of the liberals, fighting as an underdog against Batista and all his

2. Richard Oulahan, "The Bumpkin Who Turned into a Warped Wizard," *Life,* June 1, 1962, pp. 86–90.

gangsters, seemingly the hope of democracy in Cuba. Batista was a perfect villain, and anyone who fought him had, by contrast, to look like a hero. When the dictator fled in 1959, taking his millions and his henchmen with him, it seemed that a new era had dawned for Cuba; Castro was in the position of Sir Lancelot liberating people from a dragon-guarded castle. A year before coming into power, he had reassured Americans by declaring himself: "I have never been and am not a Communist. If I were, I should have the courage to say it." This seemed enough. But three years afterward he said in a speech, "I am a Marxist-Leninist and will be a Marxist-Leninist until the last day of my life." The "mob trials," purges, expropriations, and his alignment with Soviet Russia left little doubt that this was his true position. It is not really known to what extent Castro was driven into this position[3] and to what extent he planned it all along, but the about-face shattered the humanitarian image, and the scales fell away from the eyes of liberals, who now saw him as a bloodthirsty dictator along the lines of Stalin. He had offered the United States a "Trojan Horse," which at one time might have been accepted.

Charles Lindbergh, idol though he was, violated his type in 1938 in a way that almost cost him his pedestal. He accepted the Order of the German Eagle from the hands of General Goering at a dinner in Berlin at the home of the American Ambassador. Though Lindbergh was embarrassed by the honor and it would have been a diplomatic discourtesy to refuse it, still many Americans were convinced that he was sympathetic to Nazism. This also seemed confirmed by his isolationist speeches shortly after Germany began war in 1939.

3. Sheer overdrive from war may have helped Castro fracture his his own type image. During the revolt he looked good as a fighter, but humanitarian ideology requires that when you become an administrator you stop fighting and become a welfare worker, combining benevolence with rational justice. This, apparently, Castro could not do, ideology or no ideology. His own temperament and his people, as well as United States antagonism, may have forced him to violate the liberal type.

A book written by his wife, *The Wave of the Future,* was seen
as a panegyric of racism and fascism. His honorary membership in the Lafayette Escadrille was rescinded, and proposals
were made to remove his name from various public schools.
After President Roosevelt criticized him, Lindbergh resigned
his Air Force Reserve colonel's commission. In sum, he had
been "stamped with a Swastika."[4] To some, the former stainless
symbol of young Americanism was now "the most dangerous
man in America."[5] Only well after America's entrance into
the war did the old picture of the air ace begin to be restored.
News stories told how Lindbergh, while flying a civilian mission
for the Army, had destroyed a Japanese plane. As a reward
for his services as civilian adviser to the Air Force, in 1954,
thirteen years after he had surrendered his rank, he was rein-
stated as a brigadier general in the Air Force Reserve.

This image decline had a background, however. It was
really the third stage of a process that had begun shortly after
Lindbergh became a national idol in 1927. The first stage was
a period of alienation from the press and public resulting from
his refusal to play the hero in the way the public wanted.[6]
He was elusive, even unco-operative. Once he flew over a field
at which people had gathered to meet him and landed at an
empty one (his explanation was that he had not wished to
endanger persons congesting the landing area). He had a feud
with reporters, especially at his wedding. His reticence, originally seen as charming modesty, began to be reinterpreted as
unfriendliness or vanity. Editorials and magazine articles asked,
"What's Wrong with Lindbergh?"

The second downward step for Lindbergh's public image
took place in 1935, when he announced his intention to quit

4. Dixon Wecter, *The Hero in America* (New York: Scribner, 1949),
pp. 435–39.
5. DeWitt Snell, *The Lindberghs* (Schenectady, N.Y.: privately
printed, 1941), pp. 1, 7–8.
6. James Thurber parodied this role conflict in "The Greatest Man
in the World."

the country to live in England, after the tragic kidnapping of his son. Although people were sympathetic, they could not avoid the feeling that there was something wrong in this decision. Did he prefer Englishmen to Americans? Why did he not stick it out in the land that had nurtured him and made him famous? Many condemned his behavior as a kind of disloyalty, a disgrace to the nation; he was called such names as "quitter," "coward," "Herod."[7] The swastika crisis was only the climax of this trend.

This, then, was a type violation in three stages. It damaged but did not permanently destroy the status of a major national hero. One reason, of course, is that Lindbergh was eventually exonerated from all these suspicions, not convicted as were Estes and Castro. But, in addition, at a late stage of its development it is hard to dislodge an image, especially when important functions hang on it (as in the case of cult leaders and major heroes). Lindbergh had passed the time of probation and was enshrined as a living immortal, and it would have taken more than this to dislodge him. Many famous heroes have had ups and downs, playing for a time the scapegoat but ultimately staying in the hero's niche, for example, Wellington, Cromwell, Lincoln,[8] and Washington (who was once threatened by a mob of ten thousand people in Philadelphia who wanted to drag him from his home).[9]

But national heroes do fall if a role violation is serious and occurs early enough. For example, Lord Cardigan, who had led the charge of the Light Brigade, returned to England to be toasted and adulated; the sweater he wore became famous. He had been one of the few actually to reach the Russian guns and survive the attack, and he seemed a figure of pure valor. But

7. *Time,* January 6, 1936, pp. 34–36 ff.
8. It is hard to accept now the names Lincoln was called, even by northern newspapers: "Despicable tyrant," "The Ape," "Illinois Beast," "cringing, crawling creature," "assassin," "savage," "The Fiend." (Herbert Mitgang, *Lincoln as They Saw Him* [New York: Rinehart, 1956].)
9. Dixon Wecter, *The Hero in America,* p. 126.

in the countercharges, investigation, and libel suit that followed his return to England, certain facts were soon brought out. He was a total egoist, who had shown "callous lack of responsibility for his men" and in the attack had in a real sense deserted them, had lived on a yacht with a chef apart from the army, and cared for nothing except his own reputation. Brave though he was, he could be a "personification no longer" of the glory of the Light Brigade. England had no real hero for that episode.[10]

Cardigan's hero image was nipped in the bud. The same facts ten or fifty years later would have had much less effect, just as today a debunking biography of General Custer does little to diminish the glory of the hero of the Little Big Horn. But the collapse of a long-established image, when it comes, is bitter and devastating because so many people have come to depend on it. People will cling to an image tenaciously and let it go only when forced. They prefer a legend that does something for them to a truth that does nothing. When an established image is destroyed, people may turn in revenge against the leader who has let them down, and he swings from hero to scapegoat; they accuse him of falsehood and treason and strike him down.

This phenomenon is illustrated by the fall of Mussolini, lynched by a mob while trying to flee Italy. Mussolini had established himself as a strong man by his March on Rome and his grandiose posture for over two decades. But his close followers saw through him, and many despised him for his weaknesses (he was a stuffed shirt, anyone could bully him, and he lived in fear; he had temper tantrums, stomach ulcers, and syphilis; he was a ladies' man). The task of the Fascist party

10. The charge was ordered by Lord Lucan, who misunderstood orders from Lord Raglan, who died in the Crimea of fever while Lucan got most of the blame. Cardigan could have been the hero if he had not been what Americans would call "a heel." See Cecil Woodham-Smith, *The Reason Why* (New York: Time, Inc., 1962; original ed., 1953), pp. 250–91.

was to hide his real character from the Italian people; his followers protected him from public scrutiny by policemen disguised as admirers.[11] Perhaps if things had gone well politically the sham might have continued. But the Germans openly treated Mussolini as a stooge; Mussolini himself said, "I am tired of acting as Hitler's tail-light!" When the people finally turned against him, the cause seems to have been not only blame for military reverses (other leaders have lost wars without being lynched) but also outrage and shame at being taken in by him with the proof of his falsity and guilt implied by his ignominious flight in disguise. (Hitler's "last stand" could not be similarly interpreted by the Germans.[12])

A classic disaster to a long-established image was the "Bloody Sunday Massacre" of 1905 in Russia. A crowd of unarmed men, women, and children, led by a priest, Father Gapon, marched to the Winter Palace of Czar Nicholas II, singing "God Save the Czar" and carrying banners and ikons. They wanted only to present a petition for improvement in working conditions and relief from police oppression. As they approached the Troitski Bridge, the Czar's troops opened fire, killing hundreds and wounding thousands. Though the revolution came later, this was the act that shattered the bond between the Czar and the people. They could no longer believe in "The Little Father," that he meant them well in spite of being surrounded by bad ministers.

Such collapses seem plain enough. They are the blowouts, and in most cases they are caused by a spike. Let us turn now, however, to the more minute punctures and frictions that can cause image trouble. One of these is illustrated by the Ingrid Bergman scandal of 1949–50. While making a film in Italy, this movie star became the mother of a baby boy, whose father was not her husband but the director of the film, Roberto Rosselini. Thereafter, she divorced her husband and married

11. Paolo Monelli, *Mussolini* (New York: Vanguard, 1954).
12. H. R. Trevor-Roper, *The Last Days of Hitler.*

Rosselini. As a result, women's clubs and movie fans all over the United States threatened to boycott her pictures. She became "box-office poison," and her Hollywood career was finished. Even in Sweden, audiences were so unkind that Bergman turned on them bitterly from the stage, saying, "The Swedes begrudge anyone who attempts to rise above the crowd."

The curious thing about this scandal is that many stars have behaved worse without incurring such public displeasure. Bergman was puzzled, as shown in her effort to blame it on jealousy. Why should anything so small as a baby out of phase with a remarriage cause a hubbub in an industry that had produced stars like Gypsy Rose Lee and Mae West? The answer must be sought in the peculiar status that Bergman had acquired as a result of starring as a nun and, particularly, as Joan of Arc. She had been typed as a symbol of purity, and the public was not to be so easily cheated. It might be all right for others to flout public morality but not for Bergman, who had become a moral leader, a model of rectitude. Catholic countries have saints and nuns, the Far East has holy men and women, but Protestant countries must take their models of rectitude where they find them. Sometimes athletes (like Bill Tilden) are surprised to find that they have this status, and this, I think, is also the key to the furor evoked by the Eddie Fisher–Debbie Reynolds–Liz Taylor love triangle of 1959. Debbie's idyllic marriage to Eddie had become fixed in the public mind as a symbol of the way marriage ought to be; Liz's intrusion, then, put her in the role of the temptress entering the Garden of Eden.

As another example, note the repercussions felt by Franklin Delano Roosevelt after a remark he made while casting his vote in 1944. After he entered the curtained booth, the voting-machine handle was heard being jerked irritably back and forth and then a voice familiar to the nation said, "The God-damned thing won't work." This language went like a wave over the country. The Glendale Ministerial Association sent a letter asking Roosevelt to apologize for his "shocking profanity":

> We . . . do hereby express to you our deep grief over your regrettable breach against God and the conscience and hopes of millions of people of this and other lands. . . . We earnestly pray that you may feel . . . contrition . . . and reassure faithful constituents and friends the world over whom you have so greatly grieved.

Roosevelt's feeling may well have been that it is enough to be President without having to be a saint too; but one peculiarity of the American scene seems to be that the President and First Lady (unlike Vice-Presidents, congressmen, and their ladies) have to provide leadership in morals and taste as well as politics. (In England the Crown has this function, but the Prime Minister is free to be human.) The wife of the American President must expect criticisms like the following:

> Mrs. Kennedy is one of the most gracious ladies our country has ever known—a wonderful example to hold up to our growing daughters. Therefore, I consider the picture of her seated on a swing in India with her dress hiked above her knees is very poor taste.

A similar explanation can be found for the unexpectedly severe reaction to Governor Rockefeller's divorce and remarriage, premised as it was on his image as a possible moral leader for Americans.

The lesson is that if the expectations of a status are very high, a relatively slight fault can cause image crisis. Just as a surgeon who operated without washing his hands would be severly criticized, so a leader who has the role of moral exemplar must operate at a higher level than do other popular favorites and be prepared to bear with this "unfairness."[13]

13. Of course, carping and criticism are the lot of almost anyone who appears much before the public eye, because so many groups are watching. He is in the predicament of trying to please everybody. As one television performer quipped, "Say 'Happy Mother's Day' and people will write in, asking, 'What's the matter? Don't you like your father?'" But the point is that the favorite who is a moral leader is doubly subject to such carping.

RESISTANCE OF THE IMAGE TO CRISIS

We turn now to the other side of the coin. While some leaders are excessively criticized for small faults, we find the paradox that others "get away with murder," remaining popular as they do things that would ruin the reputation of an ordinary man. We can trace this immunity to at least two general sources.

First, each role has its privileges. John Barrymore was a notorious drunkard and rake. Rudolph Valentino was rumored to have been at one time a pimp. Errol Flynn cavorted from one amour to another, ending with a nineteen-year-old girl. Tallulah Bankhead, as a "bad girl"—the part she played so well on stage—was expected to say shocking things in public and lead a private life that would have been deeply deplored for Mary Pickford or Ingrid Bergman. Such behavior did not appreciably hurt the popularity of these stars. Indeed, one can make a case that their box-office appeal was enhanced. Again, when Gene Krupa, the jazz drummer, and Robert Mitchum (a movie actor who specialized in vagabond and soldier-of-fortune parts) were convicted of narcotics violations and sent to prison, some predicted that their careers were ended, but it did not turn out so. Loyal fans greeted them upon their release from prison; they remained as popular as ever, perhaps more than they would have been without this publicity. Likewise, for playboys like "Ruby" Rubirosa and General Raphael Trujillo, Jr., their romances, seductions, divorces, and obvious fortune-hunting or wastrel living do not seem greatly to offend the public. Indeed, the question might well be, why would people care to read about them if they were not as they are?

The public actually expects them to act as they do and would be disappointed if they did not. It would be something like reading a story about Don Juan and finding no seduction, or of Robin Hood without the Bishop's being robbed or the

Sheriff's being defied. The "great lover" role played by men like Barrymore is entirely consistent with the life of a roué; indeed, news-readers would follow his personal affairs with the eager expectation that more was forthcoming. Likewise, the use of marijuana was in character for a jazz musician (it is believed in some quarters to have a beneficial effect on his playing), whereas in a bank executive or the mother of small children it would be shocking. The point is that when a celebrity becomes established in a certain part, he is expected to play it off stage as well as on stage. It was no surprise to learn that George Raft hobnobbed with gangsters and gamblers; indeed, the public would have been disappointed if he had not. So we must say that if a celebrity becomes popular by a role that infringes morality—even as a "favorite villain"—he has a greater privilege to play that role in real life than does an ordinary man.[14]

A second source of immunity for misbehaving public figures is in the elements in their image that compensate the public for whatever faults they possess. Success in a more important role makes up for the fault displayed. A classic case is in Lincoln's report to the critics of General U. S. Grant's drinking, to the effect that more of them should do as Grant did. The reckoning of what is "more important" is based not on logical or realistic considerations but on sentiment. Thus, it might be more important to some people that as Jesse James went through a train he gallantly kissed some of the women while taking their valuables than that he shot a man getting on. This is essentially the immunity of a Robin Hood, something he does pleases public sentiment more than his misdeeds shock; indeed, the crime may seem like a technicality. It was constantly said in Louisiana during Huey Long's regime that though he played fast and loose with public funds, he did it to build bridges,

14. I do not try here to analyze why an immoral role should make a person popular but only to note that his privilege comes from consistency with a role so earned.

schools, and hospitals for the people. A political boss may be known to be crooked, yet as long as he does favors and fills breadbaskets, people may find it in their hearts to forgive him.

Such compensation seems to apply to irritating personality faults as well. A great performer is permitted to be a "prima donna"; a "genius" is allowed, even expected, to have eccentricities that would be more severely criticized in an ordinary man. One of the most important compensating elements in the role of a "bad actor" is comedy; make it funny enough and you can get away with murder, and that is the license of the comic rogue. Falstaff was a coward, a glutton, a drunkard, a liar, a thief, and a fraud, but it was psychologically impossible to see him as a villain. It is interesting to note that for a long time Americans failed to see any threat in Huey Long. His tomfoolery disarmed them, he was a folksy wisecracker who finally came to be called the "Senate clown," and the galleries filled with people who came just to hear him. It may not be out of place to recall that for too long Americans dismissed Hitler as not really a menace; one could not take seriously a man with such a moustache. To some extent, the same was true for "Uncle Joe" Stalin.

But though certain roles carry a privilege that makes their possessors immune to some kinds of criticism, it is also probable that every role has its Achilles' heel. A symbolic leader might be given leniency in many fields and then find that a trifling incident caused great embarrassment, even a real crisis in his own image. To refer again to the redoubtable Huey Long, a minor accident in his career showed that he could be discredited even in the eyes of his loyal followers among the poor whites of Louisiana. At Sands Point, Long Island, in 1933, Huey made an unseemly remark to a lady at a dance; her youthful escort caught him in the washroom and slugged him over the left eye. The newspapers heard of it, the story spread, and the whole country chuckled; irreverent grins followed him everywhere. He was laughed at and booed in his home state, a medal was struck by his opponents to the hero who socked Huey Long, and many papers published his political obituary with black edges. The "Kingfish" had been labeled a coward. Two personal challenges were offered him by rivals wishing to exploit his predicament, one by Mayor Walmsley of New Orleans, offering to fight him "any place, any time." The Long machine suffered its first major defeat since he had become governor, losing the New Orleans mayoralty election. Though the event did not stop Long, it had an effect out of all proportion to its material consequences.

From that time on, Huey Long worked under a symbolic disadvantage from the fact that as a man he inspired no physical fear. The epithet of coward cast a black shadow over his reputation.[15] To be typed as a fool (a coward and weakling) in this way had an especially damaging effect on Long's status as a popular hero because he could not maintain his image of "Kingfish" if he let an ordinary man get the better of him or, even worse, if he showed the white feather. Such a fool role cancels a hero role. He might as hero connive, use force, play the clown, even the prophet, but as a coward a very important element of his popular appeal had been impaired. One may surmise that it would not have taken many such incidents to put Huey out of business almost as effectively as did the assassin's bullet.

The search for an Achilles' heel should be an important part of the propaganda against any public figure by his opponents. Indiscriminate muckraking and scandalmongering is not nearly as effective as finding exactly the thing that contradicts a public image, that violates the specific functional role on which the public depends. One cannot contradict a great-lover type by finding him guilty of marital infidelity, nor would toughness and meanness hurt a boxing champion publicly if that was the character he displayed in the ring. On the other

15. Forrest Davis, *Huey Long: A Candid Bigraphy* (New York: Dodge Pub. Co., 1935), pp. 201–28.

hand, a leader whose popularity depends on being a "good Joe" could be seriously damaged by a story about his meanness (as in the case of Arthur Godfrey). If a political or financial boss has a reputation as a "smart operator," evidence of skilful dishonesty may merely confirm his status; but clumsy bungling, or being taken in by a little man, could hurt. For military heroes, athletes, cowboys, western gunfighters, and such, a central feature of their role is, of course, valor. Any cowardice or unfairness in a fight could contradict this.

The last remark is illustrated in a famous image crisis, the "slap heard round the world" administered to a private soldier during World War II by General George S. Patton. One of the most popular of American generals, Patton had been conspicuous as a tank commander whose rough-and-ready, swashbuckling ways and brace of pearl-handled pistols had established him with an image not unlike that of the young Theodore Roosevelt. Riding the crest of popularity after a successful invasion of Italy that promised to place his name in history, he made a trifling misstep that jeopardized his whole career and showed what a bully role can do to a hero's status. While on an inspection tour of a military hospital in Sicily, Patton saw a soldier sitting on his cot weeping and asked him why. The invalid replied, "It's my nerves, I guess I can't stand shelling." Whereupon Patton, in rage, upbraided the sick man profanely as a coward and a "yellowbelly" and struck him on the back of the head with his hand. After more remarks along the same lines to the other patients he then left the hospital.

It soon became evident that the general had committed more than a *faux pas*. The man he struck was not a malingerer but a good soldier who had refused to leave the front until ordered to do so, and, at the time he was slapped, the soldier was delirious from malaria. When the story spread, it caused a furor that shook the Army from its top brass to its lowest rank. Discipline promptly descended on Patton; he was forced to make personal apologies to the patient, to the medical com-

mander of the hospital, and to every division of the Seventh
Army and its officers. Notwithstanding the apology, deeper
questions remained. Should Patton be more severely punished?
Was he one of those detestable types, a sadistic bully? The
newspaper *PM* called for a court martial, the Senate delayed
his promotion, then under consideration, and the whole nation
discussed the incident. But opinion polls showed that most
Americans, knowing Patton's character and the special circumstances, found it possible to excuse the outbreak as due to
nervous tension. No doubt his established reputation helped
him. *PM* called for a court martial, but its editor had to admit
that his mail was running almost 5 to 1 against such action;
a Gallup poll showed that 70 per cent of the people preferred
keeping the General at his post. Typical explanations were:
"He's too fine a commander to be removed just for that one
mistake." "He had to put up with so much. No wonder he lost
his temper." "His action was inexcusable—but he would be
hard to replace." "He has proved himself qualified to lead and
that's what counts."[16] Even servicemen backed him 2 to 1.
After a delay, the Senate finally confirmed his promotion to
major general.

Patton was saved, but the incident, small as it was, came
close to destroying the reputation of a national hero. It did so
because the bully image directly contradicted that of the valiant
commander.[17] What saved him? In part, it was his established
reputation; people found it hard to believe that he really was
a bully. Then, too, we must consider the climate of feeling and
the corresponding role needs: "War is hell on everybody. We
must have tough men to win. Patton is the kind of man for the
job."

In other words, in some situations and for some men it is

16. The Gallup Poll, *Washington Post,* December 15, 1943.
17. This might be analyzed into the following components: (1) the
chivalrous obligation of the strong to help the weak, (2) a commander's
paternalism toward his men, and (3) avoidance of unfairness that could
imply cowardice.

appropriate to be tough. And no small part of the redemption was due to Patton himself. Deeply conscious of how the incident had hurt his reputation and fearing that the war would be over soon, he pleaded for a chance to redeem himself: "For God's sake . . . you've got to get me into this fight before the war is over. I'm in the doghouse now and I'm apt to die there unless I pull something spectacular to get me out." Given a new command, his brilliant action in Europe, beating the Russians in the race to Berlin, wiped away the sting if not the memory of the episode.[18]

This case involves the interplay of "hero" and "villain" roles. Patton, with his image in crisis from the imputation of a villain role, had to do something oppositely good to counteract it. He had the dramatic sense to know that the middle ground of satisfactory performance would not be enough, that it takes an extreme to counteract an extreme, and he chose precisely the kind of role that would reaffirm his hero image. Such a dramatic instinct has saved many a great man from going down in history as a villain.

The more general conclusion we are seeking is a formula that would apply to any celebrity's popularity and the kinds of things that are, for him, privileged or disadvantageous. The first generalization is that what is involved is a matter of the central role. A celebrity should not contradict the thing for which people admire him or that they expect from him. In other areas there may be license, especially if the misconduct

18. His superior, General Omar Bradley, speculated about how much of Patton's urge to redeem himself dramatically had to do with the winning of the war: "I've often wondered how much this desire to square himself with the American people produced Patton in his spectacular race across the face of France. For certainly no other commander could have matched him in reckless haste and boldness. Someday a definitive biography of Patton will go into the issue more exhaustively than I. Until then I shall go on believing that the enlisted man whose face he slapped in a Sicilian hospital did more to win the war in Europe than any other soldier in the Army." (Omar N. Bradley, "The War America Fought," Part II, *Life*, April 16, 1951, p. 192.)

is somehow a logical outgrowth or privilege of the established role. But one must first find this role—the central one on which the public depends—since the requirements for a saint are very different from those of a popular rogue. Staying in character means that there is vast tolerance for "more of the same."

Second, the events that will produce a type violation are just as specific as the central role itself. Not generalized "bad behavior" but only certain acts are the arrows that can enter the Achilles' heel. But these arrows are different for different kinds of images. They must be determined logically and, as far as possible, empirically. A table of "opposites" can, however, be set up from theory alone.

If the central role is that of a . . .	*then it violates the type to play the part of a . . .*
tough guy	softie, weakling
brave man	coward, bully
saint, incorruptible	profligate, crook
lover, sexual object	prig, prude
playboy	hard worker, self-made man
hard worker	playboy
good Joe	mean guy, introvert
favorite villain	good Joe
democrat	authoritarian
big shot, top dog	stooge, yes-man, figurehead, democrat
champion	loser
big brain	ignoramus, simp, easy mark
smart operator	easy mark, square-shooter
clown	straight man
good sport	poor sport, whiner

It may be that, in general, any villain or fool role contradicts any hero role, but we must be more specific in order to understand why some heroes are hurt by a particular villain role and others are not.

A third generalization: if a celebrity contradicts his central role and throws his image into crisis, he should immediately reaffirm his status by an extreme, dramatic action along the lines of his central role, that is, he should go on doing what he had been doing, only more so.

But suppose we are dealing with the comparatively rare case of a leader who can do practically anything he pleases without violating the confidence of his followers. Some leaders seem to be above the law, to have a charismatic privilege beyond logical criticism. We need not suppose, then, that the nice contradictions outlined above will inevitably result in a type violation. It may be conceded that at a late stage in development (legends live for thousands of years), and especially where strong faith and major functions depend on a leader, he may be virtually indestructible. Even leaders still living can have this invulnerability; things that should harm them do not or they are simply not believed. This is especially likely to be true of cult leaders, like Father Divine, Elijah Muhammed, or Krishna Venta (who was accused of immorality and wife-seduction by two cult members, who then blew him and themselves up—but not his image). Aimee Semple McPherson's followers remained loyal to her after scandalous escapades, law suits, and, finally, her suicide; they just could not believe it of her—or perhaps they needed her too much. It can be said that loyalty blinds such followers or that they see but cannot change their image. After all, people even found it necessary to whitewash George Washington by expunging from his letters passages such as "don't give a damn."[19] This is far short of fanaticism, but enough to reject the truth.

In short, there is probably a turning point at which images become immune to criticism, depending upon the length of time they have been established, whether the leader has found a true niche, the strength of faith they induce, and the importance of the functions that depend on the image. Our concern, however, is with the stages at which dramatic action does make a difference and crises are a real possibility.

19. Dixon Wecter, *op. cit.*

Breaking Out of a Type

The more firmly established an image, the harder it is to break out of it. There are, of course, occasions when a celebrity wants to destroy his reputation rather than keep it. His problem, then, is either to find a new type the hard way, by dialectical selection, or to seek the Achilles' heel of his own image in order to pierce it.

A common instance is among movie stars and other entertainers who are vexed because they are fixed into a certain type and cannot break out of it. Nelson Eddy, for example, finds that almost twenty years after playing the role, his imprint in Royal Canadian Mounted Police garb is still firm in the public consciousness:

> Not too long ago, an English nightclub owner wanted us to come over, which was fine except for his quaint suggestion that I do my whole act wearing a Mountie uniform. I said thanks but no thanks. It's incredible the way this concept hangs on. I haven't worn the Mountie uniform since the movie, "Rose Marie," and that, to the astonishment of people who think it was just last week, was way back in 1935. I'm beginning to believe my own line—I was a teen-age Mountie.[20]

Another movie star, Ronald Reagan, comments:

> Actors starting in the business often try desperately to be typed. . . . [They] welcome this pattern of casting because producers . . . will call on them again and again. . . . [But] I know a few fellows who are sick to death of playing cowboys and gangsters on television and in the movies, but that's the image they're stuck with. . . . One of the reasons television is such a boon to actors is that it allows them to spread their wings, as it were, to play many different roles, to break out of their type.

20. Donald Freeman, "Point of View," *San Diego Union*, July 28, 1962.

The hard way of breaking out of type is illustrated by Frank Sinatra, who made a second hit in a different medium from that of his first, as a crooner to bobbysoxers. He had a failing movie and his record sales had fallen off; people were saying gleefully that he was through; his marriage to a famous star had given him the disadvantageous role of "Ava Gardner's husband." He persuaded Columbia Pictures to cast him as Maggio in "From Here to Eternity," for a low salary and over objections that he was already tagged as a "has-been." The resulting hit won for him an Oscar as the best actor of the year and a new type as a dramatic actor rather than a crooner.[21]

Another star of "From Here to Eternity," Ernest Borgnine, also broke out of his type the hard way. After a convincing hit as Fatso, the sadistic bully, he re-established himself as a genial good guy by an Academy Award-winning performance as Marty in 1955. Likewise, Jackie Gleason, long typed on television as a comic loudmouth, was able to break out by his brilliant performance in "The Hustler" (1962) as a heroic, slightly tragic pool champion.

But for public performers there are less strenuous ways to escape a type than the heroic one of seeking a hit in a new role. It is possible to fracture images by rather trivial things, such as publicity stunts that have the appropriate contradictory and colorful ingredients. One example is the famous midget-in-the-lap photograph of J. P. Morgan, Jr. An over-zealous reporter, seeking a story, pressed upon the financier an introduction to a twenty-seven-inch circus midget during a hearing before a Senate Banking and Currency Committee investigating business and tax malpractices. "Mr. Morgan, this is Miss Graf." Morgan looked startled, but rose and shook her hand with dignity. Then, after he sat down, a press agent suddenly swung Miss Graf onto the banker's lap. Flash bulbs blazed. "The expression on Morgan's face was one of heroism

21. Louella Parsons, syndicated column, "Tell It to Louella" (1962).

rather than delight," an eyewitness said. Then followed a rather silly conversation before a Morgan aide could shoo the midget and her press agent away. It was thought at the time to have been most unfortunate for Morgan, plagued as he already was by the evil reputation of his father as a munitions maker and international capitalist. But actually it was a blessing; the unexpected result of this incident was to humanize him in the public eye, and in later years Morgan's image mellowed into that of a somewhat stuffy but certainly kindly old gentleman."[22] The midget had defeated the villain.

One of the most practical reasons, of course, for wanting to destroy an image is to escape a position in which everyone hates you. If the hard way is to make a hit as a popular hero, the easier way is simply to act in such a way that it is difficult for people to think of you as a villain. One such way is the "humanizing" escape route. Since a villain is basically an inhuman type, maudlin or even ridiculous behavior can contradict it, even if one does not succeed in making one's self popular. An example is the much publicized court-martial of Marine Sergeant Matthew McKeon in 1956, which attracted national attention because of the officer's extraordinary brutality in ordering a night march of recruits that resulted in the drowning of six men in a swamp. Much of the credit for saving McKeon from a severe sentence goes to the public relations tactics of his lawyer, Emil Zola Berman, who, besides expertly handling the press and witnesses, arranged such scenes as a television appearance of McKeon's pregnant wife with a group of attractive Marine women making an appeal for sympathetic witnesses to come forward and McKeon photographed on his living-room sofa frolicking with his baby son and talking genially to reporters. One said afterward, "I was sure McKeon was a first-class son-of-a-bitch. Now I say you couldn't ask for a nicer guy." Newspapers that had previously pictured the Sergeant as a sadistic brute began to yield to the impression

22. Sherwin D. Smith, *New York Times,* May 31, 1963.

that he was an unlucky victim of circumstance. Such a change in his image was one factor in getting him an unexpectedly light sentence.[23]

I have already discussed the ambiguously skilful way in which Richard M. Nixon broke out of the villain role, attributed to him by political enemies in 1952, by his famed television apology for his $16,000 expense fund;[24] I wish here to show how it illustrates the effectiveness of the humanizing technique for breaking down a villainous imputation. Nixon's talk was not important for its purely factual elements (which would not themselves have produced dramatic effect) but for the story of Nixon as a man, how he had worked in the family grocery with his four brothers; how he had worked his way through college, and then, "probably the best thing that ever happened to me . . . I married Pat" (TV camera follows cue to show her sitting); how he had served in the Navy while Pat worked as a stenographer; his career in law and as a Representative and a Senator; his home, heavily in debt, and a home given to his parents, also in debt; a two-year-old car and only a small life insurance policy; and then the cocker spaniel—"our little girl Tricia, the six-year-old, named it Checkers. And you know the kids . . . love the dog, and . . . regardless of what they say about it, we're going to keep it." By this time the drama had changed from that of a suspect clearing himself to that of a victim—a family of victims at the mercy of spiteful accusers who were mean enough to want to take a dog away from children.

Such details had no logical bearing on the case, but they were entirely relevant to the dramatic transformation of a villainous suspicion in the public mind into sympathy for a man who was being unfairly treated. Critics called it straight soap opera, but *Variety,* the magazine of show business, commented

23. Joe McCarthy, "The Man Who Helped the Sergeant," *Life,* August 15, 1956, pp. 51–52.
24. The event has been fully analyzed in Stanley Kelley, *Public Relations and Political Power,* pp. 177–84.

that soap operas had for some time achieved the most consistently high ratings known on radio and television. Within forty-eight hours the Republican National Committee had received 110,000 letters and 126,000 telegrams overwhelmingly in favor of Nixon's candidacy. Incidentally, the issue temporarily drove the Democratic party from the front pages of the newspapers.

Besides "being human," another way of breaking out of a villain type is to belittle one's self publicly. This is again illustrated by Morgan's episode with the midget, for he had not only been humanized by that association but made also a fool. Many public men might prefer to stay villains rather than undergo the humiliation of playing the fool just so people will not take them seriously enough to hate them. Nonetheless, it has often been possible, and advisable, to disarm wrath by displaying total incompetence, simplemindedness,[25] feminine frivolity and weakness, mental confusion, antic humor, and so on. We have already mentioned how Huey Long's clowning kept people from suspecting him of worse things. If Mussolini had only managed to make a bigger fool of himself, Italian vengeance might have deteriorated into indulgent scorn. The point is that one cannot be simultaneously a fool and a villain. If one is willing to pay the price of being fool enough, he can escape the villain's role.

Likewise, if one tires of it, one can break out of a fool part easily. As a facetious example, throw a rock through a window and you will find that people will take you quite seriously and it will literally be no laughing matter. This is exactly what had happened to "Fatty" Arbuckle in the early days of the movies, and it also seems to have happened in the Charlie Chaplin paternity suit; both men became unfunny. The trouble is, of course, that the villain role is no improvement. In general, it seems much harder to move up in public opinion than to

25. Note the tactic of Good Soldier Schweik in the famous Czech tale.

alternate between these two degraded roles. But for those who professionally want to keep the part of clown, it is important to avoid doing anything publicly that will cause people to take you seriously. This applies to good deeds as well. Jack Benny for years has played the part of a small-time tightwad and chump; he belittles himself, people get the best of him, he cannot really play his fiddle, he pinches pennies and drives an old Maxwell. Behind all this he subdues his private life, in which he is a shrewd manager, a millionaire, and is said by those who know him to be quite generous. Likewise, Bob Hope, who by his zeal for benefit shows and public service comes dangerously close to the role of do-gooder, does not allow this role to obtrude; fresh from a five-thousand-mile trip to give a free show, he instantly becomes the flippant, smiling wisecracker, with no trace of the do-gooder visible in anything he says. It simply will not do for a comedian suddenly to appear as a major political candidate or a serious protagonist of an idea or reform. Such things would be out of character.

Regardless of the direction of possible image change, one generalization seems to be sound and to apply equally to easy and to hard routes: one cannot switch from what the public wants to something it does not want, and one cannot remake one's type arbitrarily along lines of his own choosing. This would violate everything observed about societal selection. Even an image failure goes into something the public needs as a result of the failure—for example, in the case of the Czar or Mussolini. Every sudden image change is along the lines of types already established in the public mind, for the simple reason that really new images take time to develop and a certain economy applies to using old parts from the public repertoire wherever possible. If you throw your type into crisis by acting out of character, the public must grope with the question, "Well, then, what *is* he?" But it is not likely to grope for long if a type is at hand—like a traitor or a crackpot—to fill the vacuum. If there are two or more publics (as there are more often than not), sudden image change—say, from hero to villain—may be due simply to bearing two burdens for two audiences who see the same event with opposite interests. A person does what is right for one segment of the public but throws his image into crisis with another—indeed, does exactly what they want of a villain. So every public, in a sense, gets what it wants. But the public man is, to a considerable extent, the victim rather than the master of these forces and definitions.

This chapter has explored some of the sources of crisis and resistance to crisis in images. But drama itself is the crucible and real master of image change, and this will become clearer after the following chapter on role reversals.

CHAPTER SIX

ROLE-REVERSALS

"I want a clean cup," interrupted the Hatter: "Let's all move one place on."

He moved on as he spoke, and the Dormouse followed him: the March Hare moved into the Dormouse's place, and Alice rather unwillingly took the place of the March Hare. The Hatter was the only one who got any advantage from the change; and Alice was a good deal worse off than before, as the March Hare had just upset the milkjug into his plate.

LEWIS CARROLL, *Alice in Wonderland*

In Spanish-speaking countries a bullfight is normally an occasion when people turn out to see a gallant and graceful matador face a ferocious animal that weighs perhaps a thousand pounds. But before all the gallantry and grace can be displayed, picadors have weakened the bull and made it possible for a man carrying only a rapier to meet such a beast on reasonably equal terms. The ratio of apparent forces still favors the man as hero, though the cards are really stacked against the bull.

In spite of these precautions, the drama is not completely controlled. Several possibilities are open: the bull can become a hero or a victim and the matador can become a villain or a fool. (There can also be defeat with honor or, by special arrangement, an honorific ceremony without defeat for either.) If the bull were small and sickly or the matador armed with a machine gun, the drama would be spoiled on several counts: the style of attack by the matador would seem cowardly and brutal, the style of the bull would suit a victim, and the ratio of forces would favor making the matador a villain. The crowd wants the show to go properly, which means that the man remains a hero and the bull has a choice of two roles: "good bull" (a noble beast that fights fairly and suffers defeat with honor) or "bad bull" (a tricky beast that is smart to the ways of the ring or has a dangerously eccentric style, in dramatic terms a villain so unfair that it is almost a shame to risk the matador against him). This second possibility spoils the art, though the crowd may be thrilled by accidents, and it surely displeases the matador. But it sometimes happens that the drama gets out of hand and a strange reversal of roles takes place. *El toro,* a noble, straight-charging beast, becomes the hero, and the torero who makes clumsy passes, sticks the bull inefficiently or even backs away or runs from a good charge, becomes the villain. The crowd rises in rage, hisses, and throws everything in sight—in some cases the bullfighter has been literally driven from the arena by jeers and flying objects.

The point is that, however set the tradition, however carefully arranged, the bullfight—or any sporting event—is a drama with possible shifts in which antagonists may leave with roles opposite to the ones they came with. This is more the case when dramas are "open," as in politics; lacking a manager, the actors, scenes, and audiences may shift independently without reference to a common script, and *contretemps* are brought about by rivals seeking to embarrass one another.

I shall analyze here several role reversals in public drama, in which events involving the interplay of reciprocal roles and styles, timing and other elements, can be seen. My object is not to explain them fully as historic events, but I shall advance a number of hypotheses in analyzing them.

1. A person who acts out of character (violates his type) or uses the wrong style presses the audience to recast him.

2. Sufficient change in the ratio of apparent forces makes it impossible for him to keep role X and forces role Y upon him, in turn giving role X to somebody else.

3. Whatever emerges from a drama is a result of the re-

ciprocal relationships of all the actors in a situation; the whole governs the parts.

4. Change in emotional climate favors change in roles.

Let us look first at the much discussed election upset of Thomas E. Dewey by Harry Truman in 1948, which derived from its dramatic pattern—a "plot" which neither party intended.

THE TRUMAN "MIRACLE"

Truman's election as President came as a stunning surprise, even to those who had voted for him. It was hailed in the press as a "miracle," a "major political upset of our time." Post mortems offered various reasons to account for the outcome itself and for the pollsters' failure to predict it; it was said that there had been a last-minute swing, especially among the "undecideds,"[1] that Republicans had been complacent with their apparent winning margin and had relaxed too soon, that the power of the press (favoring Dewey) had been overrated, that Truman's campaign had been extraordinarily effective,[2] that Americans always favor the underdog.

I do not dispute these considerations but wish to add some others, especially concerning the dramatic action. After all, underdogs don't always win; undecided people can swing in a

1. As shown by Campbell, Converse, Miller, and Stokes in *The American Voter* (Wiley, 1960), two-thirds to three-fourths of voters make up their minds before the campaign begins, but 10 per cent remain undecided until the last two weeks. This, according to Stuart Chase, helped account for Truman's surprise victory. (*American Credos* [New York: Harper, 1962], p. 111.)

2. Truman "was not defeated. Two things had happened to prevent that defeat. The first was that Truman had been successful in his attempt to convince people of his determined loyalty to the New Deal tradition. . . . What made the difference was Truman's campaign. Seldom had one man, against so great odds, influenced so vast a body of public opinion in so short a time." (Elmo Roper, *You and Your Leaders: Their Actions and Your Reactions, 1936–1956* [New York: Morrow, 1957], pp. 138, 140–41.)

given direction, but they are not required to do so. A change of opinion about a public figure is, in fact, likely to be a matter of social typing; we should ask, How did principals type-cast themselves by their reciprocal actions? Also, the ratio of forces and styles of encounter led to an unwitting pattern that neither party intended. Truman did just the right things in dramatic terms; he could not have performed better with professional coaching. Further, Dewey's role was at fault; he played directly into Truman's drama rather than into the one he wanted.

This espisode began (as many such do) with a hero who has no chance to win. Even Truman's own party had deserted him as a lost cause; in the last stages of his campaign he had to carry on more or less alone. The National Press Club, of which Truman was a member, voted 50 to 1 against his chances (and Truman himself cast the dissenting vote). Betting odds were 15 to 1 against him at the beginning of the vote count on election day. Dewey had already announced his cabinet and his plans for when he entered the White House.

When the results came, one fact besides the consternation of the experts was especially worth noting: a subdued but distinct feeling of satisfaction in the public. Somehow everyone had received what he deserved; certain parties had been too confident and a little man had shown them up. Truman's humility and surprise that morning were admirable; he did his best not to gloat.

With the advantage of hindsight, we may reflect that the least imagination could have seen the makings of a story in the campaign, a story that had been a favorite for thousands of years: the proud had been humbled and the lowly had risen to a position in which he could be generous to those who had laughed at him. The ending was perfect for this pattern, and so also were the earlier stages—if anyone had noticed them. Let us try to distinguish them now.

Act I might be designated as the period of humiliation following the death of Roosevelt, when people began to speak

of President Truman as "the little man in a big pair of shoes."
The contrast with his predecessor was painful. It was fair game
to make fun of "Harry the haberdasher": "to err is Truman,"
"don't shoot the piano player, he's doing the best he can."
When Truman's name was mentioned, people would often
smile. A series of political mistakes gave ammunition to critics
and caused Presidential advisers to wince. It was a time for
greatness in foreign policy, said William C. Bullitt, but Truman
was "a little man who knew nothing about foreign affairs."
Democats began to wonder about the harm he would do to the
party before his term of office expired.

Truman's errors carried right into his campaign for re-
election. Harry was outspoken and careless. Twice he appeared
in pajamas before crowds that had gathered at his train. He
said Joe Stalin was "a nice enough fellow"; in Los Angeles he
said, "This sunshine . . . makes Florida look like thirty cents";
and in Idaho he dedicated an airport to the wrong person. The
press used such headlines as, "The Truman Train Stumbles
West." A cartoonist was assigned to the party just to satirize
the trip and its absurdities. A nearly empty auditorium for a
speech at Omaha was early taken as a sign that the campaign
was hopeless. This phase of the drama defined Truman as a
fool.

Act II developed when observers began to notice, toward
the end of the campaign, signs of growing interest in the candidate, with larger crowds turning out to see him. Hindsight
enables us to see that Truman's luck was beginning to change
because what he was doing had become attractive and significant to many people. The defection of his supporters disposed
people to see him as a victim. His response to the effort of his
party to "dump" him—"I was not brought up to run from a
fight"—brought out his attractively pugnacious instincts. He became reckless and cast about for ways to dramatize himself,
with a deliberate policy of aggressiveness. He recalled the pre-
dominately Republican Congress to special session, demanding

that they consider an eleven-point program that they would not have passed if they had sat for a year; he tweaked the lion's tail by flailing out at "gluttons of privilege," "Wall Street reactionaries," "the special interest boys," and the "rich man's tax bill." Crowds filled halls to hear him and (in a manner reminiscent of Huey Long's audiences) called out, "Pour it on, Harry! Give 'em hell!"—to which he responded, "Oh, I'm pourin' it on, and I'm gonna keep pourin' it on!" He made frequent bitter references to the campaign of "national belittlement" against him:

> They have been telling you a lot of things about your President, that he doesn't know what goes on, that he can't handle the government. It is perfectly legitimate for me to come out here and talk to you and let you find out for yourselves, whether I am just the kind of a bird that these columnists say I am.

This phase of the drama heralded the emergence of a new public image of Truman; if fool he was, he was a fighting fool. His role could even be seen as the last stand of an underdog fighting alone against hopeless odds. Added to this, he had the homespun style of Will Rogers; anyone could see that he was a plain man from Missouri.

At this point we should look at the correlative role of Dewey, for the Republicans had unwittingly maneuvered themselves into a part in Truman's drama. From the nominating convention on, they had given the impression that everything was well planned and "in the bag." Public attention had been drawn to the "panzer divisions" (teams of public relations men) working to put Dewey over; he was well groomed and coached, and thus placed himself in contrast to the homely style of Truman's bad taste.[3] When Truman in Chicago com-

3. "When Thomas E. Dewey ran for the Presidency for the first time, Republicans reeled sadly under Mrs. Longworth's description of him as 'the man on top of the wedding cake.' This was giving aid and comfort to the enemy with a vengeance. And the GOP had to grin and bear it." (Inez Robb, *San Diego Union*, September 9, 1959.)

pared him with Hitler, the Dewey camp maintained its "high level" policy of not replying to such low blows. But being above such issues was not altogether to Dewey's advantage dramatically, for it gave him the appearance of being smug and over-confident. His caution in avoiding issues also robbed him of initiative and gave rise to the charge of "me-tooism": did Dewey have nothing new and exciting to say? All in all, this policy of moderation placed him in contrast with Truman's recklessness. In a number of ways they were precise dramatic opposites. Who, then, was to be the hero?

Contributing to the contrast and working against Dewey was the fact that his overconfidence and caution had unfortunate dramatic possibilities. The former made Dewey vulnerable to the charge of pride (in dramatic terms, the role of Cinderella's stepsisters or Joseph's brothers). The latter possibility was more unpleasant: "playing it safe" could be interpreted as pussyfooting or cowardice, or that he was "too nice" to step down into the arena and fight (in other words, a sissy); "one man used bare knuckles and the other wouldn't get his hair mussed." A still more sinister implication of caution was insincerity. Some people did not like Dewey's manner, even the way he combed his hair; his operation seemed too slick; one of the nicknames applied to him was "Hudson River eel." This impression was helped by an unfortunate incident at the beginning of the campaign: Dewey's "no deals" announcement when he was nominated. If he was managed, if he was not acting on his own, then who was he acting for?

Even if we disregard these more unfavorable interpretations, we must recognize that Dewey's role had basic disadvantages in style and ratio of forces. He was passive and cautious, while the underdog was active and pluckily aggressive. Dewey was with his crowds; Truman fought alone. From such facts as these, Dewey was in a position to be recast from the favorite (the conquering hero) to the proud rival to be defeated (the pompous fool) or even worse, the villain (though his restraint largely protected him from the Goliath/bully role).

Truman, on the other hand, while originally cast as a fool, had shown much hero stuff. Such contrasts in role made it easy for a great many people to change their minds, or finally to make them up.

The last scene of the drama took place on election morning, when Truman awoke after an apparently good night's sleep to find himself the winner. The worm had turned, the dark horse had come from behind to upset the favorite, Cinderella had shown up the proud stepsisters, Joseph as overseer had confronted his brothers. Truman played up to his part perfectly; indeed, it fitted him much better than the "great man" shoes he had inherited from Roosevelt.

What had happened? To answer this we must speculate, since the data needed to determine what people really thought at that time will never be collected. My interpretation is that a role exchange took place because the dramatic pattern strongly suggested and invited it. The change began subtly in the minds of the audience but crystallized to decision after the polls were over and before the last curtain went up. An irrational and largely unconscious popular hope had arisen in the latter days of the campaign. "Too good to be true," in view of the odds, but—why not? Wouldn't it be a perfect ending? And doesn't the unpromising hero always look bad before the upset? The public was sentimental enough to want romance to triumph over statistics. After all, it took only a pull of the voting-machine lever to make Cinderella's dream come true.

Incidentally, this outcome not only made Truman President but resulted in a permanent new status for him—an enhancement of his image and self-confidence that has persisted to this day.

VILLAINS TO MARTYRS

We turn to another kind of conversion, exemplified by the Sacco and Vanzetti case—one of the greatest *causes célèbres* ever to come from American courts, ranking in significance at least with the trials of Scopes, Loeb and Leopold, Hauptmann, and Aaron Burr. It has been much discussed in legal, ethical, and social terms, but it awaits, so far as I know, a dramatic analysis. I see in it an example of a role reversal in which criminals (who are normally villains) became heroes, and judges and prosecutors (who are normally defenders of justice) became villains.

This was a curious outcome for a routine criminal court case, deserving a few lines in the newspapers, involving the conviction of two men in 1921 for a payroll robbery and murder in Braintree, Mass. But this case became a social issue that by 1927 had rocked the nation, indeed, the world. Its literary consequences were tremendous; hundreds of articles, books, poems, and dramas were published. It also evoked a social movement, a crusade to save Sacco and Vanzetti; thousands paraded, worked, talked, and went to jail for the cause. American diplomatic offices abroad were bombed by sympathizers. The case was compared with that of Dreyfus, John Brown, even Socrates, Joan of Arc, and Jesus. Romain Rolland charged that America had committed the judicial murder of two martyrs who represented the "sacred rights of all humanity."

Neither the men themselves nor the legal issue as such was sufficiently unusual to explain the uproar. It would never have become such a *cause célèbre* had it not possessed a dramatic pattern of unusual power and perfection.

The usual explanations are inadequate, in my judgment. The standard view was that a miscarriage of justice, due to prejudice, had resulted in the "judicial murder" of two men whose guilt was never proved. So argued jurists like Roscoe Pound and Felix Frankfurter.[4] I do not dispute that there were such legal faults,[5] but a miscarriage of justice, even a gross one, is not by itself capable of explaining the enormous social

4. See Felix Frankfurter, "The Case of Sacco and Vanzetti," *Atlantic,* CXXXIX (1927), 417, 432.

5. A recent study suggests that the miscarriage was not as gross as some supposed; that Sacco, at least, was guilty of the robbery, and that

impact of this case. The popular mind is not unduly sensitive about justice and does not get excited over technicalities. We live in a society in which all kinds of evasions of rules and corruption by self-interest are accepted. A brief review of legal history would show that dozens, perhaps hundreds, of innocent men have been imprisoned, even lynched and executed, without stirring up such an uproar. Why then (of all the aliens mistreated at the time) Sacco and Vanzetti?

Some attributed the furor to the fact that Sacco and Vanzetti were not like other criminals but were rather unusual men—they were philosophers acting on principle—and Vanzetti, especially, showed remarkable poetical ability in his court speeches and letters. Yet these qualities do not seem sufficient to mark them off from other men equal or greater in ability and stature—say, Oscar Wilde or Eugene Debs—who, eloquent in their own defense, did not win popular sympathy from so large a proportion of their contemporaries.

It was also fashionable, at the time, to blame the stir on "agitation" or "propaganda," the determined efforts of ethnic and radical groups on behalf of Sacco and Vanzetti. Yet a moment's reflection shows how inadequate is this explanation —how many are the causes that have been agitated with equal vigor and skill but have not won appreciable acceptance!

If we are to understand what happened, the dramatic pattern must be added to all these other facts. Indeed, it is my opinion that, even with men other than Sacco and Vanzetti and with different legal issues, the case would have had the same outcome. Neither ethical, legal, nor social issues nor the intrinsic merits of men make villains out of heroes or the reverse; only dramas of certain kinds, which it is our purpose in this book to analyze, accomplish these ends. The dramatic pattern in the Sacco and Vanzetti case was strong enough to have given the same role to any men who acted as they did

---

the trial was not the kangaroo court it has been painted by its legal critics. Francis Russell, *Tragedy in Dedham* (New York: McGraw-Hill, 1962).

circumstances. Not only did Sacco and Vanzetti
with the drama, but so did the other principals.
e judge, prosecutor, even the governor, acted as
y had been coached and were as eager to be villains
as _ efendants were to become martyrs. And the legal
process—not so much from its technicalities as in its length
and tortuousness—became a setting for a drama of torment.
Without such a situation, Sacco and Vanzetti might have
stirred a little support but surely would never have been discussed in the most impassioned and elevated terms and likened
to Socrates, Joan of Arc, and Jesus.

Analyzing this drama, one may judge that the time (1921)
was ripe for a witch-hunt (and, indeed, it began in that fashion) but not necessarily a martyrdom. The successful revolution in Russia had inspired a wave of radicalism throughout
the world. America was troubled by strikes, with demobilized
soldiers glutting the labor market, an "open-shop" campaign
of industrialists against the union movement, and the terrorist
activities of the IWW. Thirty-six bombs had been intercepted
by the New York post office addressed to prominent people
like Supreme Court Justice Holmes and financier J. P. Morgan.
The policy of police in dealing with troublemakers was to
"treat 'em rough"; hundreds of aliens were imprisoned or de-
ported. The popular feeling was that they deserved such treatment.

How, then, could it happen that among so many receiving
rough treatment, two should be selected to play martyrs? On
the surface they had all the earmarks of villains; besides being
convicted of robbery and murder, they were—as it abundantly
appeared at the trial—aliens, anarchists, terrorists, and draft-
dodgers.

The first thing that must be considered is the conduct of
the trial itself, which had serious dramatic as well as technical
faults. The latter were early observed by jurists, who studied
the record and pointed out that the men had been convicted

not by evidence but by prejudice. Yet technical faults do not make a martyrdom; many have gone to prison wrongly without becoming heroic martyrs. On the dramatic side, there is more evidence to help us understand how Sacco and Vanzetti could have been early defined as victims. The trial was carried out in an atmosphere of flag-waving. The prosecutor made speeches such as, "Do your duty. . . . Stand together, you men of Norfolk." The judge showed, as Frankfurter said, "a spirit alien to judicial utterances," and told the jury to "act like the true soldier"; he once referred to the defendants as "anarchistic bastards." The jury, dominated by a former police chief, were "so violent against me," said Vanzetti, that "they would have found me guilty of a dozen charges." The foreman had been heard to remark outside court, "Damn them, they ought to hang anyway."

Such features were quickly noted by groups with reason for special sympathy with the men: the foreign-language press, minority groups, labor unions, and radicals, but they had yet to sell their cause to the general public. A defense committee, formed largely of Italians, worked heroically under the slogan, "Save Sacco and Vanzetti"; many gave up jobs and mortgaged their homes to help. They publicized the case through the foreign-language press (though big American newspapers paid no attention to it); the news spread quickly to other countries while most Americans were as yet unaware of it. Indeed, the *New York World* announced itself as "at a loss to explain" the widespread concern that was developing internationally. Finally, the newspaper "conspiracy of silence" broke down, and millions of Americans began to ask, "Why are we so unpopular?" The external shock had done what the internal stimulus could not, and the threshold of public indifference was crossed.

Yet, if Sacco and Vanzetti had been promptly executed, it is safe to say that the affair, however unjust, would have involved no great international martyrdom. As it was, the defense carried on, assisted by over seventy thousand dollars raised by the defense committee, and began to develop a theatrical pattern of its own. As a clue to this pattern, consider the view the public had of the prisoners when they appeared in court, heavily manacled, surrounded by many guards, placed in a steel cage as though they were ferocious animals

This picture confirmed their status as dangerous criminals, but from a dramatic standpoint, something was wrong. It was an appropriate setting for melodrama but not the setting a court is supposed to provide. If a judge is to be the hero of a drama, he should be as fair-minded, noble, and merciful as possible, neither a bully nor an indifferent, cold-hearted Pontius Pilate; all such bad features should be left to the accused. But this is not what the people in charge of this particular drama accomplished. In their zeal to control their dangerous prisoners they overplayed their parts and fell into postures strikingly like those of the old-fashioned persecutor, the Inquisitor, the witch-burner. They were too zealous to defend the public weal; they forgot that a hero, when he does what he thinks is right, must also act like a hero. The actors representing the law in this case were unwittingly doing their best to appear the very opposite of "good guys"; the extraordinary caution with which they handled the defendants fits better the dramatic part of the nervous tyrant, the coward, the gang of bullies tormenting a helpless victim.

Many writings and cartoons of the period show that such pictures were held by the public. In one cartoon, we see Judge Thayer as a pale Inquisitor in a black cowl, barricaded by statute books and surrounded with bayonets, sentencing the prisoners; he is likened in poems to Pontius Pilate and Caiaphas the high priest; cartoons show him reading a book entitled *Theory and Practice of Refined Torture,* or with men in the background holding blackjacks and clubs. Sacco and Vanzetti's long imprisonment was compared with Poe's "The Pit and the Pendulum," as it dragged on for seven years while Judge

Thayer rejected five motions for retrial and the state dallied but finally refused pardon.

This allowed plenty of time for popular imagination to work. It was the agents of justice, acting out of character for a hero, that began a conversion in the public character of Sacco and Vanzetti, who were themselves comparatively passive. The basic principle here seems to be that when a persecutor appears in a drama he throws the weaker parties opposed to him into the more favorable role of victim or underdog; from this it is only a step to martyrdom—especially when there is skilful symbolic interpretation and enough time for the drama to unfold.

During the years from 1921 to 1927 popular support grew steadily in America. As early as 1923 a major change in complexion of the case had been noted as liberals and middle-class people took up the cause and began to outnumber the radicals and minority groups who had first shown interest. A highly paid attorney was hired to replace the volunteer radical lawyer who had made the early defense along "class" lines. As the connection with radicalism and violence was disclaimed, primary emphasis was placed on liberty and justice.[6]

The times, too, were changing. As the case went on, it seemed a barbaric affair, out of keeping with the optimism of Coolidge prosperity. The specter of revolution had vanished, and the nation was at peace, but Sacco and Vanzetti were still in prison. Americans saw fair play in football games, but Sacco was being force-fed after a hunger strike. These were strange notes in a world "safe for democracy."

The hunger strikes by both prisoners (Sacco went on one of thirty-one days in 1923 and another of seventeen days shortly before his execution in 1927) added greatly to popular interest in this pathetic and dramatic picture. Here is a point at which the defendants helped create their own role. It began

6. Max Schachtman, *Sacco and Vanzetti: Labor's Martyrs* (New York: International Labor Defense, 1927), pp. 38–39, 47–50.

to shape the lines of a classic martyrdom, helped by the more
or less conscious role-playing of the prisoners and their supporters. During their thirteen-day wait in the death house
chanting crowds marched and kept vigil outside. Nor did stays
and delays of execution gain the state any credit for clemency
but merely looked like a cruel political "cat-and-mouse game."
Judge Thayer was the tyrant who had refused five motions for
retrial; Governor Fuller was a Pilate who had washed his hands
of the prisoners at the last opportunity for pardon. It is interesting to note, also, that when the American Federation of Labor
proposed asking for a commutation of sentence to life imprisonment, the prisoners' defense committee rejected the sugges-
tion on grounds that it would have meant an admission of guilt
and "living death" in a prison cell, and held out for either
pardon or execution. At such a point the question becomes
acute: Did these men deliberately choose to conform to the
ideal pattern of the martyr rather than spoil it to protect themselves? Vanzetti's gestures and speeches were always appropriate, especially his last words, thanking his jailers for their
kindness to him and forgiving *"some* people for what they are
now doing to me."

In analyzing this case in terms of role-playing, I have not
meant to cast doubt upon the integrity of the participants,
most of whom were presumably sincere. Judge Thayer's suicide suggests the price he had to pay for doing what he thought
was right. He apparently did not realize that his very con-
scientiousness would make him, like Cotton Mather, one of
history's great villains, just as it ennobled Sacco and Vanzetti,
with some injustice perhaps to all. This case illustrates again
that unless men are masters of their public drama, they cannot
be masters of their public characters. Man proposes, but
drama disposes.

We have here a role conversion in a drama that lasted
seven years, whose very length was a factor in the result. In
this drama, the formal heroes changed into villains (the per-

secuting judge and the heartless legal system), while the con-
victs (normally villains in the public view) became first
underdog victims and then martyrs for liberty and justice, as
people were moved by the developing drama and saw its resemblance to classic martyrdoms of the past. It was not
primarily legal considerations that caused this resemblance or
changed the public attitude, though it may be admitted that
statements by the jurists helped to arouse the public. Nor
could Sacco and Vanzetti by their own acts—even assuming
the martyr pose—have brought about the conversion unless
circumstances had co-operated; many suffering from persecu-
tion have claimed martyrdom without achieving it. For one
thing, the state agencies themselves unwittingly staged the
drama and invited the villain role. The ratio of forces was
important, since it showed massive state machinery oppressing
two helpless men. The time factor worked in favor of role
change, since it permitted the image of protracted torture to
develop and created a different emotional climate, in which
people were no longer hysterically afraid of "radicals." Such
dramatic and situational factors, then, bring us closer to understanding why the "tragedy in Dedham" became a *cause célèbre*.

THE PURSUIT OF PANCHO VILLA

We turn now to an earlier incident from American history,
just before World War I, in which General John J. Pershing
played a part versus the redoubtable Pancho Villa. In this
episode, an interesting role change occurred in which Pershing
lost his status as hero and Villa lost his status as villain. The
bandit became in the eyes of many Americans (to say nothing
of the Mexicans) an intriguing rogue, even a "clever hero,"[7]
and the American Army force headed by Pershing came dan-

7. See my analysis of this basic folk and popular type in "The
Clever Hero," *Journal of American Folklore*, LXVII (1954), 21–34.

gerously close to being made fools, in a pursuit that began as melodrama but came, as it was reported in newspapers, to resemble a "Keystone Cops" comedy.

The facts were these: A bandit gang headed by Pancho Villa crossed the Mexican border in March, 1916, to raid the town of Columbus, N.M., killing seventeen U.S. soldiers and civilians, and then escaped back into Mexico. Villa had, shortly before (in January), aggravated public dislike by taking nineteen gringos off a train in Chihuahua and shooting them. These atrocities destroyed the long-suffering patience of the American public with bandits, and the cry went up, "Catch Villa, dead or alive!" An American Army punitive force was organized to enter Mexico, with the consent of the Carranza government (which was having its own troubles with Villa and wished him put out of business).

Before these misdeeds, Villa had been on reasonably good terms with the United States government, in no small measure because he was the *de facto* ruler of a disordered country in which American interests were threatened by civil war. The government had even negotiated an "agreement" with him to stop brigandage and to guarantee the safety of United States nationals. Official relations with Villa were cordial; he had congratulated General Scott on his appointment as Chief of Staff of the United States Army, he had been invited by the El Paso chamber of commerce to meet President Wilson, and he had even had a short biography read in the United States Senate. To the public he was a rather romantic figure—train-robber, high-liver, woman-kidnapper, a rough-and-ready Don Juan. The public was entertained by stories of his colorful activities; newsmen stayed with his staff to report how he had ordered a $1,000 bathtub from a firm in Chicago, how a woman had attempted to kill him, how he had taken his first drink. Even movies had been made of his life. He was, in short, about as famous a figure in America as Buffalo Bill, and, among Mexicans, of course, he was even more highly respected. Their opinion of him is summarized by the saying that Pancho was the kind of man who could "march 100 miles without stopping, live 100 days without food, go 100 nights without sleep, and kill 100 men without remorse."[8]

Thus Villa's misdeed and fall to villainy had been preceded by something rather close to idolization. But there is no question that he was hated by the American public at the time of the chase. General Pershing was brought in to head the punitive expedition, and for dramatic purposes he became the hero of the piece. A born cavalryman fresh from victories in Philippine and Indian guerilla fighting, he seemed an ideal choice to enter Mexico and catch Villa, wherever he was.

Then began a lugubrious and finally comic chapter in United States–Latin American relationships. One week after Villa's raid, Pershing crossed the border with a small army of ten thousand men. The public was agog with the prospect of an exciting continued story. Newspapers described in detail the army's equipment, including the latest machine guns, wireless radio, and airplanes. Photographs showed Pershing "on the trail" in a staff car, followed by another car full of reporters.

Almost immediately after this auspicious beginning, the story slowed down. It soon became apparent that there were serious difficulties in the way of catching Pancho. The Mexicans protected his trail, giving brazenly false and misleading information, even saying frankly that it would be a national disgrace if the Americans should succeed. A delay in following Villa, due to negotiation with Carranza (the nominal head of the Mexican government) had given him a week's head start. The stage across which the pursuit took place consisted of the mountains, mud, and deserts of Chihuahua, to which "snow, sandstorms, tropic heat and sharp cold added to the misery

8. We must take into account the *macho* theme in Mexican culture in evaluating this statement; Mexicans inordinately admire the virile man. See my "Mexican Social Types," *American Journal of Sociology,* LXIX (January, 1964), 404-414.

of the actors."[9] It began to look less like an exciting Wild West chase than a game of hide-and-seek with an antagonist who seemed more a will-o'-the-wisp than a man. Pershing's first communiqué, a few weeks after crossing the border, hinted at these difficulties: "Our troops seem to be pressing him, but I won't hazard any predictions. Villa is no fool—it may be that the campaign has just started."

He could scarcely have known how right he was. All the wiles Pershing had learned from the Indians, Chinese, and Filipinos were brought into play. One account says: "Villa was not to be found. They chased him up hill and down dale, in and out of the mountains, through and through the cities. He was here, there and everywhere. He was nowhere at all. He was not to be found."[10] Aviators were sent out to check countless apocryphal reports, even to locate Pancho's supposed grave. Frustration became prominent and replaced the early mood of confidence. The soldiers began grumbling not only because of hardships but because they suspected that the foe was somewhere else than where they were looking for him. An officer described the search as "like trying to catch a coyote in Wyoming with a stripe down his back." One scout said, "It's like trying to catch a rat in a cornfield."

From this point on, the story clearly began to shift from melodrama to picaresque comedy. The *New York Telegraph* called it a "wild goose chase." Fantastic stories told how Villa was killed one day and alive the next; he showed a wonderful omnipresence and vitality, appearing in various parts of Mexico and the United States, including such remote places as Manhattan. Sometimes he was resurrected in time for the evening papers, after having been pronounced dead in the morning edition; there seemed to be several bandits operating under the name of Villa. The expedition was becoming a joke, though a

9. H. A. Toulmin, *With Pershing in Mexico* (Harrisburg, Pa.: Military Service Pub. Co., 1935), p. 17.
10. G. R. Durston, *My Boy's Life of General Pershing* (Chicago: Sealfield Pub. Co., 1919), p. 171.

sorry one. "A whole army is kept at a man's heels killing him continuously, and yet that man never dies."[11] It was "one of the strangest situations that ever a commander was called on to face. We actually did not know whether there was a Villa anymore."[12]

Pancho's character showed an interesting change. He was now "the Fox of the Sierra Madre," and this seemed a credit to him rather than proof of his villainy. The difficulty in catching him by summer, only a few months after the start, made the situation painfully embarrassing for Americans. Pershing's force had increased to one hundred twenty-three thousand men. By winter, there had still been no contact made with Villa by this enormous posse. A press dispatch approved by Pershing put it bluntly: "The United States Punitive Expedition directed against Pancho Villa has apparently come to a standstill." Editorials began to urge recall of the expedition. The Mexicans, too, beginning to tire of American intervention, had the effrontery to issue an ultimatum that war would result from "any movement of the Punitive Expedition except in a northerly direction."

As a result of the "cramped tactical position," on January 24, 1917, ten months after the beginning of the hunt, a War Department order came for withdrawal. The movement was embarrassed by closely following Villistas and Carranza forces and the circumstance that airplanes had to be used to cover the American rear from possible attack—which gave the appearance of retreat. Thus came to an inglorious end a national effort that had begun ambitiously. The slogan, "Villa, dead or alive!" was heard no more in the land.[13]

Villa boasted openly of his triumph over the American government. True, seventeen of his men had been captured

11. A. Margo, *Who, Where and Why Is Villa?* (New York: Latin American News Assoc., 1917), pp. 10–13.

12. F. B. Elser, "General Pershing's Mexican Campaign," *Century,* IC (1920), 441–42.

13. Frank Tompkins, *Chasing Villa* (Harrisburg, Pa.: Military Service Pub. Co., 1934), pp. 184, 213.

and sent to the New Mexico penitentiary, but he was free. He remarked condescendingly that Pershing never had "the chance of a snowball in hell." "Just think—it cost your government one hundred and thirty millions of dollars to try to get me— I took them over rough, hilly country. . . . Sometimes for fifty miles at a stretch they had no water. They had nothing but the sun and mosquitoes. . . . And nothing was gained."[14] The Mexicans, of course, were delighted with the cleverness of their countryman, and even Americans were able to see the humor of the situation. Will Rogers joked in the Ziegfeld Follies:

> I see where Villa raided Columbus, New Mexico. We had a man on guard that night. But to show you how crooked this Villa is, he sneaked up on the opposite side. We chased him over the line five miles, but ran into a lot of government red tape and had to come back.

The audience, including President Wilson, laughed.[15]

The public could not fail to see the romantic side of Villa's exploit, so reminiscent of Jesse James and Billy the Kid. He was no longer the villain but a kind of Robin Hood. Time mellowed his image as Americans continued to read of how he lived prosperously in Mexico—he gave two thousand dollars to rebuild a church in Canutillo, founded a farming colony for his faithful followers, and played the *patrón* until assassinated in 1923.

Dramatically, the course of events gave parts to the actors that no one had expected them to play. These parts were not determined by the actors' personal character or the intrinsic merit of their deeds, any more than with Truman and Dewey or Sacco and Vanzetti. Time, sandstorms, various circumstantial factors—especially the roles of the protagonists vis-à-vis one another—gave pattern to the drama. Both Villa and Pershing moved out of the parts with which they began. Through

14. Louis Stevens, *Here Comes Pancho Villa* (New York: F. A. Staples, 1930), p. 299, pp. 3–4.

15. Betty Rogers, *Will Rogers* (Garden City, N.Y.: Garden City Pub. Co., 1943), p. 164.

no fault of his own, Pershing was made to look almost like a fool; surely his expedition had been a fiasco. The situation gave Villa a grand chance to play the fox, to turn to the Robin Hood pattern. Without such a drama, he might have gone down in history like other unrelieved villains, and at least his blame would not have been softened as it was in American eyes.

The picture was changed into a comedy that, viewed abstractly, had the following basic components: a big cop baffled by a little crook, an unfavorable balance of forces followed by fiasco for the stronger. Such comic frustration makes a fool; it is basically the formula of the Keystone Cops. By this drama, Villa's public image changed from hero to villain, then from villain to hero. The factors governing such role-changing were, I believe, largely situational.

But, situational or not, this eventuality might have been foreseen by United States officials alert to dramatic possibilities, avoiding great costs in American prestige as well as dollars. How might a large nation handle such a problem with a small nation and an unfavorable balance of apparent forces? Perhaps some Mexicans could have been pitted against Villa. Surely a small but determined force, like the Israeli agents who captured Adolph Eichmann, might have accomplished as an adventure what an army in full publicity could not do.

PRINCIPLES OF DRAMATIC CONVERSION

There must be many possibilities of role conversion, of which these examples show only a few. The main dramatic types—hero, villain, fool, and victim (each with dozens of subtypes)—suggest that there may be hundreds of possible combinations and routes of role change. But the possibilities are not limitless, and the rules governing them can be set out.[16]

16. One student of drama, Georges Polti, suggests that there are only thirty-six basic dramatic situations and that all possible plots are

The three patterns that have been presented here are (1) an overconfident rival that is upset by an underdog (familiar enough as the plot of the "unpromising hero"); (2) villains that turn into martyrs, and (3) a villain that becomes transformed into a kind of clever hero by the comic frustration of his large opponent. These few examples do not allow us to formulate with any finality the rules of dramatic conversion, but the laws we seek are suggested, if not proved, by the cases.

One of these laws is that the role of any actor is dependent upon the reciprocal roles of other actors. One implication of this law is that one cannot play a role unless he has the right dramatic partner. Another implication is that a marked change in one role can result in a change of role for others whether or not they wish it or knowingly change their behavior. For example, one person acting the fool may bring the status of another (who was soberly minding his own business) into jeopardy. A person can have a part forced upon him,[17] although he cannot force a role upon another (still less upon a whole group) unless the total situation favors it. So, with the help of the situation, Pancho Villa forced a role upon the American Army, but the court of Massachusetts could not

---

combinations of these. (*The Thirty-Six Dramatic Situations* [New York: The Writer, 1945].) Another, David Malcolmson, also points to the way a small number of basic themes occur again and again in literature, drama, and life. He analyzes certain transforming plots, such as "Cinderella," "the persevering tortoise," "the ugly duckling," "the patient Griselda," and "the sly fox," "stories forever repeating themselves on the street and in written pages." (*Ten Heroes* [New York: Duell, Sloan and Pearce, 1941].)

17. Anselm L. Strauss has discussed status forcing, saying that "the very nature of interaction implies the forcing of status. It is worth remembering that interaction not only puts everyone concerned in danger —actors and audience alike—but equally exposes everybody to transforming experiences that are more positive and creative in implication. . . . Status-forcing carries an explosive potential for bringing the encounter to a close in a different place than it started. . . . The interaction must be all the more precarious when one or more persons intend or need to change their relationships." (*Mirrors and Masks, the Search for Identity* [Glencoe, Ill.: Free Press, 1959], pp. 82–84.)

force the villain role upon Sacco and Vanzetti because it played the wrong role and helped create the wrong situation. Did Sacco and Vanzetti force the villain role upon Judge Thayer? More probably, the total drama conspired to this effect.

Of course, there are times when a single person by changing his role manages to change those of other actors. Truman probably did more by changing his own role to turn the 1948 election drama in his favor than did any other actor, but the desertion by his own party, the national ridicule of his inability to follow in Roosevelt's footsteps, and so on, set the stage for his decisive act. We need to study the conditions under which a single actor can change dramatic situations and the roles by which he does it. I think that most of the time this result will ensue from a tipping of the balance of several factors.

Second, if a part has some power to change the whole, it is also true that the dramatic functional whole is greater than the sum of its parts, so it can never be inferred merely from knowledge of particular parts (one's own, or those of others). New relational elements may intrude or emerge to upset one's thinking. An outstanding factor here is the ratio of apparent forces (cited several times in preceding chapters). Such patterns of the whole situation govern the whole. If a person "forces" a role upon another, it is presumably because his particular act changed the whole situation, not merely his own role. In the "quixotic" cases described in chapter ii sincere idealists achieved hero, villain, or fool roles, that is, widely varying outcomes, although their personal inputs were not very different. Thus personal input in terms of actual character, intention, even deed, seems to be indecisive in determining the dramatic role that one will receive; a very evil man can get a hero's role or a good man become a villain or fool just because the situation was wrong for him. The total situation governs.

A third principle is actually part of the second: Changes

in climate can cause changes in role, whether or not the principal actors have really changed. In the Sacco and Vanzetti case the lapse of seven years, a change of mood from morbid fear to optimistic liberalism, had a great deal to do with their conversion into martyrs. The censure of Senator Joseph McCarthy by the U.S. Senate reflected not so much a change in McCarthy as a change in the situation in which he was acting. The country was tired of his kind of role, and people who had formerly seen him as a hero investigating the evils of communism now saw him as bully (see also chap. Seven). The war mood and fear of Nazism in the United States similarly caused Lindbergh to fall into disfavor by his comparatively harmless action in accepting a medal. On the other hand, a season for heroes can bring popularity to certain kinds of men who fit the mood, and there is reason to believe that Lindbergh benefited from this mood in flying across the ocean the way he did at the time he did. The emotional climate is only one element of the dramatic situation, but it is extremely important because it indicates what the audience will perceive and select, the need for specific symbolic functions.

Granting the effect of emotional climate, we should nonetheless not overestimate the mental "set" (the bias, prejudice, interest, or other subjective factors) of the audience in the dramatic making of heroes, villains, and fools. It is all too easy to say that Italians favor Italians, Catholics favor Catholics, and so on, just because they have class, race, nationality, cultural background, interests, or attitudes in common. But the perceptions of hero, villain, and fool are not organized along such lines. The Sacco-Vanzetti case could never have become a *cause célèbre* if its interest had been confined to people with special group biases. Within two years it lost its "ethnic-radical" complexion and involved thousands who had no special reason to be identified with Italian anarchists. Indeed, the history of Christianity is proof of the dramatic power of martyrdom to go beyond special audience sets to that which is fundamentally human.

On the whole, then, special prejudices are as often ignored as followed by audiences in identifying with heroes. Certainly in literature an African or Indian can become a hero to whites; upper class to lower or lower to upper; animal to human—it seems hard to find a boundary that has not been crossed as many times as honored. Let us attribute this to the universality of drama itself. By this power, an audience can come prepared to identify with one "hero," then find itself compelled by the drama (the ratio of forces, turn of the plot, etc.) to sympathize with another. In other words, a fourth rule is that what is important in dramatic conversion is what happens on the stage and merely what the audience comes prepared to accept. That is why this book analyzes dramatic patterns as though all audiences were the same, an assumption made here for the sake of simplicity, although it is not wholly true.

When we ask what is involved in "sets," a fifth important principle from the study of social types emerges: What an audience is likely to see in a drama is limited by the cultural type repertoire. If an audience is familiar with the David/ Goliath or Cinderella patterns, it will lean to such interpretations (as it happens, these patterns are so common in folklore that they are probably culturally universal). Again, the "fair play" concept that is implicit in traditions like that of King Arthur and his Round Table must affect the power of the ratio of apparent forces. It is hard to see how the drama of Don Quixote could be effective with Eskimos who have no idea of chivalry or romantic love. Thus the choice of dramatic definitions made by any audience occurs within the limits of the stock of available types, which also provide the alternatives for the likely events. The freedom of the audience in redefinition comes, in good part, from the number of types and familiar plots that are available, making many crises and recombinations possible. A public man should know this repertoire well if he wishes to predict, let alone control, the career of his public image.

A sixth proposition concerns role conversions for any given

type: The number of "turns" or reversals is limited by the kind of type (and its reciprocal, or dramatic, partner). That is, if a big person is set against a small one, it is hardly likely that the large person can convert into a triumphant Cinderella. Again, if an individual has been typed as a clever hero, it would be comparatively easy for him to convert into a tricky villain but harder to become the Lancelot type, who always fights fairly and doesn't stoop to tricks, or the ingenue or charming simpleton. If a person is typed as a saint, he can suffer a sharp fall in public opinion through behavior that would not be condemned in another.

We are concerned here, then, with type vulnerabilities, which we discussed earlier in terms of the Achilles' heel. Any type can move dramatically within the broad framework of "hero," "villain," "fool," or "victim," but each has certain subtypes as vulnerabilities. If a big man is self-important or severe in carrying out his duties, he is vulnerable to the type of "pompous fool," whose fall is a delight to audiences of almost any society. He is also vulnerable to the big-villain types of bully or oppressor. Or, if he becomes a hero, it is likely to be as a "conquering hero," a man on a white horse, King Richard, Samson, Achilles, who overbears those standing against him (but not if matched with small opponents). This is where style (not what one does but how he does it) is enormously important in suggesting the kinds of roles one can play. Some of these vulnerabilities were more fully described in terms of type violation in chapter v. If many examples of role conversion were collected, possibly by sociodramatic experiments, the details of probable and possible changes could be worked out. Such vulnerabilities would be part of elementary tactics for anyone playing the public game.

A seventh and final proposition relates again to role-forcing: If an individual acts out of character, he can produce a role crisis for himself, and perhaps for someone else as well, by making it impossible for the drama to go on as defined and expected. It may occur because the audience can no longer believe in him in the part or because he sabotages his partner's role. For example, a person receives a gift but shows injured feelings or resentment rather than gratitude; or he is supposed to be the fool but makes people sorry for him, thus breaking down his role as the butt of the joke and embarrassing the jester. In such cases, the drama itself breaks down and the audience has to redefine all parties in terms of the available repertoire. In such redefinitions, a turnabout is quite likely, depending on the ratio of forces and other elements of the situation. Such an outcome could be a disaster or a lucky break for any actor in it. Thus one who is tired of his public image and wishes to renovate it—to give it a "new look"—will try to produce a crisis by acting out of character, by violating his role in its most crucial aspects, perhaps by seeking confrontations where such crises are likely.

These seven principles are, at best, a hint of what we may expect from further systematic study of role reversals. They suggest that we are on the verge of an art or science of role strategy, of controlling public dramas so that a man can predict and determine the roles of others, can set up situations in which the outcome is likely to make him look good and perhaps make someone else "look bad." Such an era of managed drama has been anticipated by writers like George Orwell, with a dire picture of its result for human liberty. I do not know how it would actually work. It might merely make the show more interesting, with a greater variety of outcomes. Another result might be that looking behind the props of public dramas would make audiences more sophisticated and harder to manage. But, in any case, I do not doubt that there are regularities in this field of which we can and will take account. Whether or not the winds and currents can be controlled, there is weather and therefore there must be a meteorology by which public men can sail.

CHAPTER SEVEN

HOW TO
BE UNPOPULAR
WITHOUT REALLY TRYING

Given the hazards of dramatic confrontation, it seems that anyone should be able to lay out some rules for avoiding situations in which one is likely to be made a villain or a fool. I should apologize for doing so, were it not for the number of clever people who have gotten into trouble because either they did not really know the rules or they forgot them at a crucial time or their enemies knew them better than they did. Plainly there are laws that, if flouted, lead to ruin, in drama no less than in physics.

The following principles are, no doubt, only a few of those that will prove important. The problem, baldly stated, is this: What are the surest routes to becoming a fool or villain or making somebody else one? And how can they be avoided? I will first consider the conditions that make a villain and then the more laughable predicaments of the fool.

Routes to Villainy

1. Resemblance to Established Villain Types

The United States Davis Cup Tennis team, while on world tour in 1963, found itself rebuked in the Australian press for unsportsmanlike behavior. Three of its stars were called "the most hated trio tennis ever produced."

> They have insulted their way from Mexico City to Delhi and left behind them fewer friends than anybody who ever came that way before. In Australia they have combined arrogance, rudeness, and childishness to a degree never achieved before by any group in the game where nobody expects a top performer to behave like an adult.[1]

The Americans, of course, minimized the charges, and they were even defended by some Australian newsmen. It would be hard to show objectively just how much rudeness had been displayed, though the Americans admitted that they had been "foolish" and lost their tempers on some occasions. But whatever happened was not mere "foolishness," for some people apparently disliked the Americans enough to hate them. Often the things that make people really angry are not substantive injuries but "little things"—like the conceit of a "prima donna" or the insolent attitude of a witness. If the public's attitude becomes hostile enough toward someone, it is defining him as a villain and wishes to treat him as such. A symbolic theory of what makes villains must take account of the "little things" that arouse hatred.

A dramatic law of the utmost consequence finds expression in the generalization that the hatred an individual receives bears little relationship to physical realities (to consequences, real causes, actual deeds, or real qualities of the man). One who has done little substantive harm may act in such a swaggering, sneering, insulting, or sneaky manner that people think shooting is too good for him. On the other hand, he may have committed a serious crime, with grave injury to persons and fortunes, and, for some logically unaccountable reason, people want to let him off (an engaging swindler, a romantic desperado like Pancho Villa, or a benign little old lady who poisons

---

1. Frank Browne, quoted in the *San Diego Union,* December 23, 1963.

people). This is because the dramatic circumstances—the style, pattern of drama, personal appearance, dramatic partners—were symbolically wrong (out of character) for making a villain. Someone who needs a villain is likely to turn in his choice to the kinds of people who look like villains as he conceives them. This, in turn, depends on the common stock of symbols that function as reservoirs of hatred in his society. *AT THAT TIME*

We must direct our attention, therefore, to the prevailing villain types. Our proposition is that the amount of blame and hatred one receives depends not on the harm he does but on how he resembles a type of villain and the "hatred quota"[2] of that particular type. The first practical rule, then, is this: Avoid resemblance to villain types. This, in turn, calls for familiarity with the social types (or stereotypes) of the villain in American society, the most important of which I have surveyed elsewhere.[3]

While it is not possible to describe them here, the main classes of American villains include the following: desperado, rebel, moral flouter, rogue, troublemaker, oppressor, authoritarian, snob, selfish grabber, intruder, suspicious isolate, monster, sneak, traitor, chiseler, parasite, shirker, and corrupter. Each of these has subtypes and variants. A public man might, for example, adopt a mustache without being aware that it connoted "slyness" or "Latin lover" propensities in some sections of the country. He might compromise or stand firm, be friendly with everybody or aloof, be uncouth or smooth, and find that his style has antagonized people without having displayed such obviously undesirable traits as snobbishness, overbearingness, or sneakiness. Of course, the people he comes in contact with—his dramatic juxtapositions—are quite important, as I have pointed out in chapters iii and vi. His social position (as insider, outsider, stranger, intruder, marginal man,

2. This quota needs to be determined for each villain type by empirical research. At present I assume that certain types (say, traitors) are more hated than others (say, snobs).

3. *Heroes, Villains and Fools,* chap. iii.

leader, high-status holder, eccentric, etc.) has also much to do with whether he will be defined as a villain and what types will be assigned to him. His personal features—over some of which he has little control—may suggest unpleasant things about his character ("five o'clock shadow," built-in scowl or sneer, heavy eyebrows, eyes close together, the shape of his nose). More easily remedied is the symbolic handicap of certain names (Peugh, Chisler, Hiss, Tough, Slick). Some of the "little things" that a public man feels quite justified in disregarding may be the very ones that get him into trouble.

In addition to surveying carefully his image for potential villain traits, a public man can strive to contradict (violate) any villain type to which he is vulnerable. Being very rich, of course, makes him almost automatically subject to animosity against a "moneybags" or "profiteer," and he can try to offset this type by being a "good Joe," by emphasizing the fact that he began as a poor boy and has not really changed ("I never did have time to learn good English"). By being emphatically plain and common, he contradicts the type of the snob (even though he sends his daughter to an expensive private school). Or perhaps he becomes a public benefactor and adopts as his motto that of Daniel Guggenheim: "He who gives when well gives gold, when ill gives silver, when dead gives lead." Again, if he belongs to a disliked ethnic minority, he tries to be as unlike the stereotype of that minority as possible. By such contradictory traits a public man makes it hard for people to think bad things of him.

Another application of contradicting potential villain types is the reverse of movie type casting: if there is nasty work to be done, put the least likely appearing person into it, someone as unlike the prevailing concept of a villain as possible. For example, one furniture company employs for its repossession crew a motherly woman who goes to the customer's door to tell him that the company has come for his furniture. Her appearance disarms suspicion and potential resistance while a husky man waits in a van outside. Likewise, a comely woman on a motor scooter as a "Meter Maid" somehow makes it nicer to get parking tickets. A jovial Santa Claus type can be employed for such purposes as saying "No" to loan applicants, disciplining and firing employees, or bouncing drunks out of cafes. While such tactics, widely used, may produce symptoms of confusion in the public, they avoid, for the time, the overt unpleasantness of meeting villains. One comes away from the encounter finding it hard to hate.

For further principles of avoiding villainy, we shall look at the career of the late Senator Joseph McCarthy, which provides illustrations of what not to do.

2. The Perils of Mudslinging

Denigrating political opponents by slanders, slurs, innuendos, rumors, invective, or embarrassing charges is both a deplored and a time-honored practice. Many prominent Americans have suffered severe abuse. The method is politically attractive[4] because it is cheap and easy. Rumor has the advantage of anonymity and is almost impossible to combat effectively; name-calling is cheap because it gathers up a battery of vague charges into one ball that can be hurled. The damage is done without a chance for defense. How can one refute a name?

For all its apparent advantages, a practical case can be made against mudslinging, especially when it is against prominent men, even when the pressure is urgent, the chips are down, and the stakes are high. It is apparently not effective against important people who have some other solid basis of reputation. Any number of American political leaders (Washington, Jefferson, Hamilton, Jackson, Cleveland, Lincoln, Wilson, both Roosevelts) have come handsomely through scur-

4. See Leo Lowenthal and Norbert Guterman, *Prophets of Deceit* (New York: Harper, 1949), for vilifying tactics and themes of agitators.

rilous abuse and rumors, and so have many movie stars and other celebrities. One reason seems to be that the public is really more, and more permanently, interested in the *positive* things celebrities do or stand for, and finds it convenient to forget or overlook scandals, however momentarily interesting. (Note that by this reasoning a little man who has no other basis for reputation is more likely to be hurt by mudslinging.) Another reason for the ineffectiveness of scandal against "big" men was pointed out in chapter v: it is often impossible to find a name denoting the specific type violation that will bring him low, that will contradict his central role.

For example, private scandals involving women seem not very damaging if a public man has taken a popular stand on some more important issue. We need to know more, also, about the comparative value of negative images. Presumably, certain types (like "ladies' man" or "grafter") would not hurt a politician as much as something like "sneak," "bully," or "coward." Even a crime would not necessarily damage the reputation of a Napoleon. But perhaps the most important thing is the dramatic consideration that, if one throws mud, he may place himself in a worse role than he is trying to give the one he attacks. That is, there is little advantage in proving that his opponent is, say, a philanderer, if it proves at the same time that the name-caller is a sneak.

We have something to gain by looking at the conditions under which scapegoating and mudslinging backfire, and here is where we can learn from Senator Joseph McCarthy. His role of "investigator" worked for a time; he was a hero to many people, and there was serious talk of running him for President before he was officially rebuked and fell from popular favor. Some of the reasons he went wrong can be pointed out; they should discourage future demagogs from following the same route.

It is not easy, at best, publicly to call a respectable man an evil name and make it stick. The accuser must have high authority and/or convincing evidence to offset the symbolic risk that he himself undergoes.[5] The great advantage of a congressional investigation is its mantle of sovereign authority. But against this is the disadvantage that anyone who rakes and hurls mud, even in official proceedings and especially if he gets his information from informers, is playing the role of "sneak." Wearing the mantle of authority may itself imply cowardice or a reluctance to fight fairly in man-to-man encounter; the investigator may himself be obliged to give evidence as an informer or may be publicly associated with tattletales, eavesdroppers, stool pigeons, and the like.[6] He may bully or injure a weaker party, thus creating a victim who will gain sympathy and take it away from him. He may, by some kinds of character evidence, seem to strike a low blow and establish himself as "a man who would stoop to anything." Too much familiarity with evil may imply close association with it and (as has happened to some witch-hunters) he may be tarred by his own brush. In other words, it is a dirty business, and it is a wonder that anyone gets away with it.[7]

McCarthy succeeded remarkably, considering his essentially ugly part, because, for a time, he avoided its symbolic risks. He tirelessly reiterated his patriotic duty and his legisla-

5. Harold Garfinkel has defined some of the conditions under which a denouncer can succeed. He must be publicly identified with "suprapersonal," "ultimate" values in whose name he has the right to speak and must "ritually separate" the accused one from the legitimate order, make him an outsider. ("Conditions of Successful Degradation Ceremonies," *American Journal of Sociology,* LXI [1956], 432.) I have identified some of the "stranger" types that are easily made villains in *Heroes, Villains and Fools,* chap. iii.

6. Of course, culture and political climate make a difference here. In a country like the U.S.S.R. or China, where there is no presumption of innocence, no emphasis on fair play, and informing is encouraged as a patriotic duty, one would not expect the "sneak" to be vilified as readily as in America.

7. Other professions that require the collection of damaging information (claims adjuster, social caseworker, bonding company investigator, parole officer, work inspector) seem to suffer a similar symbolic disadvantage, often finding themselves being called tattletale, stooge, squealer, spy, or snooper.

tive mandate. His tough tactics and direct style of confrontation (nose-to-nose, as many pictures showed) had a certain virile quality. And he chose obvious villains as his main targets, so there was little chance of a backfire by having them become popular victims.

But time was against him. And his failure, it seems to me, was hastened by the fact that he became careless in avoiding the symbolic risks of his perilous course. One mistake was in setting up his own spy system rather than relying on other, official agencies of investigation, such as the FBI, to do the dirty work. McCarthy used two young amateur investigators, Roy M. Cohn and G. David Schine, to collect damaging information about federal officials, which involved them in a junket around U.S. Information Agency bureaus in Europe in 1953. Cohn was especially helpful to McCarthy in public hearing by his skill as a lawyer, but his image was defective. "Few who ever saw or heard him," said *Time,* "will forget the malevolent, heavy-lidded stare with which he pinioned witnesses, the adenoidal snarl as he closed in for the kill against a suspected communist. . . . Cohn was the sort that many people love to loathe."[8] He made legions of enemies by his combined tactics of snooper and hatchetman. Small wonder, then, that people were just waiting for the kind of scandal that developed when Cohn tried to get special privileges for his drafted friend, Schine; this information, brought out by Army Special Counsel Joseph Welch during televised hearings, forced Cohn to resign and is credited with having much to do with McCarthy's own downfall.

The general principle is that it is almost impossible to sling mud successfully or to carry off any basically nasty role, even if protected by official authority, unless every effort is made to avoid resemblance to villain types like the sneak and to avoid associates who resemble them.

8. September 13, 1963, p. 27.

3. Big Party versus Little Party

McCarthy also violated the principle of the ratio of apparent forces. He browbeat witnesses of official and physical stature smaller than himself, some of them obviously innocent.[9] He was physically of the hairy-chested "slugger" type; he had, in fact, gone in for boxing in college. Thus he naturally cast himself as a bully in his own show.

> Said John Steinbeck:
> "Have you ever seen McCarthy on television?"
> "Sure."
> "Just remember," said my friend. "He sneers, he bullies, he has a nasty laugh and he always looks as though he needs a shave. The only thing he lacks is a black hat. McCarthy is the BAD GUY. Everybody who saw him has got it pegged. He's the BAD GUY and people don't like the BAD GUY. I may be wrong but that's what I think. He's finished.[10]

Presumably McCarthy thought of himself as a defender of the right, but in his zeal to attack public enemies he went too far; he overplayed his hand and turned dramatically from prosecutor to persecutor. Attacking a few obvious Communists might not have had this effect, but by flailing at everyone within reach he was almost bound to strike some victims with whom the public would sympathize.

It is surprising how easily public men can make such mistakes. One need not be a slugger like McCarthy or a bully like "Bull" Conner or a rigid man like Judge Thayer to run afoul of the principle of not abusing the little party. For example, at one point in his 1948 campaign, Presidential candidate Thomas E. Dewey was embarrassed by a dog wandering onto

---

9. See Kurt and Gladys E. Lang, *Collective Dynamics* (New York: Crowell, 1961), pp. 455–56, for the case of an innocent young man abused by McCarthy. In one famous confrontation, Army Counsel Welch managed to make McCarthy look ashamed by the question, "At long last, have you left no sense of decency?" Although conclusive data are lacking, "the incident was played up by the press and generally interpreted as having hurt McCarthy."

10. "Good Guy—Bad Guy," *Punch*, September 22, 1954, p. 378.

the stage during his speech. The story got out that Dewey had ordered the dog off in a needlessly cruel manner, and that offended the dog-lovers. His managers thought that they must publish a retraction the next day; what Dewey had really said, they claimed, was, "Hello. Would you like to come up and join us? He's just like the terrier I had as a boy in Owosso, Michigan."[11] Likewise, critics of Franklin D. Roosevelt laid themselves open by attacking unnecessary expenditures on his dog, Fala. Roosevelt promptly turned the tables on them in a classic speech: such men were contemptible to persecute a little dog; they were calling Fala names, and Fala didn't like it. Whether or not, as some said, it was the greatest speech Roosevelt ever made, "he had treated the problem perfectly. It was no longer a danger to his candidacy."[12]

These incidents illustrate a general dramatic principle that it is not only the ratio of apparent forces that is consequential but also the power of the little party in role-forcing (the dog actually had some power to make a fool or villain of Dewey). The director of a popular radio forum, "Meet the Press," expressed a similar idea: "We never load the panel against the man being interviewed, because people are always for the underdog. Why, with a loaded panel, I could take the worst man in the country and make him a martyr."[13] The martyr automatically makes his opponent a villain. International relations are crowded with crude violations of this principle, perhaps because nations are afflicted with "group egotism." One need only mention such things as the events at the Berlin Wall, by which the East German police seemed to be doing their best to cast themselves in the eyes of the world as bullies.

11. Jack H. Pollack, "How They Get Your Vote," *This Week,* June 12, 1948, p. 5. Note the similar difficulty of President Johnson when he pulled his beagles' ears, May, 1964.

12. Frances Perkins, *The Roosevelt I Knew* (New York: Viking, 1946), p. 114.

13. Martha Roundtree, *Time,* March 5, 1951, p. 89. It might be added that likewise the best man in the country could be made to look like a villain.

4. Never Attack a Popular Hero

A third principle violated by McCarthy was in choosing men of high respectability—even national heroes—for his targets. Perhaps he was taking on the "big shots" with the idea of casting himself in a David/Goliath role, but he certainly chose the wrong Goliaths. The impression in retrospect is that of a drunken hunter scattering buckshot in all directions. Among those whom he savagely assailed were President Truman ("the son-of-a-bitch ought to be impeached"), Secretary of State Dean Acheson (for being corrupt, soft on communism, and hiring traitors), and General of the Army George Catlett Marsall ("a man steeped in falsehood," who lies "whenever it suits his conscience," "part of a "conspiracy," "always and invariably serving the Kremlin").[14]

Similar mistakes have been made by other extremists in America, such as Robert H. Welch, Jr., leader of the John Birch Society (who accused President Dwight D. Eisenhower of being an agent of the Communist party) and General Edwin A. Walker, whose list of targets reads almost like a "Who's Who in America," including Eisenhower, Eleanor Roosevelt, and Secretary of State Dean Rusk.[15] It should also be noted that Richard H. Nixon, though not an extremist, was rebuked in Howard K. Smith's controversial televised "Obituary" for having "applied the word traitor" to Harry Truman, Adlai Stevenson, and Secretary of State Dean Acheson.[16]

It is hard to imagine a less effective way of winning popular support than attacking the persons most people like most. At best, the attacker will split his following or at least put their loyalty to test and generate ambivalent feelings. (McCarthy apparently did split Republicans in his own state, Wisconsin, by

14. Richard H. Rovere, *Senator Joe McCarthy* (New York: Harcourt, Brace, 1959), pp. 12–15.

15. *Time,* April 13, 1962, p. 23.

16. Telecast by American Broadcasting Company, November 11, 1962. This, in turn, laid Howard K. Smith open to charges of having slurred a respected man, Nixon.

attacking President Nathan Pusey of Lawrence College.) At worst, he will lose all his support if loyalty to the hero is universal and strong, and his attack may backfire and make him the villain.

It may be, however, that the attacker does not care whether he gets the status of villain. This was the key to the policy of Westbrook Pegler, whose journalistic spleen seemed directed at almost anyone whom many other people liked (such as Franklin and Eleanor Roosevelt, whose personal features he described insultingly). He carried enormous insurance against libel suits to permit himself the needed immunity. But Pegler was not trying to win approval. He had the status of a popular villain—someone you like to be mad at—and did not really care whether his following liked him or not. Thus, it cannot always be counted as a mistake indiscriminately to attack popular heroes.

Most often, however, it is the error of an outspoken and careless man. One of Harry Truman's "bobbles," for example, was a casual reference to the U.S. Marine Corps as "a propaganda machine that is almost equal to Stalin's." This seeming slur on the heroes of Guadalcanal aroused national ire; there was widespread editorial protest, and housewives held indignant meetings. Truman realized his blunder and quickly apologized to the Marine commandant, regretting his "unfortunate use of language" and praising the Corps for its magnificent history since its establishment in 1775.

An attack on a hero may come from a well-meaning man doing what he considers his public duty—perhaps in loyal opposition or as a gadfly stinging the public into action. But if so, he should remember that it usually is much easier to blame the gadfly than the horse and that calling a popular hero a villain is a highly probable way of becoming a villain one's self. He should be prepared to pay the price in popularity and influence for having made such charges, which—unless an Achilles' heel can be found—usually roll like water off a

duck's back away from a well-established hero.[17] Psychologists
have long known that people listen to what they want to hear
but evade or resist what they do not want to hear. Thus, trying
to make a villain out of a popular hero is like trying to lift a
stone out of quicksand; you may find yourself in deeper than
before.

Such a rule holds, indeed, for attacks on any common value,
from the sanctity of motherhood to the new look in fashion.
William Graham Sumner said long ago that values in the mores
are protected by a special pathos. John Stuart Mill analyzed
it as a handicap of minority group status; people holding an
unpopular opinion are peculiarly exposed to slander

> because they are in general few and uninfluential, and
> nobody but themselves feels much interested in seeing
> justice done them; but this weapon is, from the nature
> of the case, denied to those who attack a prevailing
> opinion: they can neither use it with safety to them-
> selves, nor, if they could, would it do anything but
> recoil on their own cause.

Parents suffer such a disadvantage in attacking the teen-age
peer group, for they are, whether they know it or not, a
"minority" in the eyes of youth, and all that is likely to result
is that the carping adult is quietly put down as a "cornball."
The reason for the futility of attacking popular values is that
it is almost impossible, except in the most calamitous circumstances, for a group to see itself as villainous—or its attacker
as anything but a villain.

How, then, is incisive social criticism possible? The answer
is rather a tragic one; those who wish drastic reforms must be
willing to suffer the role of public villain or fool as a way of
dramatizing their cause, possibly as a wedge for an opening
that others will use.[18] A contrast between the tactics of the

17. Openly seeking for the "Achilles' heel" is itself symbolically
dangerous, for it puts one into the role of Paris.

18. An interesting collection of cases of public men in America who
suffered because they ran counter to prevailing opinion is provided by
John F. Kennedy in *Profiles in Courage* (New York: Harper, 1956).

Urban League and the Congress of Racial Equality (CORE) will be useful here. The Urban League has long pushed quietly for racial integration in industry and housing, without assuming the role of "troublemaker." For example, one policy was to choose highly acceptable Negroes to enter a profession or neighborhood first, proving by example rather than by disputatious claims. In contrast, the CORE freedom riders took a more aggressive (though "non-violent") role, which, while earning for some the kudos of heroes, also brought them much blame. Of course, it is possible that dramatization of a conflict by martyrs will further a cause faster than will more gradualistic tactics. But the success of a "troublemaker" in gaining popular sympathy rests on a number of dramatic conditions that will define him, say, as a "little party" or martyr against a cruel tyrant or bigot, and not as a traitor, Red, lawbreaker, etc. It is a gamble that by no means always pays off, especially if the "big party" is also skilled in playing dramatic roles.

In addition to this painful route, there are privileged statuses that allow some people to rebuke the audience itself. George Bernard Shaw once remarked that people liked him best when he insulted them, but this—like all Shavianisms—needs to be taken with a grain of salt, the salt being Shaw himself and the fact that he had the privileged position of jester in a situation in which the people were waiting to be amused. In some societies the parish priest or paternalistic chief is allowed to say things that will cause people to hang their heads. But what is the state of the public conscience these days? More than ever, in our changing, pluralistic society, it is becoming risky to seize this prerogative, for it puts an accuser in the role of "bluenose," "moralizer," "spoilsport," "authoritarian," "revengist," "witch-hunter." The more fragmented and pluralistic the moral order, the more vantage points there are from which to say "villain" or "fool" to someone who tells others they are wrong. This is small comfort to the critic or reformer who—as an outsider, with neither paternalistic position or the jester's privilege to protect him—tries to critize the public. For him there seems left only the more uncomfortable statuses of villain and fool.

If it should be necessary to stand up against a popular hero or the values he represents, it would seem best to try to get another popular hero, or an impeccable authority, to do the work in the fairest and mildest possible manner. Pitting one hero against another splits public opinion without leaving an obvious villain. This can become, then, a contest of champions of rival views.

5. Don't Count on the Same Wind Forever

At least one more principle is illustrated by the case of McCarthy. President Truman observed that "some feeling of the times"—not merely individuals like Joseph Welch and Senators Flanders, Watkins, and Morse—finally defeated Mc-Carthy. A general mood enabled the Senate to stiffen into a majority that had not been available earlier. "It took a little while to get that majority convinced of what they ought to do. When they were convinced, they did it."[19] McCarthy's official condemnation by the United States Senate in 1954 was a token of the fact that the tide of public opinion had turned against him. Though a hard core of McCarthyites remained loyal, with the rest of the country "he was finished. He was no longer a serious force in American politics."[20]

Two principles are involved here. One, well enough known to students of public opinion, is the instability of popular moods and mandates. The other principle is that, whatever causes these tides, it is not usually the actions of particular men. Rather, a public man succeeds because the tide is moving his way. An

19. Harry S. Truman, *Truman Speaks* (Morningside Heights, N.Y.: Columbia University Press, 1960), p. 126. This is an insight by a man who has proved to be one of the country's most successful public role-players.

20. Conversely, the White House, which had quietly worked against McCarthy, "became a tower of strength." Rovere, *op. cit.*, pp. 231–38. McCarthy commented: "I wouldn't exactly call it a vote of confidence, but I don't feel I've been lynched." *Ibid.*

important action may appear to have produced a mood, but it is more likely that it seems important because of the mood. McCarthy may have spoiled his welcome and withered the feelings that supported him for a time, but public interest would probably have shifted anyway, even if his role-playing had been impeccable. Polls have shown that Americans are normally not greatly concerned about the Communist menace,[21] so we should not have been surprised—although McCarthy apparently was—when interest in uncovering Reds and traitors dissipated. This obtuseness was, if anything, in not realizing that the public was getting fed up with him. A canny public actor knows when to bow out or change his act long before he is booed off the stage.

6. The "Troublemaker"

The role of "troublemaker" as a villain type is a special hazard to the inner-directed man in a highly organized society. It is prominent in organizations that stress "getting along with others," team play, bureaucratic reliability. A "troublemaker" is one who (especially if a newcomer) talks out of turn, stirs up discontent, suggests too many new ideas, tries to run things, or throws a monkey wrench into the works. Though *moral* judgments may be losing weight in our pluralistic society, the pragmatic statement, "He's a troublemaker," is quite enough to cost a man job, friends, and support. The type easily applies to outspoken and vigorous men who find it difficult to compromise, act out their feelings ("hotheads"), take extreme positions ("go out on a limb"), "speak their minds," "don't pull their

21. In one poll, for example, 123 out of 197 did not even know what a Communist was. In another, 30 per cent could not identify McCarthy. (Stuart Chase, *American Credos* [New York: Harper, 1962], pp. 157–58.) The mass is usually described as "apathetic" toward public issues. People are interested in news but do not feel personally involved; their attitude is more like that toward an entertainment or a sports event. Mere entertainment on television often outranks significant events in popular interest. We should not exaggerate the extent of real support for McCarthy's interesting tactics, even at the height of his power.

punches." So, of course, it punishes not only rebels and criminals but many leaders who are ahead of their time. Indeed, it may seem that history is made by troublemakers, like Billy Mitchell and Nicolai Lenin. Yet this should not obscure the fact that the vast majority of troublemakers are not successful leaders and on the whole make a negative contribution to organizations. It is unfortunate that this net catches some important leaders among many others that society could do without.

Being so defined is not merely a question of whether one is "progressive" or "conservative," since both can make trouble. It is essentially a problem of the man who cannot accept organization or the rules of the game. He can be found on the playing field, in any institution, in a legislature. No group can tolerate a troublemaker; he is a universal type.

The dilemma of any public man who wants action or radical reform is that he may have to play the troublemaker role before he can earn for himself some special position in which he is accepted. He may attain a special status, such as that of jester, who has the function of stating in comic form ideas that might not be acceptable if seriously urged. He may also serve as "lightning rod" to discharge aggression against comic butts. Another special status is that of "character," a person with an eccentric and colorful personality whom people like to have around. As a symbolic leader, he may stand for such things as "Be yourself" or "It's fun to be crazy." The maverick also has a useful function in stirring up trouble when others do not wish to be embarrassed. He can stage filibusters, cast dissenting votes, hold out as a diehard when others are giving in too easily, and be a spearhead for ideas that need to be tested before the majority will accept them. It is some such function that mavericks like Senator Wayne Morse of Oregon, Vice-President Henry Wallace, Norman Thomas, and Senator Robert La Follette, Sr., of Wisconsin, have had for American democracy. A public man may have to skirt the troublemaker role and accept the risks involved if he wishes to travel as a maverick. One of the main questions is whether he has the special qualities of personality and color that will enable him to win a favorable position rather than just be written off, as most troublemakers are.

7. *Crossing the Line*

An opposite risk is encountered by the other-directed organization man ("smoothie," politician, diplomat, manipulator) who plays it safe by straddling and associating with birds of many different feathers. Straddling, when it works, has the advantage of allowing him to eat his cake and have it, too; he avoids going out on a limb and keeps friends on both sides of an issue. He often gets credit for a democratic willingness to compromise. But the straddler is inherently vulnerable to being damned by both parties, as faint-hearted, pussyfooting, even hypocritical and disloyal. Furthermore, he is flirting with one of the most dangerous villain types society possesses, that of renegade or traitor. Social types like "collaborator," "company man," "square John,"[22] "pocho,"[23] "Uncle Tom," carry some of this judgment. To the in-group, they have crossed the line and gone over to the enemy.

Some prominent Americans have, sometimes quite innocently, "crossed the line." I have mentioned Lindbergh's image crisis from accepting a Nazi medal, and his later departure from the United States to live in England for a time (following the tragic kidnapping of his son) also seemed to some Americans a kind of desertion of his country. Charlie Chaplin's departure to live in Switzerland evoked a similar reaction. When success-

22. A term used by penitentiary inmates for the convict who sincerely tries to "be good" and co-operates with the administration. See Clarence Schnag, "A Preliminary Criminal Typology," *Pacific Sociological Review, IV* (1961), 11–20.

23. A Mexican term for a Mexican who has "lost his spots," become too American, and is no longer proud of his own country and its culture. It does not necessarily imply disloyalty, however. The term *malinche* applies better to the one who collaborates with the enemy.

ful people do such things, the general feeling seems to be, "They made their money here; why do they leave?" A more deliberate crossing of the line is seen in Ezra Pound's espousal of Italian fascism and Paul Robeson's friendship with the Soviet Union.[24] But it is not necessary to join the enemy to seem guilty of crossing the line. Almost any kind of amiable contact with an outgroup—an arm thrown about another in a picture, being present at the wrong banquet, trying on a costume, living "internationally"—can compromise an individual in this manner; these acts say, symbolically, that he is on their side.

This attitude is, perhaps, an inherent risk of mobility and cosmopolitanism in a pluralistic society that has not outgrown ethnocentrism. It is aggravated by social crisis and a feeling of threat to status groups and the moral order. Upwardly mobile leaders run a like risk of betraying their "roots" and deserting their former comrades even while performing the very negotiations for which they are commissioned, unless special effort is made to show that they have remained faithful.

How can a public man safely "cross the line" internationally? One hint is given by such popular favorites as Will Rogers and Ben Franklin, who, when traveling abroad, loudly proclaimed their Americanism and took the role of official or unofficial ambassadors for their country. Thus they did not risk "losing their spots." They wore, so to speak, Uncle Sam's top hat wherever they went. Pronounced ethnic characteristics can make it seem impossible to cross the line even when in foreign territory.

8. The Perils of Cleverness

An interesting dramatic danger comes from the sheer emphasis of modern society on being "smooth"—an expert role-player, showman, diplomat, tactician. A loss of public confi-

24. Robeson's "perfidy" was consummated when he received the International Stalin Peace Prize for 1952; at the ceremony he said, in a shaky voice, "I have always been, I am, and I always will be, a friend of the Soviet Union."

dence sometimes occurs in which a leader by his very smoothness comes to be defined as a "smart operator" or "a fast worker."[25] He knows how to play the game, is adept at manipulating people, never makes a false move, and never shows his hand (even in a showdown); yet respect for his prowess is mixed with mistrust. People somehow feel that he is slick, oily, "too smart for his own good." A vicious circle sets in, in which his very skill begins to work against him, and, once loss of confidence begins, he may be unable to reassure people of his genuineness. When charm is interpreted as guile, an actor is "damned if he does and damned if he doesn't." For example, employees can come to suspect a genuinely friendly boss of manipulating them; all the efforts of "Madison Avenue" advertising have, I think, been discounted in this way by much of the American public.

An obvious concern with building "images," then, seems to have an alienating effect that offsets admiration for its smoothness.[26] Indeed, even ingenuous mistakes (like Truman's "bobbles") may in the last analysis be a surer route to the public's heart than role-playing skill, just because the real man seems to be revealed. Perhaps "mistakes" could be staged to build an image of sincerity; can cleverness be buried inside of innocence? In any event, it seems true that, however many coats of paint one uses, he must keep showing what the public thinks is the basic color or he will seem a chameleon. Such are the perils of cleverness.

These eight routes to villainy are a few of the dramatic

25. See Frank Gibney, *The Operators* (New York: Harper, 1960).
26. We should bear in mind, on the other hand, that the public admires a "clever hero" who "puts things over" on rivals and brings big men to a fall. (See "The Clever Hero," *Journal of American Folklore,* LXVII [1954].) The difference may be chiefly in the direction in which cleverness is displayed: against the public itself—a villain-making trait—or against someone the public dislikes—a hero-making trait. One moral would be that a public man should minimize, rather than publicize, the presence of public relations men on his staff.

risks that a public man must run as he plays his role. Straight-forward action as much as devious maneuvering can put him into the villain's part.

We now turn to another aspect of unpopularity, seen in certain fool roles that cause the public to laugh at rather than with a man and "write him off" as a serious influence.

PLAYING THE FOOL

It is not easy (or always desirable) for a public man to avoid the role of fool. Anyone can have a rug pulled from under him or slip on his own banana peel. Anyone can be placed in circumstances in which associates are embarrassing. However shrewd he may be in one territory, there is always another in which he is a babe in the woods. High status is no protection; indeed, the high standards required of some offices and professions make it easier to be ridiculed for slight mistakes. Sometimes one has to play the fool to prove that he is a good sport. The dunce's hat fits everybody.

Anyway, how can one protect himself from nonsense, jingles, antics, mimicry, caricature, funny names?

> Jeff Davis rides a white horse,
> Lincoln rides a mule,
> Jeff Davis is a gentleman,
> And Lincoln is a fule.

> With the help of God and a few Marines
> MacArthur returned to the Philippines.

Are you aware that Claude Pepper is known all over Washington as a shameless extrovert? Not only that, but this man is reliably reported to practice nepotism with his sister-in-law, and he has a sister who was once a Thespian in wicked New York. Worst of all, it is an established fact that Mr. Pepper, before his marriage, habitually practiced celibacy.[27]

27. From a campaign speech by Congressman Smithers against his opponent. (Winthrop Sargeant, "The Art of Vituperation," *Life,* October 23, 1950, p. 40.)

There is hardly any answer to this kind of assault on dignity, unless a better joke can be devised. But if a man answers in kind, he may lose all by putting himself in the role of the fool. If he has no sense of humor, he may be almost helpless against a determined joker. If he gets angry, he may only provide more material for jest. If he revenges himself in kind, he may turn his opponent into a victim with whom the crowd sympathizes and prove at the same time that he can't take it. In America, at least, everyone is supposed to show that he is a good sport by taking the part of fool once in a while. Once when General Eisenhower was reviewing the troops of General Patton in Italy during World War II a surprising thing happened. As Patton saluted and stood stiffly at attention before Eisenhower, the general dropped his hand from the answering salute and jabbed his thumb into Patton's taut midriff. Soldiers behind could see that Patton jumped sharply and that there was a mischievous grin on Eisenhower's face. It seemed a good joke on Patton, who was known as a "spit and polish" commander.

Aside from laughing it off, the only real answer to a jest is a better jest. It takes a wit to outdo a wit. For such few, perhaps, rules are not needed. But there may be advantage to the rest of us in trying to state some of the more common situations that have made unwilling fools in American public life.

1. The Anatomy of Fiasco

Consider the career of former Vice-President Henry A. Wallace, who has been called "the most forgotten of forgotten men" in American national politics. He dropped precipitously from public view after the election of 1948. Was this merely from his own wish for retirement?

Wallace had been Vice-President under Franklin D. Roosevelt from 1940 to 1944. Then Roosevelt dropped him as running-mate and replaced him with Truman, giving Wallace the consolation prize of Secretary of Agriculture. After Roosevelt died, Truman dropped Wallace from the Cabinet. The immediate reason was a speech (on September 12, 1946) contradicting Truman's "get tough" policy with Russia, but, more basically, Wallace had become known as a political idealist, a mystic, humanitarian, and maverick. He had been derided for talking "Globaloney" and advocating a "quart of milk for every Hottentot." He was out of harmony with the Administration, especially as the "New Deal" philosophy withered under Truman.

Wallace's ouster was followed by his leadership of the newly formed Progressive party, for which he summoned a "Gideon's Army" to take over the country at the polls in 1948. The banner of this party was "Peace," and a main plank of its platform was coexistence with Soviet Russia. Wallace's campaign was an extraordinary exercise in fervor and naiveté. "He stumped the country like a tent evangelist, calling on the politically wicked to repent or face Armagedden."[28] He drew a following of zealots, left-wingers, trade-unionists, college students, and intellectuals across the country, but, unfortunately, his campaign became more and more dominated by Communist party tacticians as it proceeded. Wallace valiantly carried the civil rights issue into the Deep South and got eggs and tomatoes thrown in his face. He actually managed to poll 1,157,000 votes, but not enough to deprive Truman of victory. It was not his failure to sweep the country but the way he went about it that caused his campaign to be widely regarded as a fiasco, a discreditable display of bad political judgment. Wallace was one of those quixotic types who out of sincere idealism go to extremes that other people regard as foolish, at least at the time.[29] He left the scene as the unhorsed knight of "Globaloney." Westbrook Pegler referred to him in his usual kindly way as "Bubblehead" Wallace, and that image seems to

28. Cabell Phillips, *New York Times,* October 9, 1963.
29. Wallace commented, "Basically, I was right then, and I am right now. The test ban treaty which Averill Harriman worked out in Moscow [1963] is a belated recognition of it. Maybe I was ahead of my time." (*Ibid.*)

have been the one with which he left politics to resume his life
as a farmer in 1948.

Other fiascos have already been considered in this book:
Ford's "peace ship," Wilson's failure at Versailles, Pershing's
pursuit of Pancho Villa. Clearly, the fiasco is one of the great
formulas of folly. What are its basic ingredients?

First, it is a defeat that, however ruinous, is neither a
tragedy, disaster, nor crime; nor are its penalities severe.
Laughter hurts an ego but seldom breaks a neck. The harm
done is mostly to the fool himself rather than to the audience
and the rest of the cast. The popular verdict is: "It serves him
right for being such a fool." Therefore, the charge of the Light
Brigade, Custer's last stand, and the Athenian Sicilian Expedition, described by Thucydides, are really too serious to be regarded as fiascos. Real pain moves a drama toward victimiza-
tion, martyrdom, or tragedy. Yet, though fiasco is comic, it is
serious enough to portend the end of a public career. The public
washes its hands of the fool and no longer gives him serious
consideration.

To bring about a fiasco, one must be involved in a bold
undertaking that, however, gallantly executed, fails because
of a blunder, because of the stupidity or naiveté of the main
actor. There must also be a grandiose—or at least a dispro-
portionate—expenditure of effort and claim. A prudent man
tries a small investment first, a "trial balloon," but the fool
stakes everything. Furthermore, he announces in advance what
he is going to do, thus building himself up for a big letdown.
Ford's expedition could have been sent quietly (a few emis-
saries would have been better than a shipload of pacifists),
and Pershing could have played down his expedition against
Villa at the start instead of letting reporters make a field day
of it.[30] Publicity is dangerous at the beginning of any under-

30. This factor bears also on the psychic importance of the charge
of the Light Brigade. It was not the first serious British military blunder
but the first time that reporters had been present on a battlefield. (Chris-
topher Hibbert, *The Destruction of Lord Raglan* [New York: Little,
Brown, 1962].)

taking; perhaps it is the very stuff of fiasco. Failure in itself is not disgraceful, but it becomes so if an early and elaborate claim or buildup is permitted.[31] One cannot tell a man to avoid mistakes, but it is possible to avoid the dramatic conditions of fiasco. Here, then, is a practical principle that can be applied: avoid public overcommitment. Any amount of resources and men can be used to move things quietly, but only a small amount should show. This not only avoids dangerous dramatic buildups but also assures a favorable ratio of apparent forces.

The United States—perhaps from the very openness of its communication system and the eagerness of its citizens to make and report news and to become celebrities—is a country especially favorable to fiasco. It encourages big gestures and asks the public man to stick his neck out. The failure of the Ford Motor Company's Edsel illustrates the tendency toward large-scale promotion of a venture that may fail. The United States government, notable in its missile shots and space program, has also seemed willing to expose itself to fiasco in the race with the comparatively secretive Russians. It has proudly announced experiments and staked national prestige on them, only to have the public groan with anguish when what should have been a quiet pilot experiment becomes a public fizzle. When the United States proclaimed plans for a manned moon-landing by 1970, at a cost of from twenty to forty billion dollars, the U.S.S.R. suddenly withdrew from the contest. "Was it sour grapes or a horse laugh" that Khrushchev was giving us, asked *Life,* when it left us to "a moon race with ourselves?"

The public man may well keep in mind these common-sense rules, just as he posts instructions near the fire extinguisher. He follows a strategy of modesty, protecting himself

31. Though Lindbergh was called a "flying fool," his flight, if it had failed, could not have been a fiasco because of his pathetically small investment in plane and equipment and the apparent casualness with which he started. A certain amount of bravado or cockiness is safe in a small man because it seems proof of a courageous spirit rather than the pride and overextension of claims that make fools. He can be forgiven for failing to fell the giant and complimented for his courage in trying.

against overcommitment by minimum claims and keeping his center of gravity as low as possible (as expressed in the Chinese proverb, "He who sleeps on the floor will never fall out of bed"). Except where almost certain to succeed, he avoids bravura—which is, to be sure, a formula for both heroism and folly.[32] He does not commit himself personally or irrevocably when there is sustantial doubt of an outcome. He avoids escalation of effort and lets others plunge first and "take the rap" for the failures inevitable in any new undertaking. He uses understatement rather than overstatement. He avoids publicity fanfare, except with the most judicious timing. In the early phases of any effort, suspense created by doubt of success ("Will he make it? Has he a chance?") is better than explicit and easy confidence of success, which will only make him look doubly bad if failure does come. The general principle is that it is practically impossible to deflate someone who makes no claims.

2. Going Out on a Limb

Another mistake commonly made by extremists is in isolating themselves from support; common sense has labeled this "going out on a limb (and then sawing it off)." By contrast, the shrewd politician acts in season, hold his finger to the wind, does not push his luck too far.

It is ironical that this mistake (as with the fiasco) is very close to the stuff of heroism, to the recklessness of the one who leads the charge (of Harry Truman, who cast aside discretion, "gave 'em hell," and won the election). It is also very close to the villain-making mistake of attacking a popular hero or a

---

32. One of Babe Ruth's famous boasts—pointing to the part of the field where he intended to place his next home run—meant taking tremendous dramatic risks for huge gain; it was essentially a double-or-nothing bat. The alternative fiasco outcome is celebrated by the famous poem "Casey at the Bat." Fiasco might be called heroism-in-reverse. If a tiny force achieving a vast result makes a hero, a small result from a grandiose effort makes a fool. It may be noted, too, that mock heroism, as a satirical device, pushes a person into a grandiose claim.

majority. Indeed, here is the essential predicament of Don Quixote, who is close to hero, villain, and fool at the same time. The key seems to be the luck that an extremist has in hitting the bull's-eye of symbolic function (discussed in chap. ii). By a kind of dramatic geometry, he wins more credit for a longer shot, but he also has a greater chance of error by going to extremes.

Let us consider the case of Major General Edwin A. Walker, who seemed for a time to be a potential leader of the "rightist" movement in the United States, even (in Texas, at least) a potential Presidential candidate. A tall, fine-appearing man, he aroused in people a feeling of respect, in or out of uniform. Moreover, he was a medaled hero. His one fixed idea was that Americans were not fighting Communists hard enough. Thus, in his command in Germany he devised the so-called "Pro-Blue" program to instruct his men on the dangers of communism. He also offered them a "political index" of the voting record of congressmen that had a strong conservative bias. This action—a technical violation of Army regulations—led to efforts to "muzzle" Walker, his refusal to be muzzled, and finally his resignation from the Army. He then carried into civilian life his fight to save the country from the Red menace. Called before a congressional committee (which might have been his big chance to reach the public), he first told how he had been "muzzled" and then proceeded to assail as soft on communism a number of distinguished Americans. He charged that there was a mysterious "control apparatus" working in the United States in favor of Russia, naming Secretary of State Dean Rusk and State Department Counselor Walter Rostow as "people who think along the same lines as the apparatus."

This was too much. It not only finished him as a major right-wing leader but raised doubts as to his mental competence. Perhaps he had said no more than many of his followers were thinking, but he had gone too far, and too publicly. Said *Time*: "It was a shoddy and confused display of name-calling without evidence." He "cut a pathetic figure" in the eyes of the senators and the public. William F. Buckley, Jr., a strong conservative, acknowledged that Walker had made a fool of himself:

> Almost everyone has been heard from by now, and the verdict is that General Walker be consigned to history's ashcan, and that henceforward his name call forth the roars of contempt and ridicule of a people for whom in two wars he fought as gallantly as any man ever has in American military history.
>
> General Walker went on to fight a third war, which he lost, ignominiously. In words of one syllable, the general made himself look foolish.[33]

The prevailing image of Walker was perhaps best expressed by William Mauldin in a cartoon in the *St. Louis Post-Dispatch,* which showed him alone with his shadow, saying, "They're all around me."

The final scene of Walker's downfall, however, came during the rioting at the University of Mississippi over the registration of James Meredith. The ex-general climbed on the base of a Confederate statue to harangue a mob on their right to protest on the basis of their convictions. He was arrested the next day and charged with inciting rebellion and insurrection. The government ordered him examined by a psychiatrist.

The irony is that desperate, foolish, even mad extremists sometimes become heroes. Walker's very aggressiveness, activism, and tendency to speak out are the qualities of heroes. He apparently had a favorable chance to assume right-wing leadership. What went wrong? It seems too easy to blame his failure upon suspicion of mental instability, as though the public consisted of psychiatrists. It is more reasonable to say that the times were not disturbed enough for Walker's extremism to be widely acceptable in a symbolic leader.

3. Comic Frustration

Another important fool-making ingredient is the baffle-

33. *San Diego Union,* April 14, 1962.

ment of a large by a small force. The practical joker gives the birthday celebrant cake with chemically treated candles that he cannot blow out. A man in a telephone booth cannot reach his party, then cannot get his dime back, then finds the door stuck, and has to pound on it to be let out. This is comic frustration, a ludicrous display of ineffectuality by a powerful force. Pershing pursues Pancho Villa with an army of more than a hundred thousand men but cannot catch him.

Bureaucratic institutions seem chronically prone to an image of comic frustration because a vast expenditure of red tape seems needed to get a small result; this is also true of Congress, in its party and committee deadlocks. It is not, then, absolute defeat that is significant, but the disproportion between expenditure and results that creates the image of nothing done.

It is obviously impossible to avoid all frustration from unexpected complications, but the dramatic conditions of comic frustration can be avoided: the ratio of apparent forces that makes the effort seem larger than the result. One should not use two policemen, two agents, two dollars, where one will do; one should not use a van if he can move it with a wheelbarrow, or a big organization to do what can be done by man-to-man contact. One key is to avoid the kind of stubbornness that makes a man determined to achieve a result that it is not worth the effort.

A good tactician senses the development of difficulty in human relations before he reaches an impasse, and seeks his goal in another way. Nor does he give an opportunity to small parties to take firm stands that seem to defy or block his program, which would give "giant-killer" credit to them and make him look foolish. If a project is going to run aground, it may be better from a dramatic standpoint to ram it against a large obstacle than let it appear to be bogged down by petty difficulties. By keeping one's public effort small relative to the opposition (however large the hidden expenditures may be), he avoids the possibility of comic frustration. Thus a political party should not advertise the amount of money raised for its candidate (unless it is small), for to lose the election after a large investment can only make their man look bad.

Albert Einstein was once observed meditatively eating an ice-cream cone while watching some men unload a carload of ducks. Einstein never cared much about his public image, but an important executive could not afford to be caught in that kind of pose. The executive must guard his role by avoiding small tasks that are subject to obvious frustration; he must seem always to be occupied by major problems, leaving the little ones to subordinates and, if possible, tossing the difficult ones to his rivals. This is the dramatic side of "delegation of responsibility" and "span of control": the more important a man, the greater the issues he should seem to have on his mind.

4. Belittling Juxtapositions

To minimize chances of being made a fool, one must avoid certain personal juxtapositions. Once when the Queen of England appeared in London, a garbage collector's truck was accidentally caught in her procession, and he was fired from his job. Why did the British take such an occurrence so seriously? They were recognizing the principle that, the higher one's rank, the more sensitive it is to juxtapositions in which it is possible to infer that the statuses of unequal parties are comparable. True, a king may associate with a fool, but only on terms that preserve the difference between the scepter and the bauble. Once Lieutenant-Governor Goodwin Knight of California, while officiating at the opening of a religious center, was photographed with a Hollywood yogi. There is nothing especially wrong with a yogi, and Knight's duty called for such public functions, but the rather strained look on his face suggested that he was not unaware that association with a cult leader might have some untoward effect on his political image.

Man of the people, yes—but the people do not like some kinds of people.

Part of this danger comes, indeed, from the very poses, so common in democratic societies, of being a "good sport," of enjoying "anything for a laugh." American politicians are sometimes so eager to prove that they are regular fellows that they put themselves in ludicrous positions, as when President Truman was photographed at a piano with a chorus girl seated upon it.[34] Baby-kissing and plain-folksing have a double peril of comic juxtaposition and behaving foolishly to begin with. How does one know that seating a candidate on a stool next to a cow is a good idea? A similar danger is found in the ideal of approachability, so fashionable among executives: "Always be accessible to your men"; "Don't close the office door." Yet the price may be that the leader finds himself surrounded by hangers-on and undesirable old friends; in Truman's case, this led to the charge of "cronyism." It may be that the leader will be judged by the crowd that hangs around him; opponents of the Kennedy administration made unfavorable comments about the "Sinatra types" being welcomed to the White House. A leader's dignity, then, is in danger from some of the demands of democratic ideology.

Public association with an antic person is especially dangerous. The fool, who has the lowest dignity, tends to share his status with those in the limelight with him. Mimicry accentuates the resemblance between the leader and his "ape," as when small boys follow a man down the street imitating his gait and gestures. Moreover, there is no way to reply to an "ape" with dignity. One aggressive tactic of public relations is, therefore, to concoct a situation in which one's opponent is inextricably involved with someone who behaves without dignity. This tactic was apparently used against Richard Nixon during his campaign for the governorship of California in 1962:

34. Of course, if a man is already unpopular, a ludicrous situation can be humanizing, by contradicting the villain image. We have already commented on the midget on J. P. Morgan's knee.

Among the newsmen who swarm around Richard M. Nixon up and down the state, a recurrent figure is a curly-haired, boyish-faced man with a shoulder-strap tape recorder emblazoned with the call letters KRGT.

There is no Station KRGT. . . . A member of the staff of Mr. Nixon's gubernatorial opponent, Gov. Edmund G. Brown, Mr. [Richard G.] Tuck . . . leapfrogs along the Nixon campaign route, appraising crowds, recording speeches, organizing short-order local counterattacks and hiring bandleaders and old ladies in a process of subtle psychological warfare.

His stock-in-trade are imagination and an ingratiating personality that have kept him on such cordial terms with the Nixon organization that there has even been talk of letting him ride the Nixon plane, since he shows up everywhere anyway. . . .

He regards as one of his defter coups the contriving of something that happened at the East Boston airport the morning after the first Nixon-Kennedy debate in 1960, while Nixon aides were trying to reassure their candidate that he had done all right. As the Vice President stepped down from his plane a sweet old lady, a Democrat wearing a Tuck-provided Nixon button, embraced the candidate and recited the Tuck-framed words: "Don't worry, son. Kennedy won last night, but you'll do better next time."[35]

How could Mr. Nixon "democratically" handle such a pest? To single him out for proscription might seem unfair, might imply that the candidate was intolerant, afraid, or could not take a joke. Yet to trade joke for joke with a clown, even if Mr. Nixon were temperamentally able to do it, would probably result in a contest reminiscent of Aristophanes' play *The Frogs,* in which Aeschylus and Euripides lambaste each other with vulgar witticisms until neither has any dignity left. In my own judgment, Nixon should have gotten rid of the heckler in some quiet way, relying on the ingenuity of his advisers,

35. Gladwin Hill, *New York Times,* October 9, 1962. A similar role was played by Miss Moira O'Conner on the Goldwater campaign train in 1964.

rather than tolerate him with the notion of being a "good sport." But perhaps the fact that he did not get rid of him is further proof of how hard it is to defend one's self from this tactic.

Association with a personage of high status, the converse of such a principle, can restore lost prestige. An illustration of this principle is Charles Lindbergh's patronage of Robert H. Goddard, the rocket pioneer, who had become a laughing-stock by his efforts to "reach the moon" and numerous experimental failures. A visit from Lindbergh in 1929 changed the picture for Goddard. From then on, people took him more seriously. The only trouble with this path, of course, is that the person of high status risks lowering his own prestige— especially if involved in a fiasco.

5. Faces of the Fool

I am well aware that the treatment here barely begins to chart the predicaments that make fools and the routes by which one can fall comically (or by which one may be "saved"). As with villains, it is not so important what one does as it is to avoid resembling the prevailing types. That fact, in turn, requires a survey of the types recognized in our society. Some fool types, of course, may benefit an entertainer, but for a serious man it is different. Did not some of Adlai Stevenson's image trouble, for example, in the 1952 and 1956 Presidential campaigns, come from his humor? Did people take him less seriously than they might? Were they more impressed by his jokes than by his wisdom? Did not even the comic title "egghead" have something to do with this humor? At any rate, a public man has to measure what he gains against what he loses by comic typing—whether it will make him seem an antic fool or pay off the way it did for Will Rogers.

I lack space to treat in detail the various types prominent in American society, but I have tried to describe them elsewhere.[36] Briefly, they include the following: clumsy fool (e.g.,

36. *Heroes, Villains and Fools*, chap. iv.

bungler), naïve newcomer (greenhorn), rash fool (daredevil, hothead, wastrel), dupe (easy mark, chump), weak fool (sissy, ladies' man, yes-man, crybaby), coward, dude, old fool (cornball, old fogey), small-minded fool (tightwad, stickler), pompous fool (stuffed shirt, windbag, boaster, showoff), upstart, comic phony (humbug, fraud), freak (deformed fool), strange fool (queer, oddball, character, square), rigid fool (diehard, fanatic), high-minded fool (idealist, do-gooder), antic fool (clown, cutup), jester (the fool-maker), and comic butt.

CONCLUSION: PLAYING IT SAFE

I have tried here to show some of the dramatic risks run by public men from resemblance to the faces of the fool or the villain. They are not so obvious that common sense is sufficient always to protect a man. More attention should be paid to such considerations as the ratios of apparent force, co-relationships in dramatic situations, the style with which a role is carried off, the amount of buildup or claim, and the all-important factor of timing. There are even risks in how a man looks that need to be further explored by scientific symbolic analysis.

It is clear that one can achieve a certain amount of dramatic safety from fool roles by a strategy of modesty, making few claims and avoiding early buildup; by not committing one's self totally when there is the possibility of fiasco; by keeping a favorable ratio of apparent forces in all transactions; by playing only in familiar territory; by avoiding small tasks or obstacles that offer the possibility of comic frustration and belittling juxtapositions; and by staying away from clowning unless one has enough wit to make it work for him. We have noted the perils of villainy in mudslinging, in the opposition of big party and little party, in attacking popular heroes or majorities, in acting "out of season," in troublemaking, in crossing the line, and in being "too smart for one's own good."

Two more general remedies are suggested. One is to study very carefully the faces of villains and fools as they are conceived in popular culture. The other is to undertake continual image (type) analysis, in order to keep abreast of those faces and take account of the symbolic liabilities (image troubles) that may have developed from recent roles. Such feedback can correct a dangerous trend while there is still time.

There is an important area of role strategy remaining, however. Suppose one cast aside concern about "playing safe" and sought the grand prize? What does it take to make a popular hero? We turn to this problem in the next chapter.

CHAPTER EIGHT

HERO STUFF

The plain man is the basic clod
From which we grow the demigod;
And in the average man is curled
The hero stuff that rules the world.

SAM WALTER FOSS

In his younger days, Goethe was better known as an eccentric than as a genius. He wandered about the countryside with the abstracted manner and dress of a poet, while peasants stared. The local opinion was that he "had a slate loose in the upper storey."[1] No one supposes that these affectations were the basis of Goethe's stature as a national hero, but the question is always relevant: To what extent do such things contribute to the making of a public "genius"?[2] Henry David Thoreau provides another illustration of the problem. People knew him far better from his personal ways—as the man who lived in a hut alone for a year, who went to jail to avoid paying a one-dollar tax—than as a writer. Likewise, Bertrand Russell has won more popular fame by "maverick" stands favoring "free love" and "coexistence" than by his classic *Principia Mathematica*. Do great men add to their luster by colorful gestures, a flair for the dramatic? This leads us inevitably to a more

---

1. Emil Ludwig, *Goethe* (New York: Putnam, 1928), pp. 6, 42.
2. Wilhelm Lange-Eichbaum, *The Problem of Genius* (New York: Macmillan, 1932), and *Genie, Irrsinn und Buhm* (Munich: Reinhardt, 1928).

basic question: Is hero stuff extrinsic? Can it be added from the outside to any man?

The theory of symbolic leadership is that such leadership derives from meaning, and meaning is always extrinsic. If a man makes the right impression and does not contradict it publicly, he can become as a symbol almost anything he pleases (or that fortune pleases). The actual possession of qualities would be crucial only if, and at the point where, they were required for a key public performance. But, since a "buildup" can create public images, even a performance is not absolutely necessary.

We need not suppose a communication monopoly like that depicted by George Orwell in *Nineteen Eighty-four* for this line of reasoning. Buffalo Bill is often cited as an example of an American popular hero who was to a large extent fabricated by zealous fiction writers and expert showmanship. He was not a fraud, but he was not different enough from hundreds of other buffalo-hunters and Indian-fighters to justify his extraordinary status.[3] The extrinsic nature of hero stuff is even plainer in legendary and semilegendary heroes, of whom we have no way of knowing whether they were really what people thought they were. By citing the possibility of total buildup, I do not contradict any earlier contention (in chap. three) that leaders must strike the right symbolic function or nothing will happen. This only requires us to ask more pointedly: What are the kinds of performance, or buildup, or personality most likely to strike the popular imagination?

We need not try to turn a completely ordinary man—a nobody—into a popular hero. Suppose we have someone of considerable ability but without talent for dramatizing him-

3. Richard J. Walsh and M. S. Salisbury, *The Making of Buffalo Bill* (Indianapolis: Bobbs-Merrill, 1928). A. L. Guérard takes somewhat this position about Napoleon; he suggests that his legend was in large measure due to the work of writers, especially the St. Helena group who began to promote him after his death. (*Reflections on the Napoleonic Legend* [New York: Scribner, 1924], pp. 134, 171–72, 196, and *Preface to World Literature* [New York: Holt, 1940], p. 74.)

self;[4] what can be done to "put him over"? Some of the contents of hero stuff have worked since the time of Sigurd, Homer, and King David. Why should they not work again? There may be public relations gimmicks yet to be discovered, but it is fair to assume that there are rules for hero-making that will work for almost anyone who uses them properly, in almost any country.

The catch, to be sure, is that they must be used "properly." No theoretical principle tells us the precise circumstances and way in which it is to be employed, as philosophers have long pointed out. Nor does it perform the creative task of suggesting the new twist that will make an old principle work more effectively. Furthermore, a single-minded effort to play the hero is itself comic, the very stuff of satire; if people know what you are up to, your public relations goose is likely to be cooked. Two popular definitions of such a man are probable—a pompous fool who thinks he is great, or a pretentious phony. For such reasons alone, a public man should be circumspect about trying to heroize himself, even if he knows how or has somebody do it for him. But the fact remains that some very crude mountebanks have imposed themselves on the public by strutting, posing, and dramatizing themselves. How is this done?

COLOR AND ITS USES

First, what can be done to make a man more interesting? Here the study of the careers of popular heroes provides suggestions. Many good men seem to suffer, for example, from a

---

4. For a realistic example, consider the "dark horse" candidate for the Republican Presidential nomination in 1964, Governor William Scranton of Pennsylvania. He is described as an effective executive and politician but "there is little color. There are few anecdotes. Pressed for 'Scranton stories,' the people closest to him just sit and stare. They have none to tell—Scranton fails to sparkle on TV." (James Welsh, *New York Times,* January 18, 1964.)

lack of color, yet almost anyone, however dull, has something colorful in his life that can be brought out. Often it has nothing directly to do with his official work. For example, a certain mayor had finished his term of office without a striking deed to leave in the memory of the public he had served conscientiously. On the eve of his retirement from public life, the following story became known. He had held a reception for a visiting political figure. The guest of honor had arrived with a woman on his arm who was neither wife nor established friend but apparently a lady of pleasure. The mayor met him in the anteroom, saw his friend, and said, "My wife and other ladies are here. You can't bring her in. She'll have to wait for you in the car or someplace." The guest insisted, but the mayor stood firm, risking the collapse of his reception, to say nothing of his political connections, if the guest walked out. The honored guest then gave in and went out to explain to his friend that she would have to wait outside while he attended the reception. This kind of story would have greatly improved the image of the mayor if it had occurred earlier in his term of office. As it was, it was like a firecracker exploding on the fifth of July.

A good story is by no means always moralistic. It has specific earmarks: spiciness, novelty, vividness, simplicity,[5] thematic significance, and "human interest."[6] One of the first steps in "coloring" a man, then, is to search his life for the stories that fit him, point up his good qualities (and even a

---

5. Gordon Allport and Leo Postman, in their well-known study of rumor, use the term "sharpening" for the simplification of rumors in the direction that the public likes, leaving unwanted details out. (*The Psychology of Rumor* [New York: Holt, Rinehart and Winston, 1947].) The point here is to look for the kinds of things in a story at its beginning that the public is crudely trying to get by sharpening. Considerable investigation is needed, not only of rumors (which, by definition, usually do not last), but of folktales, hero legends, best-selling biography and fiction, and hot news, to find the essential ingredients of a "good story."

6. See Helen M. Hughes, *News and the Human Interest Story* (Chicago: University of Chicago Press, 1940).

few "bad" ones), and create an unforgettable tale. There is literally no end to a good story, because people not only keep repeating it but cannot forget it. The general direction is clear: if you are going to give a man color, find something lively, avoid the clichés of goodness, and take a little chance.

Color involves risk because it derives essentially from eccentricity. The key is not in great achievement but in a peculiar or lively style. We may learn from flamboyant celebrities of past decades in America. Lillian Russell, the queen of the stage during the Gay Nineties, used to appear with a Japanese spaniel wearing an $1,800 golden jeweled collar in one arm and with "Diamond Jim" Brady on the other arm. "Diamond Jim" himself lived in a style that was the epitome of color. He not only wore many diamonds but also gave them away casually. He once appeared at the Saratoga racetrack with twenty-seven Japanese houseboys. He had a Gargantuan appetite and might eat a whole leg of lamb at one sitting. Another racetrack character, "Bet a Million" Gates, made such huge bets that he used to collect his winnings in a market basket.[7] Anna Held, the famous Folies star of the 1920's, took milk baths requiring the daily delivery of forty gallons of milk to her hotel suite (a gimmick suggested by Florenz Ziegfeld, whose aim was to "glorify the American girl"). Ziegfeld was not trying to prove that Anna Held was beautiful by this trick; he was striving for a glamorous, exotic quality that would set her off from other American beauties.

Indeed, beauty, if too bland and well-proportioned, is the enemy of color. Of Sophia Loren, *Time* notes, "Her feet are too big. Her nose is too long. Her teeth are uneven. She has the neck, as one of her rivals put it, of 'a Neapolitan giraffe.'[8] Makeup, hair styling, and so on, should aim at distinctiveness, not mere beauty. The same applies to a man; he should not be

7. Marshall Smith, "Spree at Saratoga," *Life,* July 26, 1963, pp. 53–60.

8. April 6, 1962, p. 78.

too handsome, and, indeed, a certain ugliness helped Wallace Beery, Will Rogers, and Babe Ruth. Likewise in the field of music, popular singers and performers strive not for sweetness of tone but for a distinctive "sound" that will set them off from competitors and catch (even by irritating) the public ear.[9]

Color is thus an audacious, even vulgar, exaggeration, often a departure from "good taste." The driver of a pink Cadillac, the movie actress walking down the street with a leopard on a leash, the celebrity making a display of himself by heavy drinking or sex escapades, all are examples of more or less successful striving for color. Such phenomena show the basic kinship of color with freakishness, as in entertainers like "Gorgeous George," the wrestler. Insanity has intense color, and it is no coincidence that a kind of madness has made heroes, geniuses, and saints. The problem, then, is to use bizarre color, of the right hue, without classifying one's self as a lunatic.

Therefore, one rule for becoming famous is be a "character." One should not be afraid of eccentricity but should use it. Propriety and conventionality are enemies of color. This rule applies even to genius; one who wants to be regarded as a genius must cultivate a few eccentricities. Einstein had exactly the right combination of ability and eccentricity to fit the American concept. So did Albert Schweitzer, who was so distinctive that, when he got on a train, passengers, without knowing who he was, would ask for his autograph, sometimes mistaking him for Einstein.[10] On the other hand, Edward Teller looks too much like a businessman, and Robert Oppenheimer is too "ivy league" to meet the ideal requirements.

An outright pose may be helpful. The Hollywood restaur-

9. See Alfred G. Aronowitz, "The Dumb Sound," *Saturdy Evening Post,* October 5, 1963, pp. 88–95. A news columnist suggested to Rudy Vallee that "the Vallee success stemmed less from voice quality than from a distinctive individuality." "At the risk of seeming immodest," Vallee smiled, "I must agree." (Donald Freeman, *San Diego Union,* March 28, 1954.)

10. Winthrop Sargeant, "Albert Schweitzer," *Life,* July 25, 1949, p. 75.

anteur "Prince" Mike Romanoff won innumerable friends and much business by an obviously phony claim to royalty, the very audacity of which seemed to delight people. William Faulkner, according to his brother, was an inveterate poseur, who liked to play the "country squire," ordering fancy riding outfits from Abercrombie and Fitch. He also relished the role of "drunkard," which he once carried off without having had alcohol for twelve hours. We have already mentioned Hemingway's style, which had some of the earmarks of a pose.[11]

The difference between a successful character and a mere oddball is that the former is riding the crest of a wave, selling himself by color, enjoying popularity, well adjusted to being different, whereas the oddball has isolated himself by the wrong color, which for him is a debit. We do not, in recommending color, dodge the problem of societal selection, of finding forms that will be significant and functional to the public at a given time.

Even if one does not wish to become a character, there is something to be gained by using props to set one's self off, creating a style or trademark, giving cues to the audience. We may cite as examples Marlon Brando's pullover sweaters, Harold Lloyd's lensless spectacles, Paul Whiteman's and Charlie Chaplin's little mustaches, Will Rogers' twenty-dollar blue-serge suit, Winston Churchill's plug hat and big cigars, General Patton's pearl-handled pistols. Lincoln's stovepipe hat. Paganini used to perform in his violin concerts in a red-lined cape, playing like the Devil, literally. When Arthur Rubinstein comes on the stage, he has "the strange metallic look of an impassive Oriental idol about to be involved in some sinister, cannibalistic rites"; he attacks the piano "with great lunges, bouncing his hands off the keyboard until they rise above his rearing scalp," coming to a near standing position at the climaxes. When it is all over, he seems lost in a trance from

11. Did Hemingway therefore damage his image by his posing, as implied by the complaints of some of his admirers, or did he make himself into an unforgettable American celebrity?

which the tremendous ovation awakens him.[12] One is not blamed for such an affectation, conceit, or idiosyncrasy if he is otherwise successful, and his real advantage is that it distinguishes his public image from that of hundreds of competitors who may be otherwise as good.

It is not necessary to look, dress, or behave peculiarly to produce color; simple action can produce all the color one may desire and avoids the symbolic risks of eccentricity. One must act in such a way as to deliver the greatest possible thrill to an audience. A colorful actor seeks high action, plunges, challenges others (in his own game, of course), solves crisis, and performs feats.

Before concluding that this route is for those who are endowed with the energies of a Hercules, let us note that there are, in almost any field, many ways of accentuating the thrill of what one does. Richard Wagner, it is said, used to put small mistakes into his orchestrations, for example a B natural instead of B flat in the part of one player. Then, at the height of a crescendo, with all instruments sounding, he would stop the performance to point out the mistake, causing general wonder that he was able to hear a half-tone error in the din. Arturo Toscanini, while yet only a cellist, began his conducting career by a remarkable feat. When the man who was conducting quit in a huff, Toscanini stepped to the podium, quietly *closed the score,* and conducted an entire performance of *Aida* from memory. The audience cheered, and the prestige of the opera company, to say nothing of Toscanini, soared.

Franklin Delano Roosevelt once, early in his career, arriving at a political convention in San Francisco, disdained a less spectacular entrance by vaulting over a row of chairs to get to the platform in a hurry. This is the bravura principle, boldly seizing the most spectacular way, perhaps by a carefully prepared stunt. Ole Bull, the Norwegian violinist, used to play on

12. Winthrop Sargeant, "Arthur Rubinstein," *Life,* April 5, 1948, p. 101.

four strings at once, which he achieved by a special, flat bridge on his instrument. A public man may well learn from show-men and virtuosos how to seize the climactic moment for a big gesture or how to make a stunt look harder than it really it. The trumpet-player strains for a high note, the wrestler groans in apparent pain, the dancer exaggerates the difficulty of his step, the speaker pauses from the profundity of his next thought, until suspense is so great that when the climax comes the audience sighs with relief and satisfaction.

Of course, bravura is close to bravado, for example in the swash-buckling statements of General George Patton. Once he challenged Nazi General Rommel to joust in tanks. "The two armies could watch. I'd shoot at him, he'd shoot at me. If I killed him, I'd be the champ. If he killed me—well, he won't." Patton meant what he said, so he did not lose respect by this "absurd" gesture. It is not necessary, however, to go to such extremes; one can achieve bravura also by making light of any hard task. Once, while walking down Unter den Linden, the German leader Bismarck was shot at from close range. Two bullets had penetrated his clothing before he seized his as-sailant and turned him over to the police. When he arrived home, he said nothing to his waiting guests until he had retired to look himself over for injuries; then he coolly told the story, as though nothing much had happened, showing the bullet holes in his coat and shirt. Everyone was more impressed by his *sang-froid* than by the fact that he had been the target of bullets. By underplaying, he won more credit than if he had made a grandstand play of it.

Because bravura is so close to bravado, it has its fool-mak-ing risks, of seeming to be a show-off, of being "shown up," of fiasco. A remarkable series of news photographs in *Life* once showed Vice-President Richard Nixon flirting with danger by reaching into a cage to pat a lion. Finally, urged by reporters, he entered the cage to bestow a triumphant but careful caress on the movie-trained beast. This gesture provoked comment as to whether it was appropriate for a man in Nixon's position to risk his important neck.[13] Yet he had been dared, and the bravura principle does call for such action; timidity might have made him look worse. In this case, however, he had been maneuvered into a situation in which only comic outcomes were possible. There was risk but no gain to justify a display of bravura. Either the lion was dangerous or he was not. In the latter case, the act would make Nixon seem phony; in the former, it would show that he was a fool to try for bravura in a field in which he had not been trained.

Clowning, of course, is an important route to color, and there is no doubt that anyone who continually makes a fool of himself, or others, will wind up as some kind of celebrity. We are concerned here, however, only with the way that clowning can be used to give one's self favorable color and the symbolic status of a hero. In America, there are no better examples of the success of this tactic than Will Rogers, who took the entertainment route, and Huey Long, who took the political route. Both drew attention to themselves and gained status from others by clowning. Long explained how he did this in speeches:

> When I'm makin' a political speech, I like to cut around the opposition with a joke, I put the truth into what I say and then I embellish it. I like to make it so funny that the other fellow, if he's in the audience, just can't help laughin' himself. One night in Alexandria I had an opponent and his wife right on a front seat. I set out to make them laugh. They held out for a long time, but finally I see the wife biting her lips to keep it back. Then I poured it on and pretty soon she was laughin' fit to be tied and the old fellow was red in the face tryin' to hold out.[14]

Of his political opponents in Washington, he said:

> [These] spoilers and spellbinders think that Huey Long is the cause of all their worry. They go gunnin' for me,

13. June 15, 1953.
14. Forest Davis, *Huey Long* (New York: Dodge Pub. Co., 1935), p. 263.

but am I the cause of their misery? Well, they are like old David Crockett, who went out to hunt a possum. He saw there in the gleam of the moonlight, a possum in the top of the tree, goin' from limb to limb, so he shot, but he missed. He looked again and he saw the possum. He fired a second time and missed again. Soon he discovered that it was not a possum that he saw at all in the top of that tree; it was a louse in his own eyebrow.[15]

Long received an enormous amount of publicity from having "insulted" a German naval commander, who had come to pay a formal call, by receiving him in his night clothes. His green pajamas made excellent newspaper copy, for the season was Mardi Gras, and this *faux pas* seemed to have a significance not displeasing to Americans. Long noted that it was the first time the "lyin' " national press had presented him in a really favorable light.[16] When told that many citizens thought his monkeyshines were incompatible with the dignity of a statesman, Huey covered his mouth with his hand and laughed silently, saying:

> I know. It cuts both ways; it helps and it hurts, that kind of reputation. Some of them stab at me for makin' light of my enemies, but a lot of 'em wouldn't even have heard of Huey P. Long . . . if it hadn't been for the Kingfish and some tomfoolery.[17]

For Huey Long, then, the risks of buffoonery were more than offset by at least four factors: (1) it made him interesting to the public, (2) it was a smokescreen for more serious business, (3) it put serious opponents at a disadvantage, since they did not know how to handle him, and (4) it often injured their dignity more than it did his.

All colorful tactics belong to the gentle art of scene-stealing, which is well developed among actors, who may go through years of plodding until they manage to steal a scene from a star and so make their "hit." A duel between star

15. *Ibid.,* p. 121–24.
16. *Ibid.,* pp. 28–29.
17. *Ibid.*

and bit-players is potential in every scene. Public men may learn from these old hands such tricks as those explained by the movie star, James Stewart, to some extras: To a man in the part of a hotel clerk, "Why don't you casually take your glasses off . . . while I'm talking to you. Take 'em off and wipe 'em on your shirt sleeve." To a man portraying a bum sitting next to him on a park bench, "Why don't you start scratching your leg just as I turn to you? I've never seen an audience yet who wouldn't give attention to a healthy scratch."[18] Perhaps the late Senator Robert Taft benefited from such a lesson when he departed from his usually staid public role to earn the title of "Taft the Mugger," by the way he behaved on the platform during a speech by Earl Warren, then Governor of California. He was "playful as a kitten," grimacing, grinning, waving to his friends. Needless to say, Warren's words got somewhat less attention than they might otherwise have received.

Theodore Roosevelt was a natural scene-snatcher, if only out of sheer vitality. Mark Hanna called him "that damn cowboy." He was eager for the spotlight and able to make what he did seem somehow more exciting than the same acts by other men. His famous charge up San Juan Hill, says one biographer, he unwittingly appropriated as his personal exploit, extracting from it "every political advantage that it was capable of yielding." He openly claimed the Congressional Medal of Honor, saying: "If I didn't earn it, then no commissioned officer ever can earn it."[19] Franklin Roosevelt's wife once made a comparable observation about him:

> I felt that he, without intending to do so, dominated the people around him and that so long as he was in the picture it would be very hard for anyone to rise to a position of prominence.[20]

18. Edwin Martin, *San Diego Union,* February 15, 1955.
19. Lloyd Morris, "The Young T. R.," *Atlantic,* June, 1951, p. 79.
20. Eleanor Roosevelt, "This I Remember," *McCall's,* September, 1949, p. 132.

Such things in politics seem hardly more than the instinct (or is it common sense?) of the prima donna, who knows that without concentration of attention no one is in a position to be the star. It may well be that, in the last analysis, history is made by scene-stealers—that this is what we mean by "great men."

It is in the light of their contribution to color that gossip and name-calling should be considered. A public man has the alternatives of trying to live in such a way as to avoid uncomplimentary talk, or to disregard it, or to encourage it. Oscar Wilde's well-known remark is appropriate here: "There is only one thing in the world worse than being talked about, and that is not being talked about." He got the worse of this, of course, and may in later life have wished to rescind his witticism, but for public men he was surely correct. Gossip shows that a public man is lively and that his reputation is growing, while its absence means that he is not interesting enough to talk about. Malicious gossip can even do some good things for a reputation. Franklin Roosevelt used to regard the names people called him as rather an asset, since they served to highlight him in the public consciousness.[21] Many celebrities have benefited from a scandalous image (Casanova, Thomas De Quincey, Talullah Bankhead—who played up to the part of "bad girl"). Movie stars and other famous people are usually a magnet for stories, many of them scurrilous, yet their reputations seem to thrive on such ferment.

It is quite possible that what is ordinarily called a "bad" story is a contribution to a particular image. For one thing, it is a truism that bad news travels faster than good, so a slightly scandalous story may be a better vehicle for spreading one's image than a favorable report would be. It is also possible that scandal—if not commonplace and nasty—may show a man in an unusual light, as a rather remarkable man, even as a sign of character of a special sort. Dylan Thomas' or Rich-

21. Frances Perkins, *op. cit.,* p. 115.

ard Burton's excesses may thus have contributed to the making of their heroic images. On the other hand, if a celebrity plays it safe and avoids all such stories, he may only succeed in making himself dull. For these reasons, anyone seeking to increase his fame can better afford to be careless about stories —to invite gossip, name-calling, name-dropping, eavesdropping by columnists—than to discourage them.

Mystery, likewise, is an important source of color. It does not always pay to thrust one's self upon the public. There is not only the risk of "saturating" the audience with one's image but there are also positive advantages in mystery. A celebrity can often gain more by being reticent, playing hard to get, leaving people guessing. Greta Garbo, for example, did not discourage fans by her reticence; it only made them more avid for a glimpse of her. The same is true for Lindbergh's aloofness. Napoleon preferred not to be seen too often in public. He often wore mufti, avoided parties, and drove out alone. When cheered at the theater, he would draw back into his box, saying, "If I am seen three or four times at the theater, people will cease to notice me."[22] If one can combine flamboyance with mystery, so much the better. "Death Valley Scottie" achieved his remarkable reputation not merely from striking gold and big spending but also from letting it be understood that he had a mine hidden somewhere. He never told where, and people never knew; it was mystery, not money, that made his fame. Of course, the mystery tactic does not apply to all kinds of images. If a leader is a "man of the people," who is supposed to be always accessible to his friends, playing hard to get will not work. But it does fit many popular heroes, who actually gain stature by placing themselves apart from the common man.

In sum, there seem to be three basic ways for a public man to get color: (1) by a vivacious style (including flamboyance, high action, bravura, comedy, scandalous misbehavior, and

22. Emil Ludwig, *Napoleon,* pp. 113–14.

mystery); (2) by personal peculiarities; and (3) in stories. Stories are the most economical, but they are hard to control once they are released. Personal peculiarities involve the risk that their possessors will be defined as oddballs or freaks (especially with the help of caricaturists). A vivacious style may call for energy and talents that a public man does not have, though his style may be improved by the use of the proper devices. The moral, for those who may be inclined to disdain the pursuit of color, is that if one is too smooth, he may be socially acceptable but may never really capture the popular imagination.

DOING THINGS ALONE

Another rule of great help in dramatizing one's self can be stated quite simply: do things alone, do not affiliate too closely. In crucial acts, at least, be isolated before the audience. Lindbergh made his epochal flight alone, Byrd stayed at the South Pole alone, Roland made his last stand alone.[23] It helped Truman that in his campaign in 1948 he seemed deserted by his party. There is pathos in aloneness—Madame Curie in her laboratory, Robinson Crusoe on his island, one against the world—and it fulfils the dramatic condition of concentration of attention. After the first conquest of Mount Everest, the world asked breathlessly of Edmund Hillary and Tenzing Norkey, "Who got there first?" Their refusal to tell was frustrating to the heroizing impulse. Teamwork is necessary, of course, but the fact remains that the hero is inherently a soloist. He must have the spotlight to himself for the great speech, the ninety-yard run, the last act of martyrdom. Shared heroism generally waters down whatever credit there is to give.

23. Alone, that is, after his followers had fallen. Likewise Achilles fought and died apart from the other Greeks. This is a basic pattern of mythical heroes.

This principle, applied to leadership in organizations, means: do not blend. Even in a team (a musical quartet or a committee), the colorful person can manage to stand out.[24] Of course, a "front man" has been given the spotlight because his performance is supposed to earn credit for his group, but time and again we have seen this work otherwise, making a star of an unknown. The organization man's rule is that if you are immersed in the ranks, move toward the front whenever you can, do not shun the responsibilities of being in the limelight. Sociologists have made much of "centrality" of position as a key to becoming a leader in organizations,[25] but centrality for a dramatic leader would be quite wrong if it meant being in the midst of things or people rather than in the spotlight. And it by no means follows that the one who makes important decisions is the important dramatic actor.

A would-be symbolic leader shuns bureaucracy, impersonality, mechanization, interdependence, or an equalitarian mass from which it is difficult to stand out. He avoids close association with colleagues, henchmen, managers, and others who might make it hard for him to hold the spotlight alone. He especially avoids lively characters who might steal the scene from him; conversely, he prefers as co-workers colorless persons who can act as foils, or at least not steal scenes. If he is the chief of a unit within an organization, he strives to get for his unit (if not for himself) independence of action, so that what it does will be accounted separately from the rest. These are basic ground rules for symbolic leadership in any large organization. In general, there are only three favorable

24. Virtuosos like Arthur Rubinstein and Gregor Piatigorski have too much color to make ideal quartet and quintet players.

25. See Alexander Bavelas, "A Mathematical Model for Group Structures," *Applied Anthropology*, VII, (1948), 16–30; Harold F. Leavitt, "Some Effects of Certain Communication Patterns on Group Performance," *Journal of Abnormal and Social Psychology*, XLVI (1951), 38–50; and L. S. Christie, R. D. Luce, and J. Macy, "Communication and Learning in Task-Oriented Groups," *Research Laboratory of Electronics TR 231* (Cambridge, Mass.: Massachusetts Institute of Technology, 1952).

spots: on top, up front, or standing out within the ranks as a "character" or a "maverick."

A leader who is already on top and up front exercises common sense in keeping his symbolic privilege. He tries to be on stage, alone, when an issue is to be decided or when any important commitment, pronouncement, or performance is made. He does not let lieutenants execute major actions but comes forward for those scenes, being wary of brilliant subordinates, protegés, staff men, or colleagues, who might steal his thunder. He credits others generously while taking the best scenes, for this generosity does not detract from the luster of the soloist but simply earns him credit as a "good guy." When it is necessary for someone else to have the leading part, he tries to be offstage rather than visibly subordinate. In all this, a charming "accidentalness" is, of course, essential for one who seeks the center of the stage but does not wish to be disliked as a "prima donna."

AGGRESSIVE TACTICS

Obviously, it is not enough to win the spotlight, however skilfully, unless one does the right thing once he is there. There is no substitute for having what the public wants; but even if one has it, he can lose the spotlight or fail to project what the public wants, if he does not use fundamental dramatic principles. Given two equally good performances, these principles can make the difference between success and failure. Some of them can be stated quite easily, though their application is more difficult: (1) the most active person captures the most interest, (2) the one who starts something is more likely to be a hero than the one who follows, (3) the one who gives the crowd a thrill is likely to be a hero, (4) the winner (or good loser) of a fight is likely to be a hero.

All these considerations put a premium on aggressiveness,

taken in a broad sense; they give the advantage to the one who seizes the initiative, pushes where others will let be, starts a fight. Americans dislike, or think they dislike, aggressiveness, but the fact remains that fights create heroes, and one of the best ways not to dramatize one's self is to avoid controversy. The one who starts things off runs the risk of being unpopular or a troublemaker or some other kind of villain, but, unless he takes this risk, he may never find himself winning the grand prize.

Theodore Roosevelt stated this formula when he said, "It is only through strife—righteous strife—righteously conducted, but still strife, that we can expect to win to the highest levels where the victors in the struggle are crowned." When Robert Maynard Hutchins, the widely publicized former president of the University of Chicago, took office, he acted in ways that seemed calculated to make him enemies (as indeed they did). He abolished football, rocked the campus with controversies, castigated fellow educators, told businessmen to their faces that they were venal and corrupt—yet he seemed only to become more popular. Even Abraham Lincoln had a kind of aggressiveness; he used to enjoy "sizing up" with men of great height and development and was always ready to wrestle or debate. An ideal hero looks upon life as a contest, a chance to try his powers. It is no surprise that a kind of cockiness or impudence is a favorite characteristic of many folk and popular heroes.

In the light of such advice, the recommendation of one public relations expert that institutional leaders should "avoid public arguments" because "a battle of namecalling in the public press does not resolve issues" but only arouses "uncertainty and distrust,"[26] seems inexplicable, unless as a tactic to prevent change in the status quo. Avoiding controversy can only help to bury even a strong man in an obscure role.

26. Ted Newsom, quoted in Irwin Ross, *The Image Merchants* (New York: Doubleday, 1958), p. 95.

On the contrary, the formula should be to seek confrontations, to be for or against something, to challenge people—if possible, larger opponents. A candidate for popular acceptance has little to gain by pussyfooting, which may only convince people that he is insincere.[27] He should use bravura, take the risky route, not shun issues but try to be on the right side of the right issues.[28]

In taking the risky route, however, the candidate should remember that a hero's basic obligation is to knock out his opponents and promise victory without exposing his following to unnecessary risk. The hero lives dangerously; his followers do not. Ideally, he goes on the stage alone, committing himself but not his followers to battle. They share his glory vicariously; as their champion, he is their protector as well as their protagonist. To win popularity by such tactics, a public man must stir things up without really alarming his followers, only a few of whom actually want to get into the fight; the majority want to enjoy it from a safe ringside seat. Their motto is: "Let's you and him fight."

In other words, the mass is inherently cowardly. There is

27. For example, President Eisenhower abandoned a good chance to dramatize his known differences with Senator Joseph McCarthy when he appeared once on a speaking platform with him. It was shortly after McCarthy had implied that General Marshall was a traitor, but Eisenhower, with McCarthy facing him, made no mention of it. He even dropped a tribute to Marshall from his speech. The reason given was that he had already defended Marshall at a news conference and that the repetition "could be interpreted only as a 'chip-on-shoulder' attitude. By thus arousing new public clamor, I could be inadvertently embarrassing General Marshall." (*Time,* November 8, 1963, p. 101.)

28. The fact that demagogs have used this principle is, of course, no argument that good men may not do so. Morality has its own public relations, its obligation to put itself over with the public. Defenders of a good cause may not only try to dramatize themselves but may attempt to deny this opportunity to demagogs whom they regard as bad. For example, it was noted that the efforts of liberals to picket the meeting of Gerald L. K. Smith only made his crowds grow larger and gave him "incidents" to exploit—that he was courting opposition and hence that the best way to defeat him was the silent treatment. (S. A. Fineberg, "Checkmate for Rabble-rousers," *Commentary,* September, 1946, pp. 2–8.)

good psychological reason for saying that people who hate most are always fearful. A widely appealing, aggressive figure has to express the dislikes of his following without making them fearful of the very things they want him to protect them from. This was a major flaw in the extremist tactics of Senator Barry Goldwater in his candidacy for nomination for the American Presidency. He was aggressive enough to satisfy many haters in the United States. ("The darn trouble is that this Administration won't take risks. Now I don't mean we have to go to war. I just say the world's strongest nation doesn't have to go around acting like the world's weakest nation." "We should aid anyone who wants to go in there and let Castro have it." "Defoliation of the forest [of South Vietnam] by low-yield atomic bombs could well be done." "We ought to present the Kremlin with an ultimatum . . . and be prepared . . . to move a highly mobile force equipped with appropriate nuclear weapons if the ultimatum is rejected.") But some of the things Goldwater proposed involved his backers in deep soul-searching, for atomic war could be the immediate consequence, and that is not a safe ringside seat![29] He might have got as much symbolic credit, without unnecessary risk, by a challenge (paraphrasing former Mayor William Hale Thompson of Chicago) to "bust Khrushchev in the snoot."

In using aggressiveness, much, of course, depends on style, for, after all, villains are aggressive too; it may be only by style that the audience can tell the good guy from the bad guy. Villains have specific styles, determinable from a study of villain types: sneakiness, backbiting, innuendo, mudslinging, bullying, domineering, quarrel-picking, cruelty. Other kinds of aggressiveness are more attractive to American audiences: pluck, cockiness in an underdog, audacity, humor, satire, honest man-to-man slugging, non-violent pressure (including the

29. " 'Can you imagine what would have happened if Goldwater had been in the White House during the Cuban missile crisis?' asked an aide of Michigan Governor George Romney. The aide thereupon touched a lighted cigarette to an inflated balloon. Pop!" *Time,* July 24, 1964, p. 18.

hard and soft sell.) We have noted how the style of Truman's encounter with Dewey helped turn the tables in his favor. Will Rogers had an acceptably aggressive style, and he got away with it because his wit, though very trenchant, was so friendly and funny that it made people smile as they doubled up from a body blow. He never made an enemy, though in fact he criticized many people.[30]

Success in finding the popular side of a live issue is as important as style in making aggressiveness acceptable. This was Rogers' forte; he was timely; he always knew whom and what to joke about; he chose "big shots" and groups rather than individuals; he laughed with the majority, never at it. Rogers, however, was a fool-maker, and there were few serious enemies among his targets. By keeping his style funny and always choosing the right opponents, he had, as it were, a double insurance against error.

It is also possible to succeed by an angry, self-righteous attack on villains. Any number of crusaders (whether or not called demagogs) have proved this. No example is better than that of Father Coughlin, the Detroit "radio priest" of the 1930's, who had a genius for finding the right villains to attack. In one famous moral blast, a talk "On Prohibition," he chose the Drys, who in their zeal for temperance had the bad judgment to refer to American Legionnaires as "staggering drunks." Coughlin defended the American Legion against the bluenoses who had slandered a patriotic organization. "A wave of sympathy and support for the fearlessness of the cassock-garbed lecturer" swept the country. His fan mail increased until he finally needed a staff of one hundred clerks.[31] The right issue need not be world-shaking. One candidate in a

---

30. H. F. Pringle, "King Babbitt's Court Jester," *Outlook,* April 8, 1931, pp. 496–98; Patrick O'Brien, *Will Rogers, Ambassador of Good Will* (Philadelphia: Winston, 1935), p. 282; S. Trent, *My Cousin, Will Rogers* (New York: Putnam, 1939).

31. Ruth Mugglebee, *Father Coughlin* (Garden City, N.Y.: Garden City Pub. Co., 1933), pp. 183, 203.

mayoralty race won himself considerable popularity by opposing parking meters, which were irritating to citizens; thus he put the bureaucrats who had installed them in the role of villains. By finding the right villain, one almost automatically puts himself on the good side of an issue. Since the role of "bad guy" is pre-empted, there is nothing left but the role of the "good guy." Also, the more clearly established a villain is, the safer is an aggressive attack on him and the less careful one has to be about style.[32]

At the opposite pole of adroitness in finding villains was Wendell Willkie's costly remark during a 1940 Presidential campaign speech to a labor-union group in Pittsburgh. "I will appoint a Secretary of Labor directly from the ranks of organized labor," he said, adding, apparently as an afterthought, "and it will not be a woman either." He got a hand from the predominantly male audience, but the listening Roosevelt remarked, "That was a boner Willkie pulled. . . . Why didn't he have sense enough to leave well enough alone? Why did he have to insult every woman in the United States? It will lose him votes."[33] Likewise, Senator Barry Goldwater, during preliminary campaigning as a prospective Republican nominee for the 1964 Presidential race, and courting the South, got himself into trouble in Tennessee by proposing that the TVA should be abolished. Like Willkie, he had taken a careless shot and gone out on a limb. Wailed one Tennessee Republican, "TVA ranks right behind God, mother and country down here, and Barry knows that damned well; yet he still goes around shooting from the hip."[34]

"Going out on a limb" means in this context taking a chance in attacking a villain and putting himself in a bad dramatic position, on the unpopular side of an issue, or confronting a villain who has too many friends, or who is not a

32. This is apparently what McCarthy counted on, as suggested in chap. VII, but, as it happened, he did not always choose clearly established villains.
33. Perkins, *op. cit.*, p. 116.
34. *Time*, November 8, 1963, p. 25.

villain at all. This is, indeed, the hazard of Don Quixote—a fanatic who never quite knows when his following has left him. But it is also the inherent risk of the opportunist feeling his way, looking for a live issue and a good villain.

Short of an instinct that some politicians and showmen seem to possess, there seems no easy way to find issues and villains. A public man can hardly afford not to analyze opinion polls, his fan mail, audiences, and the development of his images, watching for the green shoot, the mandate from popular reaction.

For all these risks, one dramatic juxtaposition seems safest. One can take a shot—on fair and honest grounds—at almost any large party and have a good chance of getting away with it in public opinion. This is the basic dramatic advantage of the giant-killer. Even in defeat, he has the favorable dramatic alternatives of underdog, victim, and martyr. The best established leader is vulnerable to attack by a small party and risks being defined as a villain if he does not respond properly. For example, Governor Nelson Rockefeller was challenged by a college student during his campaign for nomination as Republican Presidential candidate in 1964:

> *Tate:* Aren't you a Robin Hood in a grey flannel suit?
> *Rocky:* No, I'm not. I don't take from the rich.
> *Tate:* What about in some of our states where some people are just too lazy to do anything?
> *Rocky:* Well, I don't know if you've got in mind personal friends of yours or not. But in my opinion there are very few people who fall in this category. Circumstances, in some cases, are more than people can cope with. You can't let them die in the streets.
> *Tate:* If I know I can depend on all the rich people in the U.S. to support me in my time of need, why should I do anything?
> *Rocky:* Well, if that is your fundamental belief, then I hate to think how you were brought up and what goes into your mind.[35]

35. *Time*, January 24, 1964, p. 13.

The point here is that, regardless of whether or not Rocke-feller responded properly in this case, he underwent symbolic risk in being called a "Robin Hood," and the small party had more power to injure his status and a better chance of scoring than he had in return. Moreover, the small party had a greater range of acts that he could undertake without being defined as villain. Rockefeller was walking on eggs; the student was not. Rockefeller's status was already insecure because of his un-popular divorce and remarriage, and, as a big man, he was a sitting duck for a would-be giant-killer. Though it is unwise for a giant-killer to attack popular heroes and sacred statuses, it still remains mostly true that "the bigger they are, the harder they fall."

MAGNIFICATION BY PERSONAL ENCOUNTER AND DRAMATIC CRISIS

In searching for an issue, another dramatic principle seems plain: a personal encounter, however small, is better than an abstract issue, however large. A feud can be as heroizing to an individual as a whole war or an epochal act of statesmanship; and it is much easier to achive a man-to-man confrontation than to solve a great issue on a world stage. The public puts tre-mendous emphasis on the personal; they ask why the Duchess of Windsor could not get along with Elsa Maxwell; what hap-pened to the kitten that Lindbergh took along as mascot on his flight. Such things do not reduce the magnitude of issues; rather, they make them seem larger. For an individual seeking drama, then, another rule is this: If one cannot find a per-sonal issue, he should increase scale until he can. Perhaps the microscope will find what the telescope missed.

The magnifying power of drama is nowhere better illus-trated than by crises. "A pygmy is a giant," says George Mere-dith, "if he can manage to arrive in season." Another remark, by a dramatic critic, William Archer, is equally significant: Drama "may be called the art of crises." What is this art, and how can a public man use it to deliver the telling punch at the moment when the tide of events is ready to turn?

Such a turn is illustrated by the role of General John J. Pershing as the hero of World War I. America suffered fewer losses and fought no harder than the British and French, yet received most credit for having saved Europe, a result brought about by the dramatic pattern and America's time of entrance into the war. Pershing's contribution to the drama was very real. Though the United States entered the war late, and the Allies were in difficulties, Pershing insisted on training his soldiers thoroughly, while the British and French pleaded for help practically on their knees. He refused to let Americans be used to plug gaps in other armies; they would fight by them- selves, said Pershing, only as an American Army, and when he was ready.[36] Americans admired the stubbornness with which he protected his men from Allied pressure until the situ- ation had reached its very worst and the Germans were making their last desperate effort to crush France. Both sides had suf- fered attrition to the point where they were staggering, but the crisis was real, and the Americans were the force that stopped the Germans. Thus, a conspiracy of circumstance (including Pershing's stubbornness) made the American Army the savior of the world. It was the perfect moment to come on stage—at the peak of a melodramatic crisis, with a villain ready to fall.

Is there anything unfair about this? Rather, one should ask, is not this kind of unfairness built into history?[37] Is it not the

36. This reluctance to enter battle—or was it timing?—has been analyzed by Thomas Clement Lonergan, *It Might Have Been Lost* (New York: Putnam, 1929).

37. Bismarck was once viewing a battle near Koniggratz, the out- come of which was dubious. A last minute, unexpected charge by his forces saved the day. His aide-de-camp said to him: "Your excellency, you are a great man . . . now. If the crown prince had come too late, you would now be the greatest of rascals." Bismarck did not take it amiss, but burst out laughing. (Ludwig, *Bismarck,* p. 278.)

Georgii Plekhanov calls such a gift from the historical situation the advantage of Napoleon in 1795, of Franklin Roosevelt in 1932, of any political party that takes power when things are so bad that they can only get better?

The time when things are best for playing a hero's role can be analyzed into two parts. First, the psychological moment, when drama obtains and suspense is at its height; second, a balance of material forces such that a rapid swing from crisis (or looming defeat) to victory is possible. This is the real opportunity: the conjuncture of a dramatic moment with a crisis that can be solved because forces are ready to co-operate with the hero. It is like the surfer waiting for the "ninth wave." A public man has to be "in season" in both the short- and long-run aspects of events. In the short run, there is a transitory moment of a particular drama when a certain role is playable by a particular actor and the audience is ready for him to speak or act. Such moments can come and go very quickly. In the long run, there is a social climate, such as that which for a time favored McCarthy or Sacco and Vanzetti. A public dramatist tries to time his efforts to coincide with the natural turning points in events; he comes in at the propitious moment to swing an even tug-of-war, to champion a certain bill, to prescribe a cure when an illness has about run its course. Without such a conjuncture, he stays judiciously off the scene. There may be suspense, for example, when no turning point is possible (the anguish of people watching a house burn to the ground), so that an effort would seem only foolish. There are social tides against which it is useless to struggle; to do so

---

"illusion of power" that adds stature to leaders and gives a man who may be only riding the current of events credit for having caused them. Thus, "in coming out in the role of the 'good sword' to save public order, Napoleon prevented all other generals from playing the same role, and some of them might have performed it in the same way, or almost the same way." (Georgii Plekhanov, *The Role of the Individual in History* [New York: Inter-National Publishers, 1940], p. 40.) For other analyses of conditions under which a "great man" can determine events see Sidney Hook, *The Hero in History* (New York: Day, 1943), and William F. Ogburn, "The Great Man versus Social Forces," *Social Forces*, V (1926), 225–31.

is simply to court fiasco, unless one hopes to wring from it the role of martyr. The public dramatist, unable to act, consoles himself with the thought that, just as there is always another wave for the surf-rider, there are always new scenes coming.

Waiting for "moments" and "tides" may seem like opportunism, and perhaps it is. But I do not see how a public man, of whatever principle, can avoid taking account of the fact that there is a dramatic as well as a practical time for any act that is supposed to appeal to large numbers of people. To ignore this is to say that one does not wish to influence the masses—which is by definition what no "public man by choice" can say.

Once he admits his need, he may find himself not only seizing moments when they come but trying to produce them and to manage suspense. Any event—a strike, a sports contest, the marriage of a movie star, the passage of a bill—can be handled in such a way as to maximize suspense, or at least to avoid anticlimax. The leader may use theatrical devices to build suspense, such as foreshadowing, enigmatically teasing announcements, political coyness, and preliminary events or subplots that point to a coming main event.[38] He will not nip opposition or a potential crisis in the bud if it offers possibilities for a more impressive role later; quick knockouts may be good fighting, but they are poor showmanship. He will avoid too early a buildup, cited previously as a main cause of fiasco. He may try to deepen crises by introducing a note of alarm or uncertainty into an otherwise smooth operation. For example, Drew Pearson reported that, during a dispute between the United Auto Workers and the Ford Motor Company, the labor chief, Walter Reuther, unexpectedly called off negotiations.

38. A featured aerialist in a circus troupe always missed his big trick a couple of times to emphasize its difficulty, and then, when everyone was worried, he would finally do it perfectly. One night, however, he said to the manager, "If you don't mind, I'm going to do my big stunt right the first time tonight. I've had such a trying day." (Bennett Cerf, "Try and Stop Me," King Features Syndicate, *San Diego Union,* May 26, 1953.)

Things had apparently been going too well. Reuther told the Ford negotiator: "I can't come to an agreement without first threatening you with a strike." Discussion stopped, strike news flared in the headlines, and a "deadline" was announced. Then an agreement was reached that looked like a victory for the union, though substantially the same agreement might have been reached a week earlier.[39]

BEAUX GESTES

Beaux gestes are important for a public man if he can achieve them. They consist of dramatically perfect gestures that invite interpretation and fit neatly into a certain plot. They are exemplified in the appropriate last words of a martyr, the glorious gesture in the face of overwhelming power (Napoleon, returning from exile to face an army coming to arrest him, throws open his cloak and tells them to shoot; cheering, they follow him to Paris), the apt slogan to turn defeat into a promise of victory (General Douglas MacArthur, evacuating the Philippines, says, "I shall return"). The gestures may be too good to be entirely true and arise only in legend after an event (of "the much talked about surrendering of Lee's sword and my handing it back," said General Grant, "this and much more than has been said about it is the purest romance"). Lindbergh's carrying a ham sandwich to France was a *beau geste* when combined with his remark that he would not need more if he failed; his understatement made it all the more effective.

Beaux gestes are among the most economical dramatic devices, considering their enormous impact, since they require little effort and are sometimes thrown off on the spur of the moment. The requirement is only to have poetry in one's soul, or poets on one's staff, to provide inspiration at the right mo-

39. *San Diego Journal,* October 6, 1949.

ment. A *beau geste* types a person instantaneously as "the kind of man who would do something like that." Besides its great casting power, it raises a scene from the commonplace to high drama and starts the ball of popular imagination rolling. There is almost no limit to where a *beau geste* can carry a reputation.

GILDING THE LILY

Certain symbolic themes are the "what" of "hero stuff." One can be as colorful and dramatic as he pleases, but the question remains: What does he symbolize? Answering this means either finding something new—a function indicated by a "green shoot"—or choosing from the existing repertoire of symbolic themes. That is what Estes Kefauver was trying to do in the Presidential race of 1956, with his coonskin cap, reminiscent of Davy Crockett. Sometimes a public man falls naturally into a part that has been waiting for him (as did Pershing in 1916) or accidentally into a folk pattern (as did Lindbergh in 1927, with the striking resemblance of his career to Cinderella). But if a public man does not find his part ready-made, then he has the public relations task of lily-gilding, of adding something to what is there.

One of the most effective jobs of lily-gilding of our time was the buildup of Jack Dempsey by "Doc" Kearns and Tex Rickard into more than a mere fighter, into an almost legendary figure with iron fists and an iron jaw. Kearns and Rickard used an almost poetical hokum that far surpassed the imagination of most sports promoters. "One cannot speak of Dempsey's million-dollar drawing power," says a sports authority, Nat Fleischer, "without giving the credit for his rise to 'Doc' Kearns."[40] He was the master showman who first gave to Dempsey the title of "Jack the Giant-Killer," taking advantage of Dempsey's relationship to larger fighters like Jess Willard and Luis Firpo,

40. *Jack Dempsey* (New York: C. J. O'Brien, 1936), p. 25.

"the Wild Bull of the Pampas." It was a happy thought, says Dempsey, which "caught on at once. Sports writers began to take it up all over the country. . . . I began to get uncomfortable about some of Kearns' tall tales about me." Publicity stunts—such as having Dempsey's sparring partner wear a catcher's mask and inflated chest-protector—reinforced the image. The curious idea became prevalent that Dempsey was a little man, though his height was over six feet one inch.

> Usually every detail of that sort about fighters is accurately known. That I should have been generally supposed to be an inch shorter than I actually was seems hard to believe. Jack Kearns' ballyhoo that made me "Jack the Giant-Killer" was partially responsible. Various pictures that were published of my different fights, too, added to the misconception. Repeatedly they showed me fighting against men who were inches taller than I and many pounds heavier.[41]

Dempsey's later fights were not mere pugilistic demonstrations but carefully engineered theatrical spectacles, guided by the genius of Tex Rickard, whose philosophy was that it was not sufficient simply to publicize a bout; one had to make a kind of play out of it. "We got to dramatize this one," he would say. "As soon as we got it dramatized, the newspaper boys will get hot after it every day. And that's advertising. Now, let's see what we got here." Having seen "what we got here," he would pour hundreds of thousands of dollars into a contest that some felt sure would fail to draw a crowd. His romantic touch in the Dempsey-Carpentier fight, for example, was the "Rapier" versus the "Broadsword," Carpentier as the gallant war hero of France against brute force. For this piece Dempsey obligingly became the villain. It was his most unpopular fight, but the "take" was the third largest of the million-dollar gates.[42] Dempsey's defeat by Tunney had enormous natural hokum;

41. Jack Dempsey, *Round by Round: An Autobiography* (New York: Whittlesey House, McGraw-Hill, 1940), pp. 136, 176.
42. C. J. McGuirk and Jack Dempsey, "Golden Gates," *Saturday Evening Post,* October 20, 1934, pp. 10–11 ff.

the "long count" became the "fall of the hero through treachery," and rumors circulated that Dempsey had been poisoned, the referee bribed, and so on. Fans simply could not believe that Jack was not still the giant-killer.

Following Rickard's lead, fight promoters now go to great lengths to find the thematic gimmick that will dramatize a contest—the "plucky underdog," "dark horse," comeback of the "has-been," "old man," "white hope," the college-educated "highbrow" versus the boy from the city streets. Stories are leaked concerning workouts, deals, quarrels, training lapses, illnesses, dissipation, even foul play; one promoter had both fighters publicly engage a hypnotist to make them "painless" so that people could wonder which of two invulnerable iron men would succumb first. The problem is basically no different in politics, evangelism, business promotion, or any other area of public drama. Hokum may not always be suitable, but it is in answer to a popular demand; and perhaps in this regard public relations men are doing no more than the service performed by the saga-makers of old.

Barbara Frietchie's story is another excellent example of lily-gilding—this time by a real poet. John Greenleaf Whittier sold his famous poem to the *Atlantic Monthly* for fifty dollars in 1863. He had not directly observed Dame Frietchie's historic act, but based his poem on a newspaper clipping and on conversation with some of Dame Frietchie's relatives. When doubts about certain details of the story were expressed by historians, he replied:

> The poem . . . was written in good faith. The story was no invention of mine. It came from sources which I regarded as entirely reliable; it had been published in newspapers, and had gained public credence in Washington and Maryland before my poem was written.

But the doubts included considerations such as the following: (1) Barbara Frietchie was ninety-six years old and bedridden when she was supposed to have performed her immortal act of leaning "far out on the window-sill" and shaking the flag at Jackson "with a royal will"; (2) it was 5:15 A.M. when Jackson marched through Frederick, whereas the sun did not rise until 6:45 A.M., so it was doubtful that the heroes could have seen each other; and (3)—a detail that seems rather conclusive—Jackson did not pass Barbara Frietchie's home but chose another route.[43] The story seems to have benefited from rumor and poetry, but who would prefer the paltry facts to Whittier's version?

To gild a lily, one might search first in folklore—the great storehouse of popular ideas[44]—for themes by which to improve the image of a public man; then he might create a biography stressing these themes, and then might outfit and instruct his candidate to act in such a manner. It is not possible to describe all of them here, but some of the most tried and true are as follows: the conquering hero (a man of iron with magical power who cannot be beaten and seems invulnerable to ordinary hurts); the "charmed life" (involving hairbreadth escapes and other signs that the hero is invulnerable or has a special providence watching over him); the deliverer (who comes to solve crises and avenge wrongs); the miraculous birth (requiring remarkable features of the hero's origin that foretell great deeds to come); the giant-killer theme (David/Goliath); the "Achilles' heel" theme (a good man is destroyed by treachery, advantage being taken of a special weakness); the Cinderella theme (an unpromising hero's unexpected triumph over proud rivals); the self-made man (a hard-working Puritan version of Cinderella); the "log cabin" theme (observing the humble origin of the hero); "thrashing the bullies" (a common theme in American biography, usually an early feat

43. John Clagett Proctor, "Nearby Frederick, and Barbara Frietchie," *Washington Star,* November 12, 1944.

44. I have identified some of these universal patterns in "The Folk Hero," *Journal of American Folklore,* January–March, 1949, pp. 17–25, and "The Clever Hero," *ibid.,* January–March, 1954, pp. 21–34. See also F. R. S. Raglan, *The Hero* (London: Methuen, 1936), and Otto Rank, *The Myth of the Birth of the Hero* (New York: Nervous and Mental Disease Publishing Company, 1914).

of the hero to show his promise); the clever hero (or fool-maker);[45] the "great lover" (a variant of the conquering or clever hero in the field of romance); the "Robin Hood" theme (a bad man who does good to the common people, combining popular benefactor and clever hero roles); the "last stand" theme (a fighter who will not give up in the face of finally insuperable odds); the martyr's splendid voluntary sacrifice; aloneness (the pathos of one against the world); the incorrupt-ible (a moralist or saint who stands firm and pure when others are ethically deficient); the quest theme (the solitary, dedicated pursuit of a transcendental value by a Galahad-like idealist or thinker);[46] the culture hero (a bringer of light, a great teacher, or a founder of institutions, to whom mankind is grateful); the man of destiny (who is in tune with the deeper purposes of events). Any of these themes can, with imagination, be added to a real man; and every one of them is an element of "hero stuff."

The "how" is another matter. Ancient symbols must be adapted to the modern situation—the magic of a folk hero might become the charm of a TV manner, "Robin Hood" might be seen in a politician who takes from the rich to distribute welfare, the "iron man" might be an executive who works six-teen hours a day. But the themes are so adaptable and have lived for so long that poets will surely find further use for them.

I shall close this chapter with an analysis of two lily-gilding approaches that seem practicable for politicians in America.

The "Man of the People"

Democracy puts a special strain on its leaders, for it asks

---

45. For a full analysis of this role see "The Clever Hero," *op. cit.*

46. This theme appears in the biography of Madame Curie: "Life is not easy for any of us. But what of that? We must have perseverance and above all confidence in ourselves. We must believe that we are gifted for something, and that this thing, at whatever cost, must be attained." (Eve Curie, *Madame Curie* [London: Heinemann, 1941], p. 158.)

244   SYMBOLIC LEADERS

them, whether or not they are temperamentally so inclined, to bend down and prove they are of common stuff. Some, like Woodrow Wilson, are not able to do so, while others learn how. The early Franklin Delano Roosevelt was far from a man of the people. While Assistant Secretary of the Navy under Wilson, he was described as rarely smiling and a bit of a snob. His power to win friends came only gradually and with hard work (memorizing names, socializing, cultivating ease in conversation); he literally remade his type.[47] Nor was General Douglas MacArthur the "democratic" type, but he also made concessions; when with troops, he smoked his famous old and battered corncob, but in solitary moments he preferred a long and handsome pipe.[48] On the other hand, Andrew Jackson was a natural man of the people. He would sit on his plantation porch, saying, "I love the common man," and "with a jet of tobacco juice slanchwise between the Ionic columns . . . drown a doodlebug at five yards.[49]

Vulgarity may help to establish such a type. Will Rogers used to insist on poor English in his newspaper columns: "I want it to go as she lays, even if the guy that has to set up the type has to get drunk to do it.[50] The pianist José Iturbi offended critics but greatly increased his popularity by playing boogie-woogie in a film with Judy Garland.[51] Earthy humor and clown-

47. He "really didn't like people very much." He had a "streak of self-righteousness" and a habit of throwing his head up and looking down his nose through a pince-nez while he talked. One Tammany old-timer remarked, "Awful arrogant fellow, that Roosevelt." He learned from the mistakes of Wilson, and studiously improved his social relations by "promiscuous and extended contacts," "swapped yarns, and became easy and natural." (Perkins, *op. cit.,* pp. 11–12, 20–21, 71, 324.)
48. *Life,* October 9, 1950, p. 36.
49. *Time,* October 22, 1945, p. 103, review of Arthur Schlesinger, *The Age of Jackson.*
50. Donald Day (ed.), *Autobiography of Will Rogers* (New York: Houghton Mifflin, 1949), reviewed in the *Chicago Tribune,* October 23, 1949.
51. "One day Mr. Pasternak said to me: 'José, you don't have to do this if you don't want to, but what about a number with Judy Garland—semipopular?' I thought I would be a good fellow so I said O.K.—on one condition—that it should be a really hot number. . . . You know the re-

ing also have this effect, as illustrated by the Huey Long stories previously cited.

George Washington, for all his devotion to the people, would never have told vulgar jokes—which illustrates the difference between being "for" and "of" the people. The one who uses the latter approach must come down off his pedestal, must prove he is a regular fellow, must show that there is no distance or difference between himself and others.

Dramatic self-humbling gestures also may be used.[52] The democratic hero should be easily accessible, talk on equal footing with everyone, joke to show that he is not stuffy or aloof, call people by their first names, and encourage them to use his own first name. He is well advised to get a nickname as soon as possible, since this makes people feel more familiar with him (Honest Abe, Ike, Jackie, Old Hickory, The Babe, Kingfish, Our Will). The "log cabin" and "self-made man" themes are major parts of the image; biography should represent him as having started life in lowly circumstances (Will Rogers conveyed this idea so effectively by stressing that he was one-quarter Indian that people did not realize he had attended an expensive private school). In public appearances, he should not try to hide defects or be overcorrect in deportment; simple unaffectedness and natural foibles may convince people that he is acting exactly as he would at home. Such acts may help create that peculiar bond with the people that some leaders gain and that is denied to many of apparently equal ability and stature. At the very least, the man-of-the-people approach helps overcome the distance of leadership in secondary society, the isolation of the "famous unknown."

---

sult. I played boogie-woogie, and I enjoyed it." (*Time,* May 21, 1951, pp. 101–2.)

52. Lincoln provides excellent examples of self-humbling gestures. Once he tipped his hat to an old Negro who saluted him, saying, "I would not be outdone by his courtesy." Gandhi used to remain seated on the floor while talking with important visitors on chairs. Was this just his custom or a self-humbling gesture?

The risk of this stance is not in overdoing such tactics so much as in seeming out of character while doing so. If "in character," you may stoop almost as low as you like, but, out of character, the slightest gesture may backfire. Danger lies in "folksiness," in obviously phony poses. Calvin Coolidge was once caught in a photograph that showed morning pants beneath his overalls as he posed pitching hay; in 1952, a similarly damaging photograph showed Senator Robert Taft in a business suit embarrassedly holding up a chicken some admirer (or heckler) had given him. Clearly it is wrong for such people to try to be folksy. There may be also some risk in leveling one's self too far by indiscriminate fraternizing; Truman suffered because of the cronies he chose for advisers while in the White House.

The fidelity and intimacy of TV close-ups have not shown up folksy tactics as much as one might expect. While they have made it harder for some nervous people to be warm or to fake warmth, they have at the same time made it easier for other personalities to "let go" and be human.[53]

Thus glad-handing and baby-kissing may not work for all, but they still work well when done by the right people and with the right people.

The "Great Man"

At the opposite extreme, seemingly, is the role of the Great Man, which has aristocratic grandeur and a kind of mystique associated with it. This role reverses the formula of the man of the people. Supreme talent and remoteness are the keynotes, not equality and accessibility. The role is well illustrated by Charles de Gaulle of France, or Washington, or Napoleon. De Gaulle uses tricks, such as trying to look every person in

53. For example, Jackie Gleason, Steve Allen, Art Linkletter, Perry Como, Lucille Ball, or Phil Silvers, the star of the "Sergeant Bilko" TV show, who does not even bother with a toupee to hide his bald spot. He advises, "Don't be eager to hide what you may consider a defect. If there's one thing people dislike, it's perfection." (Philip Minoff, "Those Likable TV Stars," *Family Circle,* November, 1956, p. 30.)

the eye as he passes a crowd, to give him a feeling of man-to-man contact, but he is plainly not a man of the people. A candidate for the position of Great Man must strive to set himself off by dignity, genius, spirituality, rectitude, will, miraculous powers, and so on, to show that he is not of the common stamp. It is appropriate to stand a head taller than others; people are less interested in the common roots than in the unusual flowering of the treetop. Indeed, his status has a kind of sacredness or apotheosis about it; the Great Man gets on his pedestal and stays there, and the people do not want him to come down.

Such a symbolic leader does not shun the heroic posture in fear that people will think he is vain or arrogant. He uses bravura and mystery and wears the laurel wreath as though it had been made for him. Napoleon, of course, is the supreme example of such a leader. He thought of himself as a man of destiny; he kept Caesar's bust in his study and believed that in some msterious way he had inherited Caesar's role.[54] Bismarck likewise assumed that destiny was working with him. He sought divine approval for day-to-day policies and, before a battle, would open the Bible for an oracle; once, when it thundered during one of his speeches, he shouted, "The Heavens are saluting us."[55] General Douglas MacArthur, although he possessed the common sense of an American about rank, nonetheless had some of this mystique. He seemed to be "on intimate terms with history" and to speak as though he had received a "special briefiing from heaven.[56] Of his mission in the Far East, he said, "I am here by the Grace of God. This is

54. See Friedrich Gundolf, *The Mantle of Caesar,* trans. J. W. Hartmann (New York: Macy-Masius, Vanguard, 1928). Napoleon once asked Cardinal Fesch whether he could see anything in the clouded sky. The cardinal answered that he could not. "Very well," said Napoleon, "you had better learn to hold your peace; for I can see my star." (Ignazio Silone, *The School for Dictators* [New York: Harper, 1938]; reprinted in Lewis A. Coser (ed.), *Sociology through Literature* [New Jersey: Prentice-Hall, 1963], p. 217.)

55. Ludwig, *Bismarck,* pp. 276–77.

56. *Time,* May 9, 1949, p. 32; see also Francis Trevalyan Miller, *General Douglas MacArthur* (Philadelphia: Universal Book and Bible House, 1942), p. 39.

my destiny." Winston Churchill, too, had more of the great than the common man in his role. H. G. Wells commented that he "believes quite naïvely that he belongs to a peculiarly gifted and privileged class of beings to whom the lives and affairs of common men are given over."[57] It is permissible for a Great Man to humanize himself to some extent, to show that he is of common stuff, for example, Churchill with his big cigars or MacArthur with his corncob pipe, but these small symbols do not really erase the distance that separates him from the common man; rather, they relieve it. However, he would violate his role if he went too far with tactics that a man of the people could use with impunity.

These two approaches to playing the hero provide a kind of dilemma in a democracy. Actually, people like both the demigod and the man of the people, but they are hard to combine in the same role. Such a tension can be seen in the office of the President of the United States, between efforts to shield him and to give his office stature and dignity and efforts to make him accessible to people, to submit him to free-for-all press conferences and the handshaking that approaches manhandling. If the American President could solve this role dilemma, could be either a remote man of grandeur or a man of the people, he would lead a simpler life and perhaps could do a better job as President.

In this brief survey of hero-making approaches, I have tried not merely to make the role strategist's task easier but to increase our understanding of how symbolic leaders are made and the part that people have in making them. I have not intended to write as a modern Machiavelli, instructing our modern princes (or their public relations agents) in how to manipulate their subjects. I have merely tried to state in their simplest form a number of academic hypotheses about symbolic leadership, and all these statements require much further testing and

57. Phillip Guedalla, *Mr. Churchill* (New York: Reynal and Hitchcock, 1942), p. 225.

extension. My assumption is that this sort of public discussion of any topic, however threatening to those who fear manipulation, works in the long run more in favor of the majority than of any elite. If the discussion seems not sufficiently to have illuminated either the public or the strategic problems of leadership, then my confident answer is that not something different but more of the same kind of study is needed.

CHAPTER NINE

PUBLIC DRAMA
AND
CHANGING SOCIETY

This book is about drama as it happens in public life and what it does to leadership and our society. It treats of such things as the rise of Castro, the failure of a public policy, international incidents, or a spat between two movie stars, always in terms of dramatic patterns that are basically similar regardless of the actual scale of events and persons. Some may object that such a dramatic approach reduces the complexities of public affairs to the level of a grade-C movie, but dramatically, in fact, public affairs are often precisely at the level of a grade-C movie. In this dimension, we may not read into events more subtlety than is actually present, up front where the audience can see it, nor may we ignore the curious meanings that the public may attach to what is objectively there. How much the audience sees is always a research question, but at least let us not say that what is behind the scenes has the same status as what is on stage.

It is unavoidable that, where drama supervenes, "reality" is not what the hard-headed man would like it to be; nor do events always follow his prediction. For from the moment drama begins we start to project and interpret roles, and there is an important nexus between what a thing "is" and what the audience sees that is, at the same time, the reality and the magic of drama. The "magic" is an outcome that matter-of-fact analysis could not predict—a "sentimental," "frivolous," "romantic" change of status. Thus public drama defeats material or economic determinism, for we cannot predict the dramas of a society or their outcomes from our knowledge of objective and material forces.

One important effect of public drama is that leadership is more unstable than it would be otherwise. Contretemps, upsets, follies, contests, scandals, make a feast of entertainment or a spinning political roulette wheel. Fads come and go at a dizzying pace, sparked at least partly by dramatic factors, such as television "hits." A country like the United States has an open public drama, in which new faces appear daily, there is always a contest to steal the show, and almost anything can happen and often does.

Drama has entered modern life in new ways. For example, there is a new consciousness of role-playing. Fifty years ago, the ordinary man would never ask, "What is my role?" He thought in terms of character—of what one is, not of the image one projects. He would regard "playing roles" as hypocrisy except upon a stage. Now the distinction between public drama and personal life seems to have diminished. Anyone who wants to be somebody, to have many friends, to run an important organization or project, believes that he must cultivate an image. We simply do not let roles take care of themselves any more.

This is all part of a change that his occurred in the relationship between drama and life, brought about by mass communication, increased leisure, and other modern developments, and especially, perhaps, in America. Every society, of course, has a dramatic dimension. From ancient China to Chinatown, from Australian aboriginal dance to color TV, this dimension is preserved in religion, dance, legend, storytelling, song, ritual drama, theater, and fiction. The function of the dramatic dimension in any society has always been to burst through the routines of life into the wonderful and mysterious.

TV, movies, and modern news-reporting may not have brought more magic to life than they have displaced, but I do not think one can truly say that there is less magic. It is nonetheless a different kind of drama that is involved; its audiences are different and its implications for the modern society are different. For example, audiences relatively less often form within institutional settings, such as temples, and tradition no longer sets effective limits to the content of dramas. We are oriented more toward what a live man does on a screen than toward what a dead man did. In short, there has been a movement of the dramatic dimension from tradition and local events (community audiences) to that range of things conventionally called news, entertainment, and reading, which are presented before shifting, transitory, and boundless audiences. This I call the "public drama."

The enormous importance of celebrities today signifies this new orientation. They are more important because they are the stars of the public drama. On them rests the burden of carrying on the show for a public that has come to depend on them; they are, one might say, the regular troupe, and, indeed, it is almost a profession to be a celebrity. One of the things celebrities are finding out about this "profession" is that they are leaders and have the responsibilities of leaders. But special events come and go (elections, crises, assassinations, scandals, and so on), creating new stars and villains of the moment. Amateurs crowd the footlights. A dizzying succession of popular idols (and at least some of our "faddism") is due to the speed with which scenes change.

Two points may help to explain why the public drama is unsettling to the social order. One is the size and extent of audiences. The dramas themselves are larger, simply in terms of audience if nothing else. The smallest event may become a matter of concern to the whole world, and it is almost impossible to anticipate the alignments and shifting audiences that will be created.

The other point is in the range of things that can become dramatic. Though modern man may have lost something in his own personal drama and be more submerged in the anonymity of audiences and though there are fewer community dramas in daily life, the range of events that can become dramatic and the amount of the world's territory that can be involved is enormously larger than it used to be. This increase in range is linked with the inherent transcending power of drama; through its experience people are refocused away from the ordinary structural facts of daily life. They are lifted out of their families, jobs, institutions, political parties, classes, nations, and so on.

This is not mere escapism. Of course, escape has always been a function of storytelling, but in the public drama we find ourselves thrown into strange juxtapositions and all sorts of situations that can hardly be called escape. Atomic threats, Kenya riots, Kremlin politics—along with Antarctic expeditions, moon shots, and movie stars' love affairs—have little to do with and could not be predicted from the facts of our social status. The range of identifications is great, and there is no real limit to what can become emotionally important. Because we are only loosely related to our institutions—the alienated white-collar or blue-collar worker, the mobile community member—we are strangely shaken and moved by odd dramas, fads, and other events that burst into our lives as news, entertainment, or whatever they may be called.

A central fact about all drama, as opposed to daily life, is that the role one gets is not part of his regular routine and structure. It may be part of the repertoire of roles available in the society (as when a Hopi plays "mudhead" or an American father plays Santa), but it still takes the actor out of his regular roles of church, work, and so on. Likewise, from the very nature of drama it follows that while it obtains, you are not "you" but the part you take; there is an identity-transcending character that goes hand in hand with structure transcendence. The transcending power of drama works even when the drama itself is part of social structure (as in a ritual) and has its own social structure (for example, the frontier-town setting for a "horse opera").

Along with this structure transcendance is the fact that things are happening to persons—our symbolic leaders—that could not be predicted from the facts of their social status. Looking at the mass today and their organizational leaders, one cannot tell who the stars of tomorrow will be or from what stratum they will come. What, then, allows us to predict them? The answer given in this book is in terms of dramatic factors. To whom can a drama happen? The answer is: to anybody. And who can be the audience or following? The answer is, again, and with the help of mass communication: anybody. And if dramas move people, where can they be moved? In this already mobile and rootless world, the answer is: anywhere. What, then, are the limits, within human existence, to what can happen?

We must seek for the answer to this question, I think, within drama itself, which has its own laws. Sociology, and surely politics, have long been (perhaps unduly) concerned with structures and how they control and organize the lives of men. There always remain the baffling and wayward phenomena called "mass movements." Whatever else may be said of them, of one thing we can be sure: mass movements can generate the wave that swallows up the structure. Much of what Max Weber called the force of charisma in history is really the force of drama.

Whereas drama can be subservient to organization—as shown by Goffman, Hughes, Van Gennep, and any number of other studies familiar to sociologists[1]—it is also plainly capable

1. Erving Goffman, *The Presentation of Self in Everyday Life* (Gar-

of being its enemy. This is because drama has no indigenous relationship to a particular social structure; it does not "belong" to a certain context of class, politics, or ethnicity. Drama is concerned no more with democracy than with oligarchy, whites than Negroes, Catholics than Protestants, order than anarchy. Audiences can form that unite very different kinds of people from all parts of the structure, and from other structures, in the same perspective, at least for a moment. Thus drama is inherently a solvent in its effect on structure. Every morality play is balanced by some fall from Eden. This book shows how the dramas of public life sometimes work to confirm leaders and sometimes work to stir up movements and upset leaders. It shows vicissitudes, fiascos, role failures, and reversals. Stability is hardly the lesson taught; rather, our lesson is: Watch out for what is coming!

Another name for this solvent power is "universality." Every drama has more or less universality, and in any case more than the routine from which it came. Shakespeare meant more in saying "All the world's a stage" than merely that every man has a role. He meant also that the whole world is a potential audience and that anywhere—any status or any institution— is a potential setting for a drama.

The universality of drama is based not so much on intellectual perception of general truths as on the ease with which humans identify with roles other than their own and persons different from themselves.[2] It is safer to emphasize than under-

---

den City, N.Y.: Doubleday, 1959); Everett C. Hughes, "Work and the Self," in J. H. Rohrer and Muzafer Sherif (eds.), *Social Psychology at the Crossroads* (New York: Harper, 1951); Arnold Van Gennep, *Les Rites de Passage* (Paris, 1909; London: Routledge and Kegan Paul, 1960).

2. Including a wide range of animals. Franz Kafka succeeded in making a story hero of an animal as unattractive as a cockroach, as did Don Marquis (though in a much different vein!). I was convinced of this ability of men to identify with unattractive characters by an experience I once had while shaving. A rather alarming insect flew into the bathroom and landed in the tub. No insect-lover, I reached down to scoop it out. At this moment it assumed what seemed to be a bravely defiant posture, with its "arms" outspread. I felt an immediate sympathy for this little bug, making his stand "alone against the world." I was

estimate this ability. Charles H. Cooley held that sympathy and drama are facts of human nature and are therefore basically cross-cultural, in spite of their limitations, because we have a common stock of sentiments to draw upon and because we can learn to sympathize. Indeed, our mental health and maturity are measured by our breadth of sympathy.[3] A dramatic crisis is a turning point, a moment of unpredictability and emergence. The "hero" is the one to whom we turn as a vehicle to carry us through the crisis. So by our power of identification we have great freedom to choose heroes, from various times, places, races, and statuses.

By stressing this freedom of drama, I am not denying that people often fail to identify with dramas from other cultures or social positions than their own. Class interest is so powerful that Marx considered it a major force in history, and J. S. Mill said that justice in a democracy is possible only because there is a disinterested group in the electorate who can swing the balance between interest groups—implying that interest groups cannot be expected to rise above their prejudices. We can predict voting and buying habits from class, church, and political-party membership. Yet I think our tendency today is perhaps to overemphasize ethnocentrism, reference groups, and other such limitations of audiences rather than see the potentialities of these audiences and their actual range of identifications that may transcend group barriers. It is not so much that they cannot identify outside their "interests" as that they do not because the right conjuncture of dramatic elements has not been found.

We are only beginning the study of audiences to find out

---

the giant; he was the hero; and my feeling was much the same as when reading about Roland standing off the charge of the Saracens.

3. "One's range of sympathy is a measure of his personality, indicating how much or how little of a man he is." (*Human Nature and the Social Order* [New York: Scribner, 1922], p. 140.)

what they actually do see and can identify with.[4] Let us concede the obvious, that audiences are different on account of their cultures and places in the social structure. Symbols—language, music, dance, and so on—must be understood for drama to be effective. But these cultural and structural elements are not the essence of drama; they may be instruments and, for the same reasons, may be obstacles to drama. In explaining lack of universality, we can say that drama is deformed by these various biases, contents, and symbols.

The transcending tendency of drama has a creative power to make and break statuses, to give and take prestige, to generate enthusiasm, to involve and mobilize masses in new directions, and to create new identities. Within the framework of an orderly society we have a turbulent, almost chaotic, process in which statuses are made and mass attention and alignments are shifted drastically from one subject to another. One day we may be agitated by a strike and find ourselves "pro-labor"; on the next day we may be concerned with a crisis in which our sympathy is with a President who takes an "anti-labor" stand. One day we may seem to be pro-French, pro-Texan, pro-Catholic, and the next day against these same symbols, depending on the turn of the drama. How, then, can a public policy or a stable ethic be achieved when drama is pouring like a torrent through the open sluices of a dam?

Control over mass communication might reduce this torrent to a smooth-flowing stream, with a consequent stabilizing effect on statuses and the internal social order. But we cannot close the door to disruptive dramas without sacrificing our cherished freedom of communication. Since we are not likely

4. This book is not an audience study to fill an empirical gap. It draws mostly from the public record rather than from a direct study of audiences. I do not claim that extensive documentation from the public record can take the place of audience studies, but I can only note with regret the lack. The audience should always be the last court in any study such as this.

to take this step, we find the public man embarking on the rapids with his life-preserver on, in a canoe steered valiantly by a public relations man.

In dealing with some of the rocks and eddies of the turbulent stream of public drama, this book implicitly calls into play the structural-functional theories of sociology. The theory of functionalism holds that the parts of a social system are dynamically interrelated by functions, and a function is a contribution of any element in the system to the maintenance of the whole, to its equilibrium.[5] Some functionalists hold that anything that persists with any tenacity in a society does so because of its function, that is, it "earns its keep"; otherwise people would give it up. A corresponding assumption is that anything new that grows to institutional status does so because it performs a new function or has taken over from some older institution. Malinowski held that every element of a culture should be presumed to have a function until proved otherwise.

Sociologists study organizations and other social structures, seeking functions. They distinguish between formal structures, which are comparatively rational, based on explicit rules, and obvious and intentional in at least some of their functions, and informal structures, which are stable patterns of relationship that grow up without such explicit intention and recognition. They hold that an informal structure often grows up to buttress a formal one because some function was unmet by the formal organization.[6] Some of these informal structures are *sub rosa,* even illicit. But structure and function are presumed to be interrelated and coexistent; if there is a function, look for a struc-

5. For example, instead of speaking of ritual functions for social organization, we may prefer to say (with George Homans), "The performance of ritual reawakes . . . a sense of the value of the norms. To the extent that norms are one element in the group equilibrium, ritual helps to maintain equilibrium." (*The Human Group* [New York: Harcourt, Brace, 1950], p. 310.)

6. For example, what Charles H. Page has called bureaucracy's "other face." See Peter M. Blau, *Bureaucracy in Modern Society* (New York: Random House, 1956), p. 50.

ture, and if there is a structure, look for a function. There is in such extreme and doctrinaire structural-functionalism a rather too neat lacing-together of the social system.

We find, therefore, a kind of battle in sociology between structural-functionalism and the idea of "process" as a model by which to conceive of society. If too many things are happening and relationships are unclear or do not stay fixed, it is hard to talk of structure, and the notion of process seems more applicable. An "equilibrium" of process helps to signify stability in the midst of flux. On the other hand, if change is not dismayingly apparent, it is easier to talk of structure, as do anthropologists and some students of bureaucracy.

This book deals with a process of vast importance and scope that is almost impossible to reduce to structural terms, a process that occurs within structures, using the props, settings, and symbols provided by particular institutions and cultures, but that is essentially fluid and not attached to these structures. It flows through them like water through a net. Our subject then, invokes the "process" view of modern society by its focus on the flowing stream of drama, with its structure-transcending tendencies, within the "order" of society. Governments and classes fall, but the public drama goes on. It does not require a given social structure to maintain it because its sources are in human nature.

We have in the study of emergent symbolic leaders a way of seeing how society finds and serves needs by choosing people who best symbolize something that others want or want to do. But this function is performed within a structure no more definite than an audience, though formal fan clubs, political parties, and organized movements may come out of the audience. It would be stretching a point to call a mere audience the "informal structure" of leadership. The public drama is working much of the time without building any structures at all. Moreover, it is often at war with structures, whether it generates "escapist" tendencies or a movement to change a structure. The public drama is actually working to keep society relatively structureless by its function of satisfying audiences in ever-shifting alignments, occasionally arousing movements that disturb the status quo. The paradox is that even when a public drama uses a traditional pattern (poor boy makes good, Cinderella, delivering hero), it may bring in a leader who does something quite new.

On the other hand, drama does have a structure or pattern of its own. There is surely something for structuralists in the notion of "laws" and configurations of drama, which confine and limit an actor as much as do considerations like income, schooling, and civil service rating. It is the pattern of this process, working largely as a solvent within the more formal, obvious, and static structures, that the study of the public drama helps the student of society—traditional or modern—to see.

If we look at symbolic leadership not so much from the standpoint of what it does to social structure as of what it does to identity,[7] we find an equally important dimension. If we ask what this "work" is that the public drama is doing for audiences, an obvious answer is that it is providing models of what to do and how to live. For example, the CORE demonstrators in the South provided a new pattern of behavior for both Negroes and whites. If it is then asked why traditional, institutional models do not suffice, why there is demand for the torrent of role-casting and scene-changing that I have called the public drama, the answer is twofold. First, it is precisely because public drama is presenting a wider range of models than ever before, because it is "open," that the public is also "open" in its receptiveness to new models and has come to expect them. Second, there are new problems for which people do not find old models sufficient; they are rejecting traditional models and looking for new ones. Meeting such needs might be called "positive

7. See Anselm L. Strauss, *Mirrors and Masks* (Glencoe, Ill.: Free Press, 1959).

function of faddism." It is safe to assume that a rapid turnover of symbolic leaders indicates a restless searching for identity in a society. A faddish symbolic leader represents the failure of a trial-and-error "experiment" in societal selection. He has hit a mark (found a function), but not a durable one—from the standpoint of identity, he has not found a permanently satisfying life style.

The faddism of teen-agers illustrates this well. They have an identity problem in the sense that they are still finding out who they are and may be confused about it. Changes in models and peer-group norms show that models are not supplying permanent answers to the question, What kind of person shall I be? For example, consider the most prominent teen-age fad of early 1964, the Beatles, a guitar-playing vocal quartet of English boys who, after success in their own country, came to America and were an instantaneous hit among teenagers here as well. Girls went into ecstasy at the very sight of them (following a tradition of screaming and swooning established twenty years before by Sinatra fans). The nation was inundated with "Beatle" records and pictures of the hirsute foursome.

The interesting thing is that—as experts in entertainment and even some teen-agers agreed—musically, the Beatles were not very different from, and surely not superior to, many other "rock-and-roll" combos. Indeed, it was quickly noted that it was not so much the sound as the sight of the Beatles that drove the girls into hysterics. Their long moplike haircuts produced a comic, even a gay, effect. These haircuts symbolized some of the defiance that teen-agers have always shown in hair styles. Within a week after the Beatles' American debut, twenty thousand wigs per week were being sold in New York.[8] Enthusiasm for the singers, however, reached a peak in the first

---

8. I observed teenagers reacting to a rack of these wigs in San Diego. They would go up, almost furtively, to try them on, then giggle with delight at the change in their identity.

week or so of their advent and then showed immediate signs of diminishing.

Here we have an illustration of how a fad, however brief, satisfies an identity problem. Teen-agers, by means of the Beatles, had an adventure in identity. The wigs, and later the haircuts, gave them a new picture of themselves to enjoy and derive momentary prestige from. Insofar as it was shocking to parents, it met one of the requirements of a good identity model as far as adolescents are concerned. The fad was readily acceptable because it was grafted onto the popular guitar-playing, singing model already established by stars like Elvis Presley and Ricky Nelson. Basically, however, the Beatles offered little new except a hair style that could be duplicated (and therefore cancelled) within a few weeks, and therefore they could not last as a distinctive type. Besides, they offered little that was new for teen-agers to do.

By contrast, the social type of the "surfer" can be used to show how a fad can help with a more permanent solution to an identity problem. This type offered youths not only a distinctive dress and hair style ("tennies," short pants, T-shirt or canvas shirt, bleached hair) but also a satisfying and demanding sport, social life on the beach, and, for some, a "way of life," a kind of carefree, irregularly paid profession,[9] that might persist beyond adolescence and even disrupt conventional careers. Thus faddish symbolic leadership can reorient personalities and shift socialization within our society.

Within the formal structure, then, personality changes that transcend that structure may be occurring by means of symbolic leadership. The emergence of new types as models means that socialization is not following clearly defined, routinized educational tracks. Society is fluid and open, in terms of personality structure and life style. The models actually selected by people may bear little or no relation to their opportunity structure,

9. Surfers can earn money by such things as teaching surfing and making surfboards.

and frustration may be prevalent—another reason why a society with a profusion of emerging symbolic leaders is in a fluid and relatively unpredictable state. Personality needs may be "satisfied" vicariously within all kinds of dramas, but people are in a state of tension unless the structure also allows action, so that people can do something, perhaps participate in a social movement. Then the structure gets modified, and the public drama becomes political.

This book has tried to show how public drama works as a force within out society, for politics and for changes in identity. I hope it has made plainer some of the laws that govern the ups-and-downs of celebrities, who are at the same time models for personalities and leaders of the mass. This force is more serious than is implied by the word "entertainment," not so quietly rational as implied by the words "news" and "information," nor so manageable as implied by the word "propaganda." I hope, too, that the book has made the public drama more interesting professionally to social scientists, and given them the confidence, if not the means, to explore this elusive and illusory realm for things they may have been missing in more substantive "structural" approaches.

Man's second life is now in the public drama. His dreams are taped, filmed and projected. It may not be too long, in our audience-directed society,[10] before the public drama becomes our first life—before the balance tips and the vicarious becomes the real, and what one does at the office seems only an intermission from the real show. At least, one must not discount the public drama. It is growing and finding new modes and techniques of power. It will have its players and watchers, its masters and students, its beneficiaries and probably, despite our hopes, its victims.

Let me repeat that this book was not meant to be a hand-

10. See my *Heroes, Villains and Fools,* pp. 103–107.

book but a statement of academic hypotheses. It does not claim the expertise that might have been supplied by masters of political strategy, public relations, or the theatre. If I undertake the task by their default, I am well aware that studies of food chemistry do not make one a cook. I do not really suppose that I have been telling Machiavelli anything, even if he is listening. I assume that public discussion of any topic in the long run works more in favor of the majority than of an elite, more in favor of sincerity than of technique. If a magician performs to an audience of magicians, he may find that his most winning way is not tricks but candor.

Index

265

270 INDEX

Norkey, Tenzing, 225
Novak, Kim, 17, 27

Object of desire, 45
O'Brien, Patrick, 231 n.
Ogburn, William F., 236 n.
Open public drama; *see* Drama
Oppenheimer, Robert, 216
Opportunism, 111
Orwell, George, 211
O'Toole, Peter, 37
Oulahan, Richard, 124 n.
Outcome, dramatic, 73, 76
Out of character, 149, 174, 246;
  see also Type violation
Out on a limb, going, 201, 232;
  see also Extremists

Paganini, 217
Page, Charles H., 258 n.
Park, Robert E., 21
Parsons, Louella, 142 n.
Patton, George S., 136, 197, 219
Paul VI, Pope, 77
Peabody, Eddie, 62
Pearson, Drew, 237
Pegler, Westbrook, 47, 187, 198
Pepper, Claude, 196
Perkins, Frances, 185 n., 223 n.,
  244 n.
Perón, Eva, 78
Persecutor role, 160, 184
Pershing, John J., 163-69, 199, 204,
  235, 239
Personal encounter; *see* Encounter,
  personal
Phillips, Cabell, 89, 198 n.
Piatigorski, Gregor, 226 n.
Pickford, Mary, 44
Pilate, Pontius, 87, 160, 162
Plekhanov, Georgii, 235 n.
Pollack, Jack H., 185 n.
Polti, Georges, 169 n.
Pose, 67, 216
Postman, Leo, 214 n.
Pound, Ezra, 194
Prejudices; *see* Mental "set"
Presley, Elvis, 23, 38
Pringle, H. F., 231 n.
Process model, 259
Proctor, John C., 242 n.

Props, 217
Psychological moment, 236
Pusey, Nathan, 187
Pussyfooting, 193, 229

Quest theme, 243
Quixote, Don, 173, 202, 233
Quixotic characters, 73, 171

Raft, George, 24, 36, 133
Raglan, F. R. S., 242 n.
Rank, Otto, 242 n.
Ratio of forces, 72, 85, 92, 97-98,
  148-49, 154, 163, 171, 173, 184,
  185, 204, 209
Reagan, Ronald, 141
Reciprocal relationships, 149, 170
Redl, Fritz, 51 n.
Regular fellow, 206; *see also* "Man
  of the people," Good Joe type
Resistance: non-violent, 82, 86; of
  image to crisis, 132, 140
Reston, James, 67 n., 106, 113
Reuther, Walter, 237
Reversals of role; *see* Role, re-
  versals
Reynolds, Debbie, 130
Rickard, Tex, 239
Ritual drama; *see* Drama, ritual
Robb, Inez, 151 n.
Robeson, Paul, 194
Robin Hood, 20, 133, 168-69, 234,
  243
Robinson, Edward G., 24, 36
Rockefeller, John D., 102
Rockefeller, Nelson, 131, 233
Rogers, Betty, 168 n.
Rogers, Will, 20, 23, 31, 36, 58,
  168, 194, 216, 220, 231, 244,
  245
Roland, 95, 225
Role: benefactor, 78; celebrity, 12;
  conversion, 148-75; dilemma of
  the American President, 248;
  forcing, 170-71, 174, 185; great
  man (*see* Great man role); hero
  (*see* Hero, role of); Martyr
  (*see* Martyr role); playing consciousness of, 251; reversals,
  148-75; sneak, 182; strategy,
  175, 210, 248; tragic, 61, 93;